HAALAND

HAALAND

The incredible story behind the world's greatest striker

LARS SIVERTSEN

EBURY
SPOTLIGHT

1

Ebury Spotlight, an imprint of Ebury Publishing
20 Vauxhall Bridge Road
London SW1V 2SA

Ebury Spotlight is part of the Penguin Random House
group of companies whose addresses can be found at
global.penguinrandomhouse.com

First published by Ebury Spotlight in 2023

www.penguin.co.uk

A CIP catalogue record for this book is available from the British Library

Hardback ISBN 9781529913095
Trade Paperback ISBN 9781529913101

Printed and bound in Great Britain by TJ Books Ltd, Padstow, Cornwall

Imported into the EEA by Penguin Random House Ireland, Morrison
Chambers, 32 Nassau Street, Dublin D02 YH68

Penguin Random House is committed to a sustainable future
for our business, our readers and our planet. This book is
made from Forest Stewardship Council® certified paper.

CONTENTS

PROLOGUE

There's nothing in the world quite like Borussia Dortmund's home ground, the Signal Iduna Park. On a matchday, around 80,000 people will file through the turnstiles and onto stands that seem somehow both vast and compact at the same time. On all four sides, the stadium roof is sloped so that the noise generated by the fans is sent straight back down, rather than escaping up towards the sky. And what noise. There are football grounds where the crowd come to be entertained, but in this place the fans come to make themselves heard. Dortmund's legendary south stand, a giant single terrace with a capacity of around 25,000, is one of the great wonders of the football world. Nicknamed the 'Yellow Wall', it is not so much a crowd of people as a heaving mass of scarves, limbs and souls. And it's loud, very loud.

Perhaps a young footballer, someone not quite used to being in the middle of all of this, could be forgiven for being cowed by it all – or if not, then at least affected in some kind of way. But on Tuesday, 18 February 2020, as the camera panned across the Borussia Dortmund players ahead of their Champions League knockout game with Paris Saint-Germain, 19-year-old Erling Haaland was smiling. Not the confident, cocky, arrogant smile of a star relishing the spotlight, but a boyish, uncontained grin. If anything, it looked like young Erling was doing his best to suppress a fit of the giggles. The hopes and dreams of every Dortmund fan in the stadium –

and many more of them outside of it – may well have been resting on his deceptively young shoulders, but Erling Haaland was having a great time.

And why not? Erling Haaland had, after all, quite a lot to be smiling about. In early 2020, at the age of 19, he was already one of the most talked-about footballers in the world, and this was his breakthrough season. Just over a year earlier he had left Molde FK in Norway and moved abroad for the first time in his life, joining RB Salzburg in Austria in January 2019. In his first six months at the Austrian club, his playing time was limited, but when Israeli striker Munas Dabbur left for Sevilla in the summer Haaland became first choice. He repaid that faith by scoring 11 goals in his first seven league games. When the time came for his Champions League debut, he promptly scored a hat-trick. By the end of September 2019 it was already clear that Erling Haaland wouldn't be staying in Austria for very long. There was much intrigue surrounding his next move. Some felt a transfer from RB Salzburg to its German sister club, RB Leipzig, made sense. Ole Gunnar Solskjær, Haaland's former boss at Molde, was now the manager of Manchester United and was taking a keen interest. In Serie A, Juventus was lurking. But the decision, in the end, was to move to Borussia Dortmund.

Dortmund and the Ruhr valley is an area that was once defined by mining, heavy industry, breweries and football. But after decades of industrial decline, the mines and heavy industry have mostly been consigned to history, while the breweries have either been closed down or bought up by faceless conglomerates. All of which has left football as the final thing giving the city of Dortmund an identity. Uli Hesse, a German author and journalist, wrote in September 2011, in the second issue of football magazine *The Blizzard*, that

Many places are referred to as football cities, but the term is rarely as fitting as it is in Dortmund, because almost everyone who was born or lives here cares deeply about Borussia and defines himself or herself to a large degree through the fortunes of the football team.

Dortmund fans have also learned the hard way that even having a successful football club is not something that can be taken for granted. In the 1990s Dortmund was determined to catch up with serial champions Bayern Munich, and started spending big money to bring stars and success to the city. In the short term it worked, as Dortmund won the Bundesliga in 1994/5 and 1995/6. They also won the Champions League in 1996/7, before winning the Bundesliga again in 2001/2. But the success had been achieved by spending more money than the club was bringing in, and their debts were starting to mount. When the club's performances on the pitch dipped and the team failed to qualify for European competition in 2004, the financial house of cards started tumbling down. Dortmund nearly went bankrupt, just three years after winning the league. It was clear that the club had to be rebuilt and run in a way that was totally different to what had come before. Dortmund, a club with a massive fan base and a huge cultural footprint, had to adopt the methods and strategies of an underdog.

The club was eventually reborn under the leadership of Jürgen Klopp, a charismatic leader and a man who understood how the passion of the Dortmund fans could be weaponised. Under Klopp, Dortmund filled its squad with young players, players who had the hunger and energy to execute Klopp's aggressive pressing style. Having become all too familiar with the perils of trying to out-spend its rivals, Dortmund based its football on out-running and out-fighting them instead. 'Dortmund are constantly chasing something at a million miles per hour, whether it's the ball, the opposition, space or the goal, and they rarely allow themselves a breather,' Raphael Honigstein wrote in the *Guardian* in April 2012. And under Klopp, Dortmund returned to the summit of German football, winning the Bundesliga in 2010/11 and 2011/12. The club nearly won the Champions League again in 2012/13 but was, gallingly, beaten in the final by Bayern Munich.

Since then Dortmund has remained a constant presence near the top of the Bundesliga, but the title has continued to elude the club. It has also been unable to return to the final stages of the Champions League, getting no further than the quarter-finals in the nine seasons since the club's win in 2013. The German club has come a long way since flirting with bankruptcy in 2005, and can now spend some serious money, but it still lags far behind the sheer spending power of Bayern Munich and the other financial elites around Europe. Accepting that it can't afford to sign ready-made superstars, Dortmund has instead implemented a model of signing the superstars of tomorrow. After all, it was a pivot to youth that brought Dortmund its last two league titles. And this is where Erling Haaland comes into the picture. The club has built a reputation as a finishing school for superstars, a place for young players to make the step from being world-class talents to world-class players. And Dortmund – though a big club with a big fan base – has shown that it's prepared to put its faith in young players and make them central pillars of the team. For Haaland, it was the perfect next step.

Paris Saint-Germain (PSG) is a very different kind of football club. Since being bought by Qatar in 2011, PSG has been merrily throwing vast sums of money at the transfer market, collecting superstars like they were Panini stickers. The club's squad has at times looked more like a guest list than a football team. Domestically the team has had success, but it continues to fall short in the Champions League and has been consistently criticised for being less than the sum of its very shiny parts. Even though Paris and its suburbs are possibly the greatest hotbed of young football talent in the world, PSG seems utterly disinterested in developing young players. You are, after all, never more than a few months away from the next transfer window. Dortmund's local rival is Schalke; its competitive rival is Bayern Munich. But if it is possible for a club to have a spiritual and philosophical rival then it may well be Paris Saint-Germain.

So when Dortmund took on PSG in the knockout stages of the Champions League, the game was heavily laden with subtext. For Dortmund, there is always a question of whether the club's policy of building a team around youth can ever be enough when coming up against star-studded European elites. And it's hard to think of a club further removed from Dortmund's values than PSG. Were any of these things on Erling Haaland's mind as he took to the field that Tuesday evening, under the lights, in front of the cameras, backed by some of the loudest fans in Europe? Well, no. Almost certainly not.

Most professional footballers are good at blocking out the noise, but Erling Haaland is exceptional at it. 'He doesn't care,' Erik Botheim, a close friend and youth teammate, explained to Norwegian newspaper *VG* in January 2020. 'This is the thing. He is mentally strong, and mostly he's just enjoying himself. He doesn't care.' What Botheim means by not caring is of course that Haaland is not distracted or affected by the noise and the pressure surrounding a young superstar. But when it comes to improving his game, Haaland is obsessed. Obsessed with the obvious things, like fine-tuning his remarkable physique or working on his finishing. But he is also obsessed with looking for things off the pitch that can help him become a better footballer. One of them, and something he is particularly passionate about, is meditation. 'I think it's a really good thing,' Haaland told *GQ* in January 2023, 'to relax, to try to not think too much. Because stress is not good for anyone. I hate to be stressed, and I try not to be stressed. But the concept of meditation is to try to let go of these kinds of thoughts. It's really individual, but for me it's worked really well.'

One of the many impressive feats of Erling Haaland's career so far is that whenever he moves club, whenever he goes up a level, whenever the challenge becomes bigger, he responds by scoring even more goals than before. When faced with new challenges and difficult obstacles in their professional lives most people would experience at least some kind of trepidation, but, as Botheim put it, mostly Erling is just enjoying himself.

So it made total sense for a 19-year-old Haaland to smile as the Champions League anthem rang out in the evening air, just minutes before kick-off against PSG. The pressure and expectation of the crowd, the game's significance for Dortmund's eternal struggle against the club's financial superiors, none of this would have registered much at all. Another thing that Haaland was likely oblivious to was the eyes of the football world paying particularly close attention to him that night. His rise had been meteoric, yet critics could say that so far his was a career of caveats. He scored four goals in 21 minutes for Molde? Well, that's the Norwegian league for you. He scored nine goals in a single game for the Norwegian U-20s? Yes, but against Honduras. He scored 16 goals in 14 games for RB Salzurg? Well, that was just in Austria. He scored a hat-trick in his Champions League debut? But that was just against Genk. He scored a hat-trick in his debut for Dortmund? Well, that was just against Augsburg. Here there were no caveats. This was the real deal, a Champions League knockout game against Paris Saint-Germain – with names like Kylian

Mbappé and Neymar on the opposing team. But Erling Haaland just doesn't care, and so he smiled his boyish smile.

From kick-off, Dortmund looked like the better team, but in the first half the players failed to find a way past Keylor Navas in the PSG goal. In the 26th minute, Jadon Sancho forced a good save from Navas, while eight minutes later Haaland himself drilled a shot off his powerful left foot into the side netting. Haaland was quick and looked menacing, but he wasn't fully in sync with his teammates. He hadn't been with the team for very long, and it showed. At half-time the score was 0–0. The Dortmund players were playing well but, with a return leg in Paris to be played in a few weeks, a draw at home would be a poor result.

In the second half Dortmund kept pushing. They had more possession but created few big chances, and PSG looked a threat when they countered. The pace of Mbappé was a constant worry. But Achraf Hakimi, the Spanish-born Moroccan on loan at Dortmund from Real Madrid, is also lightning quick. Playing as a wingback with the experienced Łukasz Piszczek covering behind him, Hakimi looked like the most promising outlet for Dortmund in attack. And it's Hakimi who eventually fashioned a breakthrough. Jadon Sancho played a ball to the right for Hakimi, who had been afforded a huge amount of space out wide by the PSG defence. He advanced with the ball before putting in a cross to where Dortmund's left wingback Raphaël Guerreiro had made an unexpected run into the box. His first-time finish hit a PSG defender, but Haaland was lurking – like he always does. The big Norwegian stabbed the ball home. The stadium erupted, the PSG defence appealed for a non-existent offside and meditation-enthusiast Haaland assumed the lotus position just outside the six-yard box. Grinning, he was quickly swamped by his teammates.

But PSG, whatever the team's failings may be, still has an extra-ordinary collection of individuals. Most notably Kylian Mbappé, who rarely goes a full game without reminding the world of what he can do. In the 74th minute, Mbappé had possession some 15 yards inside Dortmund's half. The Dortmund defence were all back, all in position, so this should have been a reasonably safe situation for the defending team. Except there really is no such thing as a safe situation for a defending team when Mbappé has the ball. He skipped past one Dortmund player as if he wasn't there, evaded a rash and mistimed challenge from the covering defender, and suddenly he was in the Dortmund box – albeit out wide, with a difficult angle for the shot. Mbappé instead played a low ball into a central area, where Neymar had eluded everyone and could tap the ball into an open net: 1–1. A good night for Dortmund suddenly turned into a bad one. A 1–1 draw was not a good result to take to Paris. For all their talent and youthful exuberance, Dortmund's team had been undone by the two most expensive players in world football. 'A £350-million goal,' one TV commentator noted dryly.

But Dortmund weren't finished. Roared on by the Yellow Wall, defender Mats Hummels played an incisive ball into Giovanni Reyna in midfield. Just 17 years old in this Champions League match, Reyna has a curiously similar background to Erling Haaland: like Haaland, he was born in northern England in the early 2000s, as his father, Claudio, was playing for Sunderland in the Premier League at the time. And like Haaland, he had been drawn to Dortmund because of the club's reputation for developing and trusting young players. Here, in a knockout game in the Champions League, the 17-year-old received the ball in midfield, turned and headed towards the open space in front of him. The PSG defence had left gaps and, even though Jadon Sancho was on the move to his right, Reyna was only looking for Haaland. He squared the ball, and Haaland let it run across his body before taking it on his left foot. But the ball continued to move diagonally and Haaland's touch wasn't perfect – or was it? With a couple of quick strides of his long legs the ball was suddenly in the perfect place for a swing of Haaland's mighty left boot. He unleashed a shot with such venom that it could have done serious harm to fans behind the goal – if the net hadn't stopped it first.

At the Signal Iduna Park a big goal isn't something you just see and hear, it's something you feel. A sound, a noise and an energy that pierces your skin and rattles your bones. This one shook the building to its foundations, shook the ground itself, and in disbelief Erling Haaland wheeled off to assume the lotus pose once again. Except this time his momentum is too great, and he falls over before his team-mates have time to swamp him. And this time it is not a grin on his face, but rather the moonstruck look of a teenager who can barely process what just happened and what he just did.

'For the second goal, is it confidence, is it technique, what is it?' former Swindon striker-turned-TV reporter Jan Åge Fjørtoft asked Haaland in Norwegian after the game. '*Æg tenke bare å dryla te for å vær heilt ærlege, så drylte eg an i mål så det va fint det*,' Haaland replied, in his thick regional Norwegian dialect. It's an answer that presents a challenge to translators. *Dryla* is not a word in common usage in Norwegian, except informally in a handful of regional dialects – most typically in Norway's southwest, where Haaland grew up. It typically refers to hitting or kicking something with tremendous force, most usually a ball – though in extreme circumstances one might also *dryla te* a disagreeable person (however, this is not advisable, and one will likely have a problem with the authorities in the aftermath of such an act). The most accurate and phonetically pleasing English translation is probably 'to wallop' something or someone (though again, this is not advisable). So Haaland said, roughly translated: 'To be honest, I thought I'd just wallop it, and then I walloped it into the goal so that was good.' If Norwegians were not already sufficiently delighted with seeing their golden boy put the pampered Parisians to the sword, he gained further approval by staying true to his roots and his dialect. Erling Haaland is not someone who will change the way he speaks just because a TV reporter has pointed a microphone at him. If even some of his fellow Norwegians are unfamiliar with what it means to *dryla* something, well, that's their problem. They can watch the replay of the goal, for educational purposes.

Dortmund would go on to lose the return leg and get knocked out of the Champions League. But, at least for one glorious moment at the Signal Iduna Park, the Dortmund fans had seen the wealth of Qatar be undone by one glorious swing of a 19-year-old's left foot. It was a feeling to savour and a moment to remember. As for Haaland, the thumping strike against PSG had well and truly announced his arrival on the world stage. For anyone who had dismissed the hype so far, well, it was time to sit up and pay attention. The goal was also the fully distilled essence of Erling Haaland: the power, the skill, the confidence, and not least the ability to block out all the noise and simply put the ball in the net. And while this will have been lost on the rest of the world, the goal and his post-match interview also showed Norwegians what Erling is all about: even on the biggest stage, against the most famous opponents, he will play the game more or less the same way he played it growing up in Bryne. And if you stick a microphone in his face he will speak like a kid from Bryne. Because that, when all is said and done, is what he is. A giant, unstoppable, irrepressible kid from Bryne.

1

GIFTS FROM THE ICE

When the last ice age came to an end some 10,000 years ago, the retreating glaciers revealed a strip of land on the southwest coast of Norway that looked nothing like its surrounding areas. Modern-day visitors who fly into Stavanger Airport from the south on a clear day can hardly fail to notice the abrupt shift in landscape as they approach the southern coastline. Just past the small fishing port of Sirevåg the jagged coastline gives way to a fine sandy beach at Brusand. Here, the craggy, rocky hills of southern Norway are replaced by a long, flat plain, reaching some 40 miles north, all the way to the more heavily urbanised areas around the city of Stavanger. This is Jæren, the largest lowland plain in Norway. It's a landscape that's totally different from both the country's icy north and the dramatic mountains and fjords of the west coast so beloved by tourism campaigns and cruise ship ads.

With incalculable force, the glaciers of the ice age had chiselled and smoothed the bedrock, and had left behind much bigger deposits of sediment than anywhere else in the country. In plain terms, Jæren is flat and has a thick layer of soil, making it just about the best place in the country to grow things. With its southern location, Jæren also enjoys a longer growing season than the rest of the country. But there is a catch, or rather, there were a few of them. First, large parts of the area were covered in peat bogs. With trees being relatively sparse, peat was an important fuel resource for many years. But turning bogs into farmable land takes a lot of effort. Second, with its coastal location facing straight into the North Sea, and with no mountains or hills for cover, Jæren lies fully exposed to all manner of weather. It may be milder than in other parts of Norway, but it is regularly swept by howling winds and near-horizontal rain. Third, and perhaps most significantly for the early farmers of Jæren, there are the rocks.

The glaciers may have kindly left an uncommonly thick layer of soil, but they also left rocks, an unholy amount ranging from pebbles to boulders, scattered all over the plain. Any farmer with a notion of working the land would first have to clear it of rocks, which, before the advent of modern machinery, was no small task. Perversely, come the following spring, the fields would somehow be full of rocks yet again. The soil is constantly pushing ever more rocks towards the surface. The landscape of Jæren is capricious: it gives the farmer sustenance and an income, potentially a very fair one, but it also gives rocks, endless rocks, subjecting the farmer to a never-ending test of grit and perseverance. Manually lifting rocks of all sizes out of the ground while cold, piercing winds from the North Sea blasts the landscape: well, it builds character.

Skilling-Magazin, the first Norwegian illustrated weekly magazine, visited Jæren in 1887 and concluded the following:

> The Jærbu [a person from Jæren] has labours in front of him which seem fairly hopeless. But the trials of stamina and hard graft he has withstood, the victories he has won, the

conquests he has achieved against the barren nature, give us faith that he is a man with a future. The Jærbu has a heavy task to accomplish, but he will manage it.

In the way that a landscape will always shape its peoples, it is clear that the inhabitants of Jæren came to value perseverance and hard work above all else. Local historian Svein Ivar Langhelle notes:

> The heroic figure of Jæren was and still is the skilled, able farmer. The one who further develops his land. He who through great toil and effort is able to build something, stone by stone, and in the end achieves more than his peers.

At the same time the farmers of Jæren were also keen to look to the future and possessed a strong entrepreneurial spirit. According to Langhelle,

> the farmers of Jæren were more effective than farmers elsewhere at familiarising themselves with new methods and equipment for farming, and … they were quick to adopt methods that proved beneficial.

After all, the arrival of modern machinery meant that the farmers got some help in clearing all those infernal rocks. The machines made a huge difference, changing life and changing the landscape itself: 200 years ago just 1–2 per cent of Jæren had been developed as farmland. Today, in some counties, that number is as high as 80 per cent.

The town of Bryne, which today is the municipal centre of Jæren and technically a city, was founded almost by coincidence. In the second half of the nineteenth century a railway line was being built between Stavanger, the dominant city in the region, and Egersund, an important fishing town some 50 miles to the south. It was decided to build one of the stations along the line at the southern end of a lake named Frøylandsvatnet, and when the line was finished in 1878 a village started growing around the station. It would continue to grow, as workshops and small factories serving the local agriculture started popping up. A wool-spinning mill and a dairy also arrived, as did a house of worship and a school. The aforementioned entrepreneurial streak of the locals would continue to drive development of the town: Trallfa, a factory that initially produced trolleys, wagons and wheelbarrows, would in the 1960s and 1970s produce some of the world's first industrial robots and eventually gain a significant global market share. In 1918 the Aarbakke family started a company that made horseshoes, and two generations later Aarbakke AS has had huge success producing equipment for the booming Norwegian oil industry. The outskirts of Bryne was also home to Brøyt, a company that in the 1960s was Scandinavia's leading producer of excavators. Bryne was officially declared a city in 2001, and today has some 12,000 inhabitants. This makes it only the 47th biggest settlement in Norway, but it is the commercial centre of the Jæren region.

Kjell Olav Stangeland, the former chairman of Bryne's football club, was the long-time editor of the local newspaper and has written comprehensive history books on both Bryne the town and the football club. He has no doubt that the local people have been shaped by the land:

> You have to start with the initial poverty and scarcity. People have had to work their way up from very little. For a farmer it was hard graft just to survive. What has been characteristic of the Jærbu has been to be careful of not spending more

14

than you have, and to work hard. You know that you have to work for your supper. And you should never get over-excited or get ahead of yourself. If things are going very well today, they could go badly tomorrow.

Having established that there are certain traits and qualities associated with being a Jærbu, it then becomes necessary to define terms. Geographically speaking, the lowland plain of Jæren stretches all the way north to the urban areas around Sandnes and Stavanger, but culturally people from these cities will most certainly not be considered to be from Jæren. Historically speaking, the people of Jæren would consider themselves to be hardy rural folk and would view the city dwellers from Sandnes and Stavanger with no small amount of suspicion. Traditionally, many would consider Skjævelandsbrunå, a bridge crossing the river Figgjo some 7 miles north of Bryne on the road towards Stavanger, as Jæren's true northern border. People from the northern side of this bridge should be considered city dwellers, with all the foul things this might entail. 'There is a saying here that if you want workers you need to get people from south of Skjævelandsbrunå, because they know how to work,' Stangeland explains.

> To this day you'll find people who will say this, and you'll find people who will insist that the best thing is getting people straight from the farms – because the farmers have learned that you have to get up early and work hard if you want to achieve anything.

Local band Silo & Saft take it one step further in a song titled 'Skjævelandsbrunå':

This is the story of a small bridge,
When you get there you must turn around,
Beyond it only city people and snobs live.
They insist they live in Jæren,
But God and every man knows damned well,
That a Jærbu lives south of Skjævelandsbrunå
Skjævelandsbrunå,
It's a dividing line between right and wrong
I am strong in my faith, that I live on the right side of the bridge

Still, people lucky enough to be born possessing the good sense to settle on the correct side of this bridge will have to accept that it does come with a certain stigma as far as the rest of Norway is concerned. People from Jæren are known for both a kind of stoicism and for having an economical way with words. But some may see them as dour, possibly even a bit introverted. Arne Garborg – a Jæren-born author who was nominated for the Nobel prize in Literature six times – wrote in his 1892 novel *Peace* that people from Jæren are 'a heavy folk who dig their way through life with ponder and toil'. Still, locals might also argue that there is a difference between being an introvert and simply being understated. What reason is there really for using ten words if two or three, or even a meaningful pause, can suffice? 'Understatement is very typical of Jæren, both in our daily speech and in our sense of humour,' Stangeland says. 'You should certainly never exaggerate anything. I remember when the football club had Kent Karlsson, a Swede, here as a manager in the eighties. When Bryne won 4–0 people would say "oh, that wasn't too bad." "Not too bad? What on earth?!" he would exclaim. He wondered what it would take for us to actually get excited.' But football is something that does get the people of Bryne and Jæren excited. And over the years, it's football more than anything else that has put Bryne on the map.

2

THE FARMERS

Football came to Norway in the 1880s, and the first ever Norwegian football club – Christiania Footballclub – was founded in Oslo in 1885. In Stavanger, Viking Fotballklubb was founded in 1899 and is the oldest club in this part of the country. When exactly Bryne's football club was founded is a matter of some conjecture. The official founding date is 10 April 1926, though few written records exist to confirm this. The oldest document in the club's archives is an application letter of October 1928 from Bryne Turn- og Idrettslag (Bryne Gymnastics and Sports Club) to join the regional FA. Bryne's membership was accepted, but the club had no stadium of any kind and had a hard enough time finding smooth ground to train on. Eventually a patch of land was rented adjacent to the local mill and the river that runs through town.

In the book *Ups and Downs through 90 Years: The Story of Bryne FK*, authors Reidar B. Thu and Kjell Olav Stangeland (both former chairmen of the club) provide a comprehensive and exhaustive history of the club, and outline how trying to have a football club in Bryne during these early days involved some rather unique challenges. The patch of land they had rented was at first not entirely suited for football or any other sporting activity. The ground had to be smoothed, heather and brush had to be uprooted, and – of course – rocks had to be pulled out of the ground. The pitch, such as it was, was positioned within a split in the river. This meant that errant shots had a fair chance of being claimed by the water. To make retrieval of the ball more manageable, and to avoid it being washed away downstream altogether, fishing nets were deployed. Thu and Stangeland also recount one rather spectacular incident involving a Swedish man who had settled in Bryne. This Swede had a passion for duck hunting, and one early evening, in the dusk, he mistook a rogue clearance for a feathery foe. He took aim and, in what must have been a fine display of marksmanship, shot the ball clean out of the sky. As footballs were not as easily replaced back then as they are now, one can only imagine that this outcome was the source of some frustration for the Bryne players. Towards the end of 1930, the club bought a plot of land next to the railway line, about half a mile south of the train station. This is where Bryne Stadium was gradually built up over the years, and where the team still plays.

During the interwar period Bryne wasn't much more than an average village team. Though one incident from 1935 showed what one might diplomatically describe as an increasingly competitive spirit among the locals. Regional newspaper *Stavanger Aftenblad* described an unsavoury incident that occurred during a match between Bryne and the team from the neighbouring town of Nærbø:

Everything was set for an exciting match in Bryne yesterday. There were many spectators, and the hosts had also ensured nourishment for the soul by inviting a band of musicians.

Early on, there was danger at the opposite end of the field, and Bryne's centre seized the moment and scored the game's first goal. It was quite understandable that the patriotic natives would erupt in something akin to a war dance, but that the local musicians were unable to contain themselves was nothing short of a scandal. They readied their instruments, and with the full force of their lungs they performed an entire piece of music, or a march. During this time, the players were free to do as they wished, because no one could hear the referee's whistle. From this point, the motto of the game became to stamp on your opponent. It must be considered sheer luck that there was no need for an ambulance. The game that was played in Bryne yesterday did not further the cause of football.

Thu and Stangeland observe wryly that the byline of this article was simply the letter 'R', and that it was most likely written by one Ragnvald Skjærpe – who was in fact the chairman of the opposing team. Whether this was shameless skulduggery by the Bryne side or a very early case of media bias, we will never know.

During the Second World War, Norway was occupied by Nazi Germany, which put a halt to organised football. But something very important for Bryne's football scene did happen during these years: a pair of brothers, Lauritz B. Sirevaag and Odd Harald Sirevaag, moved to Bryne with their family from Stavanger. The two were gifted footballers, and in the post-war years they were a driving force as Bryne became Jæren's premier football team. Odd Harald 'Buster' Sirevaag was a particularly lethal attacker and, with 257 goals in 385 games for Bryne, he is to this day the second top goal scorer in the club's history. In 1962 Bryne memorably beat their local rivals from Stavanger, Viking, in the Norwegian Cup. It was the first time that Bryne had beaten Viking in a competitive match. There hadn't been too many opportunities to try, since Viking at the time had played in the national top division every season since it was established in 1937, while Bryne had yet to ascend to that kind of level. However, the club was promoted to the second tier in 1964, and eventually, after several near misses, it was promoted to the top tier of Norwegian football in 1974. Of the team that secured promotion, all but three starters were from Jæren.

'I think a big part of it is that we never accepted that Viking had to be any better than us,' Stangeland remembers. 'We had no business being in the elite based on our resources, but we didn't care.' For Bryne the rivalry with the big city of Stavanger and its flagship team Viking was always a driving force. Viking had been a significant power in Norwegian football throughout most of its history: after winning the national league – the Hovedserien – in 1958 and the Cup in 1953 and 1959, the club had had a golden age in the 1970s, winning four straight league titles between 1972 and 1975, before claiming a league and Cup double in 1979. Bryne may have been the unofficial capital of Jæren, but it was also at this point a very small town with a population of just a few thousand people. Aspiring to compete with one of the powerhouses of Norwegian club football was a bit of a stretch. 'Bryne is just the right distance from Stavanger,' argues Stangeland. 'You got a lot of ideas from the city, but we didn't have the problem of the smaller towns closer to Stavanger who would lose all their best players to the city. I think that mattered a lot.'

Bryne stayed in the top division from 1976 to 1987. And, incredibly, the club finished second in the league in both 1980 and 1982. With football already popular in the area, the club's success made it a real focal point of the community both in Bryne and in the surrounding towns. 'In the 1980s there were no more than 5–6,000 people living in Bryne,' Stangeland recalls. He was the club chairman from 1981 all the way through to 1987.

> And if we had fewer than 5,000 at a home game, that was considered poor attendance. Someone made the point at the time that if this had been in Oslo and you had a similar level of interest, you would have needed a stadium that could fit several hundred thousand.

Everyone cared about the team on some level, and for little Bryne to have a team in the top division was a source of great pride.

On the pitch it was Gabriel Høyland who led the way. He made his debut for Bryne in 1972 aged just 17, and in 1974 he became the first ever player from Bryne to play for the Norwegian national team. Throughout his career he had no shortage of offers from bigger clubs, both in Norway and abroad. He turned them all down, and went on to play an incredible 596 games for Bryne and got 23 caps for Norway before he retired in 1986. Today they simply call him 'Mr Bryne'. Høyland was a skilful, elegant forward who had both flair and an eye for goal – a kind of Norwegian Kevin Keegan, if Keegan had combined football with working on the family farm. He was also compared to Glenn Hoddle, and appropriately he managed to swap shirts with Hoddle after having been an unused substitute when Norway faced England at Wembley in 1980. 'They used to say his style was not dissimilar to mine,' Høyland told the *Telegraph* in May 2022.

Høyland is also, of all things, a passionate Burnley supporter. It's not uncommon for Norwegian football fans to split their loyalties between their local Norwegian team and an English club. Decades before the Premier League became a global sporting and media phenomenon, games from the old English First Division were regularly broadcast on Norwegian TV. This started in 1969, a time when there was only one TV channel available to Norwegians. With the games kicking off on Saturday at 4pm local time, they coincided perfectly with people either settling in for the weekend or preparing for lively Saturday nights out. Exact numbers do not exist, but it has been estimated that well over a million people regularly watched these games, which was close to a quarter of Norway's population at the time. It led to many Norwegians forming an emotional connection with an English football club, and this applied to aspiring footballers as much as anyone else. Kjetil Rekdal, for instance, has 83 caps for Norway, scored in both the 1994 and 1998 World Cups, and is a fanatical Leeds United supporter. In this context, Bryne club legend Høyland being a Burnley fan makes a bit more sense. At some point Høyland had developed a passion for the Clarets, and he maintained it throughout his own storied football career. 'In the seventies, I would bring a radio to training or games if Burnley were playing,' he told public broadcaster NRK back in 2003.

A star player's enthusiasm for Burnley wasn't the only British influence on Bryne during the club's glory years. From 1977 to 1979 the team was managed by Stavanger-native Kjell Schou-Andreassen, who had previously won the league with Viking and managed the Norwegian national team. To replace the highly regarded Schou-Andreassen, Bryne turned to Englishman Brian Green. Green had previously managed Rochdale and the Australian national team, and became a popular figure at Bryne. In their exhaustive history of the club, Thu and Stangeland describe how 'the jovial Brian Green became a familiar figure around town, a town which at the time had no more than 5,000 inhabitants. He spoke to everyone, and everyone spoke to him.' People would ask Green over for dinner and he would accept, whether he knew them well or not. 'In the shops he would charm staff with his attempts at speaking Norwegian, to the point where he would receive discounts or even be absolved of payment altogether.' On the sporting side of things, the team had been well coached by Schou-Andreassen, but the easy-going Green appeared to further unlock their potential. The training sessions were lighter, and the meetings were shorter. Green led the team to a sensational second place in the league in 1980 and 1982. He left the club after the 1982 season, and Bryne stayed in the top division until relegation in 1988. The golden era peaked in 1987, when Bryne won the Norwegian Cup. Thousands of Bryne fans descended on Oslo for the final, creating the eerie, giddy sensation that the whole town was there. Everywhere the visiting fans from Bryne went in downtown Oslo that weekend, they'd run into friends, neighbours and colleagues. The game itself went into extra time but was eventually decided in Bryne's favour by a goal from Kolbjørn Ekker. It remains the club's only major trophy.

Like most football clubs, and smaller clubs from smaller places in particular, Bryne have had periods of financial difficulty. Raising funds has been a constant battle, but it's also been an area where the club has historically exercised some ingenuity. 'The thing that above anything else financed the club up until 1970 was the dance hall,' Kjell Olav Stangeland says, chuckling. In the early 1960s, massive wooden decking was built close to the stadium by volunteers so that dance parties could be hosted at the club. To extend its use beyond the summer, four walls and a roof were added soon after. *Planen*, as the old hall was called, was used as both a dance hall and an indoor training venue.

In the first half of [the 1960s], there was dancing at Planen on Saturdays and Sundays. And, if you can imagine, on

Saturdays there could be as many as 2,000 people there. There wouldn't be room for that many people in the dance hall itself, so people would go in and out. And at that time, if you wanted to drink beer legally out on the town, you had to go as far north as Sandnes. There was no alcohol being served in Bryne, not until the hotel opened in 1977. So people had to have their drinks in their inside pockets, and there would be two to four policemen trying to arrest people and empty the bottles if they found them. Inevitably there would be fights. That was the reality of it. And the profits went to the club. Even if it just cost three kroner to go in, with that many people there the money started adding up.

Though these dance parties were eventually consigned to history, the facility remained in use all the way up to the spring of 2001, when the site burned down. Generations of kids from Bryne would spend many a cold winter evening playing football on the ancient wooden decking, which towards the end of its life was no longer entirely flat and even. Underhit passes would veer off in curious directions, as howling winds tugged at the creaky old walls. The fire was no accident, but the perpetrator was never found. A couple of years later a bigger, more modern indoor venue was erected on the same spot. And about two decades after that, journalists and reporters from around the world would start flocking to this indoor training pitch to tell the story of the kids who trained in it. One kid in particular.

In 1983, Bryne decided to hire a head of marketing in an effort to expand the club's commercial horizons. One of the applications that came in was from a certain Rune Hauge, who at the time was working for German club FC Nürnberg. Hauge was originally from

Voss, in Norway's mountainous western region. He had travelled to Germany to study economics, and according to Norwegian newspaper *VG* he ended up meeting several board members from FC Nürnberg through playing at a bridge club. Hauge was, and still is, an exceptional bridge player. He was hired at Nürnberg initially as an interpreter, but was later promoted to assistant manager and had some involvement with the club's transfer dealings. Evidently Hauge liked the idea of moving back to Norway, and joined Bryne as their new head of marketing. In a year the club's non-sporting income doubled.

'He came in with inspiration and ideas from German football, and he was in many ways a wild man himself,' explains Stangeland, who was the chairman at the time. 'He had little restraint and many ideas.' At one point during Hauge's reign as head of marketing, Bryne had the highest sponsorship income in the entire top division.

> Little Bryne had more income from sponsors than the clubs from the big cities. We were way ahead of them, thanks to Rune Hauge. It was said that the shopkeepers in Bryne would run and hide when they saw him coming down the street. They found it hard to say no to him.

Stangeland laughs, before composing himself: 'Those were small sums really. But when it came to shirt sponsorship we made several hundred thousand at a time when other clubs hardly had any income from shirt sponsorship.' Bryne made improvements to the main stand and built Norway's first VIP section, an enclosed area where local sponsors could watch the team in safety from the ever-unreliable Jæren weather. Other Hauge-inspired money-spinners included a sponsorship deal with a local agricultural machine supplier, which involved the supplier showcasing tractors and other types of machinery along the stadium's running track at half-time. This proved unpopular with the fans, and very unpopular with the stadium announcer, who had to read out complicated specifications for farming machines. The club later pivoted to half-time shows involving local, sometimes national, celebrities, and at one point a famous racehorse. The business with the horse proved unpopular with the local athletics club, who feared infection as a result of horse droppings being left on their running track. Still, Hauge displayed an uncanny ability to generate money, and for him Bryne turned out to be a launch pad for an even more profitable career as a player agent. He would go on to become a hugely successful and equally notorious agent in England during the 1990s, before he decided that the real money was in selling media rights. Needless to say, he made a killing on that front as well. But it all started out at Bryne, and one of the first transfers he facilitated to an English club involved a Bryne player.

In 1991 little Bryne had no fewer than six youngsters who were called up to represent Norway at various age groups. These included Geir Atle Undheim, who would go on to play almost 300 games for the club and eventually help them get promoted back to the top tier almost a decade later. One of the other youth internationals was Janove Ottesen, who didn't make it as a footballer but instead founded alternative rock band Kaizers Orchestra. Described by the *New York Times* in 2013 as 'an idiosyncratic amalgam of Scandinavian and Eastern European folk influences filtered through high-energy blues and metal', Kaizers became one of the best-selling Norwegian bands of the early 2000s, much to the confusion of the rest of the Norwegian music industry. Of all the success stories to come out of this part of the country, Kaizers Orchestra is definitely the most outlandish. But it was, again, connected to football, as Jan Ove Ottesen is the son of

Rune Ottesen – who got 17 caps for Norway and moved to Bryne to play for the team in the late 1970s. Still, the most promising young player at the time was a quick, combative defender with clear blue eyes and bright blond hair. His name was Alf-Inge Håland.

3

ALFIE

At 19, Alf-Inge Håland was already the captain of Bryne and one of the team's most important players. He would later legally change his name to Alfie Haaland. Alfie's father, Astor, had also played some games for Bryne before later becoming the headmaster of the local secondary school. Unusually for such a young player, Alfie also had a column in the local newspaper, where he gave a player's perspective on the team's progress. Or rather, at times, their lack of it. Because while the area consistently produced promising young players, Bryne was stuck in the second tier. And it became inescapable that a player with Alfie Haaland's talent and ambition would have to move on to fulfil his potential. On 13 October 1992, Norway's U-21s played England in Peterborough. The England team featured future stars such as Ray Parlour, Steve McManaman and Lee Clark. But Norway, captained by Haaland, won the game 2–1, with Haaland playing brilliantly and scoring one of the goals. Nottingham Forest, then still managed by Brian Clough, quickly took an interest. Later that month an agreement was reached with both Haaland and Bryne. Facilitated, of course, by one Rune Hauge.

Trouble securing a work permit for Haaland meant he was unable to complete the transfer to Forest until about a year later. Because of the country's climate, Norway's football season is played in the warmer half of the year, running from early spring to late autumn. So the delay meant Haaland played another season for Bryne, a season in which Bryne missed out on automatic promotion by just four points and then lost in the play-offs. In the summer of 1993 Haaland again captained the Norwegian U-21s against England, an England side that this time featured Andy Cole, Jamie Redknapp and Darren Anderton. The game was played in Stavanger and ended 1–1, with Andy Cole scoring for England and Egil Østenstad for Norway. Østenstad, who later played for Southampton and Blackburn Rovers, was playing for Viking at the time and no doubt enjoyed scoring against the mighty England in his home stadium. By the time Alfie Haaland got to Nottingham Forest, the club had been relegated from the Premier League and Brian Clough had retired. Haaland made his debut for Forest against Leicester City on 6 February 1994, and he wasn't the only Norwegian in the Forest line-up: the skilful midfielder Lars Bohinen had joined the club in November.

'We were kind of pioneers at the time,' Bohinen told the *Guardian* in June 2023. 'We didn't make any waves, we were just constantly being professional and producing performances. I think that's why we had so many players doing well in England.' Haaland and Bohinen were part of the first wave, but throughout the 1990s more and more Norwegians found their way across the North Sea. In the 1997/8 season there were as many as 23 Norwegians in the Premier League. A good number of these had been helped on their way by the ever-enterprising Mr Hauge, though it also seems clear that Norwegian players were perfectly suited to English football in the 1990s. 'We were a decent generation of players but we were also able to adapt quickly,' Bohinen said. And he believes he and Alfie Haaland succeeded at Forest in large part because of their mentality: 'We brought a hard-working outlook. I think that was the main reason we succeeded, because there was a bit of a different mentality among the English players at the time.' Nils Johan Semb, assistant manager of the Norwegian national team during the 1990s and national team manager himself from 1998 to 2003, has pointed to two big reasons why Norwegian players were popular in England at that time: 'Good attitudes, low prices,' he told *Aftenposten* in 2014.

And if mentality and effort were the key components that gave Norwegian players an edge in the Premier League in the 1990s, well, there can be few more obvious examples of this than Alfie Haaland. Having started out as a central defender, Haaland would go on to play right-back for his country at the 1994 World Cup. He was in the starting line-ups for the win against Mexico and the defeat to Italy, but got booked in both games and had to sit out the decider against Jack Charlton's Ireland. In the Premier League he played some games in defence and some on the right, but eventually he would make a name for himself primarily as an aggressive, tough-tackling midfielder. Football was both played and officiated very differently back then, and Haaland belonged to a generation of midfielders who would two-foot you first and ask questions later. This, along with his work rate and attitude on the pitch, made him a fan favourite. He moved from Forest to Leeds in the summer of 1997, and was an important part of the team for his first two seasons at Elland Road. In his third season he had to accept a reduced role, spending periods of time on the bench. In the summer of 2000 Joe Royle brought him to newly promoted Manchester City. 'Alfie is a fantastic footballer and a great athlete,' Royle said at the time. Haaland started 35 games and played well for City that season, but the team were ultimately relegated back down to the First Division. That, however, is not what most people remember about Haaland's season at City.

'He was an absolute prick to play against. Niggling, sneaky,' Roy Keane said of Haaland in his 2014 autobiography, *The Second Half*. And one suspects Haaland would wear this description as a badge of honour. After all, as a combative central midfielder, Haaland wasn't there to make life comfortable for his opponents. If Keane had described him as a refined gentleman of impeccable manners and fine breeding, well, Alfie Haaland wouldn't have been doing his job very well. When Leeds hosted Manchester United at Elland Road in September 1997, the visitors were unbeaten in their first nine games of the season. Games between Leeds and Manchester United have always been feisty, going all the way back to the 1960s and the days of Don Revie and Matt Busby. Roy Keane had recently been made United captain and was certainly no less fired up than usual. But Keane, who had been out drinking until four in the morning just a few days earlier, played badly. Towards the end of the game, with Leeds 1–0 up, United's Ben Thornley overhit a forward pass towards Keane. Haaland, displaying his impressive athleticism, breezed past a tired-looking Keane to secure the ball, and as he passed him Keane swung a leg at him for no particular reason. Well, there was a reason: Keane was losing and he was annoyed. 'He'd done his job. He'd done my head in. He was winding me up from the beginning of the game,' is how Keane described it in his autobiography, released in 2002. And when swiping a leg at Haaland, Keane ruptured his cruciate ligament. The freshly minted captain of Manchester United had put himself out for the rest of the season trying to kick an opponent off the ball, because he was playing badly, was 1–0 down and had lost his head.

'He was lying on the ground and I just told him to "get up" as you normally do with players – nothing more than that. I wasn't trying to intend anything against him,' is how Alfie Haaland himself described what followed in an interview many years later. But the inference that he was somehow feigning injury did not go down well with Keane. What came after has become the stuff of urban legend: when Haaland faced Keane again in April 2001, the angry Irishman aimed a vicious kick at Haaland, getting himself sent off and effectively ending Haaland's career. That hardest of hard men, Keane, exacting his carefully planned revenge, is how the story goes. Though on closer inspection, there are things that don't fully add up. It was not the first time the two had met on the pitch since Keane's injury. That had been on 28 November 1998, when Manchester United beat Leeds 3–2 and Keane even scored a goal. No sign of Keane avenging anything there. They met again on 18 November 2000, with Haaland now playing for Manchester City and facing Keane and United in his first Manchester derby. United won 1–0 after an early David Beckham goal, and Keane again seemingly felt no particular need to right any wrongs, perceived or actual. But when they met in April the next year, things were different. 'Another crap performance. They're up for it. We're not,' is how Keane describes the game. Manchester United had taken the lead through a Teddy Sheringham penalty in the 71st minute, but in the 84th minute Steve Howey equalised for City. This was when, almost immediately after City's equaliser, Keane's assault on Haaland took place. For all the mythologizing of Keane as a patient avenger, biding his time to right an old wrong, it does look quite a lot like he just got frustrated and kicked someone – again.

'I'd waited long enough. I fucking hit him hard. The ball was there (I think). Take that you cunt. And don't ever stand over me sneering about fake injuries,' is how Keane famously describes the incident in his 2002 autobiography. When asked by the *Observer* in 2002 if he regretted it, he replied:

> No. Even in the dressing room afterwards, I had no remorse. My attitude was, fuck him. What goes around comes around. He got his just rewards. He fucked me over and my attitude is an eye for an eye.

Though perhaps it bears pointing out that it was very much Keane who, in his own vernacular, fucked himself over with that tired swipe at Haaland back in 1997. And when facing possible legal proceedings from Manchester City and Haaland, Keane swiftly distanced himself from his own version of events, telling the *Observer* in September 2002 that

> I have never in my career set out to deliberately injure any player. In the incident involving Haaland I was making a genuine effort to play the ball. The words used in the book represent a degree of artistic licence on the part of the author.

In a later edition of his 2002 autobiography, the wording of the incident was changed. The phrase 'The ball was there (I think)' was replaced with 'I lunged for the ball, but mistimed the tackle.' And in his later 2014 autobiography, Keane would reiterate again that there was no premeditation involved and he would insist, seemingly contradicting his first autobiography, that he never intended to hurt Haaland.

Whatever Keane's intention was, Alfie Haaland was never the same player. He did play 45 minutes for Norway against Bulgaria a few days later, and he played 68 minutes for City as they beat West Ham 1–0 the weekend after. That summer he had an operation on his left knee – not the one struck by Keane – but he never fully recovered. He made a few brief substitute appearances for City the next season, but his body was no longer able to play professional football. Attempts at bringing legal action against Keane never amounted to anything, but Haaland has continued to suggest that Keane's tackle ended his career. 'Did that tackle end my career? Well, I never played a full game again, did I? It seems like a great coincidence, don't you think?' he told the *Daily Mail* in 2008.

As his professional career came to an end, Alfie Haaland and his family moved back to Bryne. He sat on the board of Bryne FK for a time, and became the club's sporting director for a few seasons. He involved himself in both local business and local politics. For a period he worked for Aarbakke, the company that a couple of generations ago made horseshoes for the farmers of Jæren but is now a leading machining company that provides equipment for the oil industry. He then started working as a player agent. But eventually his primary occupation became looking after one of the best footballers in the world: his son.

4

THE BOY

On Wednesday, 26 July 2000, Bryne's local paper, *Jærbladet*, carried a small notice that could have been easily missed if you weren't looking carefully. Just 18 words and a number. But one suspects this tiny notice will one day find its way into a display at some kind of local museum. It read, simply: '*Leeds, England, 21 juli. Astor og Gabrielle har fått ein bror. Gry Marita Braut og Alf Inge Rasdal Håland.*' Astor and Gabrielle have a brother, signed by the parents, Gry Marita Braut and Alfie Haaland.

The sporting pedigree of Erling Haaland's father is well known, but perhaps not enough is made of his mother. Gry Marita Braut was also an outstanding athlete in her youth. In 1992 she became a Norwegian champion at the heptathlon for her age group, 17–18. Heptathlon, for the uninitiated, is an athletics contest made up of seven events, which are contested over two days. The seven events are the 100-metre hurdles, high jump, shot put, 200-metre sprint, long jump, javelin throw and the 800-metre middle-distance run. Succeeding at the heptathlon obviously requires a finely balanced physique, combining both explosive strength and speed. But becoming competitive at the heptathlon also requires huge amounts of patience and determination, as the athlete has to put in the hours to master the intricate skill involved in the events. Being a national champion at heptathlon for her age group was no small achievement. Gry Marita Braut's mother, Erling Haaland's grandmother, was also an accomplished athlete in her day. In fact, the records for the local athletics club in Bryne show not only club records for young girls set by Gry Marita Braut in the 1980s, but others set by her mother, Inger Åse Braut, in the 1960s. In addition, Inger Åse Braut's brother, Erling Haaland's great-uncle, is none other than Gabriel Høyland: the Burnley-supporting farmer who played almost 600 games for Bryne and 23 for his country. In short, on his father's side both his grandfather and father played for Bryne, and his father played at a World Cup and played for three storied Premier League clubs. On his mother's side, both his mother and grandmother were exceptional athletes in their youth and his great-uncle is Bryne's greatest player of all time. Some family to be born into. Some pedigree. As one of his future coaches would later note wryly: Erling Haaland was not designed to sit still.

Erling was born just over a month after Alfie's transfer to Manchester City had been confirmed, and with Alfie playing for City until he retired because of injury in 2003, young Erling's first steps, first run and first kick of the ball all happened in a Manchester City household. There's no shortage of photographs in which young Erling is donning a Manchester City shirt – photos that today seem amusingly prophetic. Alfie's former teammate, both for Norway and very briefly at City, Egil Østenstad, was and remains a close friend of the family, and he remembers Erling showing a competitive spirit early on. 'I've known him really since he was very small and we still lived in England,' Østenstad told the *Heia Fotball* podcast in 2019. 'I have pictures at home of him playing with a ball, both him and my daughters, because we spent a lot of time together back then when we lived in England,' Østenstad says.

> He has a temper. He has tamed it a bit now, but he could be very, very sulky when things didn't go his way. It's not that many years ago, really. But I think that temperament is something that will help him become very good.

The unfortunate and premature end to Alfie Haaland's career meant that the family moved back home, which meant that young Erling grew up in idyllic surroundings in Bryne. His fourth grade (Year 6) teacher, Andreas Vollsund, remembers Erling well. 'He was a fun kid. A lively guy,' Vollsund says. He uses a particular Norwegian phrase, '*Han hadde lopper i blodet*', which literally translates to 'he had fleas in his blood' – a common way to describe someone who is a bit restless and who doesn't particularly enjoy sitting still for long periods of time. 'He had a lot of friends, there were a lot of fun things about him. He was lively, energetic, extrovert.' Vollsund, who in 2020 became the local mayor at the age of just 34, is himself an accomplished amateur sportsman. In his twenties he helped Lye, a local floorball team – a kind of indoor hockey popular in Scandinavia – gain promotion to that sport's national top division. He recognised early that Erling had some unusual qualities:

> He had an incredible winning mentality, all the way from when he was a child in my classroom. He wanted to be the best. I remember he told me, he didn't care about school at all, because he was going to be a footballer like his father.

I tried telling him that school is the important thing and he had to prioritise school, but he didn't want to.

Vollsund laughs. 'So I told him that at least you owe me some tickets if you make it big. And he came through on that one when I went to see him play for Dortmund.'

Erling Haaland won't have been the first primary school pupil in the world to say they wanted to become a footballer, but according to Vollsund there did seem to be something more behind his words than typical boyhood dreams.

Listen, you, me and everyone could say that they want to become a footballer. But you could tell by looking at the boy that he really meant it. And that's what's so impressive, he has an incredible winning mentality and he had an X-factor to him.

As a child Erling Haaland tried different sports in addition to football, which he started playing at the age of five. He played handball for a few years, did some athletics and even tried a bit of golf. But there was never much doubt that football would end up becoming his preferred sport. He was moved up a year group and became part of a strong youth team at Bryne, with several other kids who ended up becoming professional footballers too. These included Tord Salte, who was sold to Lyon as a 16-year-old before later coming back and having a career in Norwegian club football. He played with Andreas Ueland, who later played with the University of Virginia in the United States and, in May 2023, joined Chicago Fire. And he played with Andrea Norheim, who moved to Lyon's prestigious women's team before returning to Scandinavia and becoming a league champion in Sweden with Piteå in 2018. For many years she played with the boys' team at Bryne, which she later credited with helping her reach a high level as a player. But Norheim also recalls that young Erling had to work on controlling his emotions.

'He is someone who had an infectious good mood when things were going well,' she told Norwegian TV channel TV2.

At those times he was very happy and it was fun to play with him. But if things didn't go well it wasn't as fun to play with him. He would be very sulky and unhappy. That could be a negative influence, though he did improve as he got older. He was advised that this was something he had to work on. I remember thinking that he could become very good, but not unless he stops becoming so upset when things are going wrong.

Norheim then stressed that the young Erling was ordinarily a very kind and nice person.

In addition to playing with his regular team at Bryne, Erling Haaland was also invited to spend time with a very ambitious youth team from Fyllingsdalen, a borough of the city of Bergen some 140 miles up the coast from Bryne. The U-14s at Fyllingsdalen was an unusual team: they had attempted to attract the most promising kids in the Bergen area, and when they played in youth tournaments abroad they invited certain prospects from other parts of the country as well. To create an elite group like this for such a young age group was not something that went down particularly well in the Norwegian football community at the time. 'It was as if we were going to be arrested,' David Nielsen, one of the architects behind the project, would later joke. Nielsen, a Dane, had a long career in Scandinavian football as a player and was working as an assistant manager of a team in Bergen back in 2011 when he had the idea to try to create something of an elite U-14 team. 'The regional FA, the FA, etc. They acted as if we'd done something totally illegal. But the parents who had their kids with us, for them it was as good as it could be. A perfect scenario,' he told TV2. In the autumn of 2013 this controversial outfit took part in a tournament for U-14 teams in Madrid, facing the likes of Juventus and Real Madrid.

'With the kids we had visiting, it was almost like we were a national team when we went abroad,' Nielsen says. With a forward partnership of Erling Haaland and Noah Holm, David Nielsen's son who now plays for Rosenborg in the Norwegian league, the Fyllingsdalen U-14s beat Juventus' U-14 team 2–1. Against Real Madrid they lost 3–0. 'Nothing is more important than being as close to your dream as possible when you're 10, 11, 12 years old,' insists Nielsen.

It's about finding out what level the best players are at, and what we have to do to play against them, whether we win or lose. And then you go home and train for a year and go again. When we came back from those tournaments, we knew what we needed to get better at. It was intensity, phys-ical duels, not technical stuff.

Shortly after this Nielsen became the head coach at Strømsgodset, and in 2014 he gave current Arsenal and Norway captain Martin Ødegaard his senior debut in the Norwegian top division when Ødegaard was just 15 years old.

I've coached both Erling Haaland and Martin Ødegaard, and I can tell you one thing: you don't have to wonder if those kids are any good. And you can't hold them back for even a second, and not give them opportunities against the best.

But the team at Fyllingsdalen was very much an outlier, both in terms of how youth football in Norway works and for Erling Haaland. From the age of five and until the age of 16 he played his football primarily with Bryne, and for most of those years he played under a coach whose approach to youth football was radically different to that of Nielsen and the Fyllingsdalen experiment. There is one coach who has spent more time training Erling Haaland than any other, and his name is Alf Ingve Berntsen.

5

THE PROJECT

Norway has a total area of around 150,000 square miles, which makes its landmass almost 40 per cent larger than that of the UK. But where the UK has a population of some 68 million, the population of Norway is just 5.4 million. Oslo now has just over 1 million inhabitants, but outside of the capital there are only a handful of cities with more than 100,000 inhabitants. In short, most Norwegians live in smaller cities and towns, most of which are quite spread out geographically. This has implications for football, and talent development in particular. In the UK there is typically a clear divide between grassroots, community clubs and elite clubs with their academies. In Norway it's almost all grassroots, but some of the grassroots clubs also happen to have a very good first team, and some of them play professional football.

Only a small number of clubs from the cities have academies comparable to what you would see at British football clubs. And the challenge for the rest, the small town and village clubs, has always been the same: how do you run your youth teams in a way that includes as many kids as possible, regardless of ability, while at the same time providing the challenges that the more talented kids require to develop? Typically children will start playing organised football at around 5–6 years old, and they will be coached by parents and volunteers until they are well into their teens. Some of these parents will have a solid footballing background or some type of coaching credential, but inevitably the quality of the coaching will vary greatly from club to club. Even at Bryne, a club with a proud history for its size, much of this work will be done by volunteers of varying pedigree. Though, for the generation of Bryne kids born in 1999, things were a little bit different.

Alf Ingve Berntsen was an experienced coach who by day worked as a teacher at the local secondary school teaching sports to adolescents in their late teens. But in 2006 he decided to coach youth football at Bryne. 'I fell into it because I had twin boys,' Berntsen explains.

> I had been coaching the first team at Klepp, who were in the third tier at the time. I coached them for two years and that went really well. But my boys were sad that I was always going off to coach Klepp rather than watch them. So I thought I'd do a year or two. Which ended up being 10 with the best ones, and 13 with the more recreational players.

Berntsen decided to coach the kids and to do things a bit differently. Conventional thinking would suggest that there is a fundamental difference between youth coaching aimed at making the best players as good as possible and youth coaching aimed at inclusivity and keeping as many children active for as long as possible. As many as possible on the one hand, as good as possible on the other. Berntsen rejected this, and instead embraced a supposedly contradictory motto: as many as possible, as long as possible, as good as possible.

Berntsen wasn't the only coach with a solid football background who worked with the group. Stig Nordheim and Leif Rune Salte, two players from Bryne's 1987 Cup-winning team, both had children in the group. As did Roger Eskeland, who played more than 500 games in goal for Bryne. And then there was Alfie Haaland, whose son Erling was actually born in 2000 but was moved up a year to play with the kids from the 1999 generation. Berntsen was also joined by two coaching and teaching colleagues, Espen Undheim and Arne Tjåland. 'We had a very good group of parents. The reason I've become almost a kind of spokesperson is that I was there the entire time,' Berntsen says.

> I had the UEFA A-licence before I started with them. Before that I was educated as an economist, but I got bored with that so I went over to the Norwegian School of Sport Sciences and got a bachelor's degree in sports and physiology. So I had that background, as well as experience from coaching, when I started this project.

They started out with a group of 39 boys and one girl, and the group stayed more or less the same for ten years. Out of the 40 children involved, five ended up playing for the Norwegian national team at various age groups. For 12.5 per cent of players from one such group to be called up is unusual, to say the least. In footballing terms, Norway is divided into 18 regions, and from the age of 13 onwards the most promising players from each region are occasionally invited to train and play with each other in something called a *kretslag*. Think of it as a kind of regional youth all-star team. Out of the 40 players

technique. There was a greater emphasis on drills that would resemble situations that happen on the pitch, and there would be a greater element of competition in drills. Half the time was still spent playing small-sided games, but now the coaches would be more careful to balance out the teams and start to give the more talented kids more difficult challenges. Behaviour became even more important at that age, and the coaches introduced yellow and red cards.

When the players turned 13, training started to become even more focused. In the years between the ages of 13 and 15, there was a big emphasis on increasing the tempo in practice sessions. This would apply both to passes and to regaining the ball after possession is lost. Berntsen and his coaches had an awareness that a young player who wants to go far will have to focus a lot on stops and starts, changes of direction and moving the ball quickly and accurately. Drills became more specific and more competitive.

But adolescence, specifically at this age, also brings a range of new challenges. 'When they hit puberty and really start growing, you have to hold some of them back,' Berntsen says.

Not all of them, but some will have trouble. When they're through that growth spurt you have to start with periodisation, which is when you start judging the physical load of the individual players. If a player has had a very tough session or a game the day before he can still train today, but maybe he has to train a bit less. Some people will get their growth spurt when they're 12–13, some when they're 16–17. So in a group of 14-year-olds you might have some who can handle any kind of training load, they can do whatever they want, but others have to be more careful, and others still have to be handled according to periodisation principles.

Judging all of this is part of the skill of a youth coach, and in this area, with the coaches we had, we were very strong. So when Erling now is big and strong, but also athletic and dynamic is his movements, part of that is because he's done this his entire life. Start-stop, high intensity, variation.

One of the most easily recognisable and remarkable things about Erling Haaland now is his speed and how he combines his imposing size and strength with rapid sprints. While watching Haaland in full sprint, there can be a part of your brain that struggles to accept that a player that size is moving at that speed. But Berntsen points out that speed is only one part of the equation. 'His acceleration is one thing, there are a lot of athletes out there who are big and who can accelerate,' he says.

> Usain Bolt is very fast over 100 metres, but after the 100 metres sprint he needs 40 to stop. Erling can only use 1 metre to stop and then he has to change direction. That's something you can practise, and something that's important to practise. What is unusual about him is that he is able to translate his physique into football movements. I think he has trained very smartly in key periods. Especially when it comes to start, stop and change of direction.

With a very strong group of young players, Berntsen and his team always resisted the temptation to put the best ones together and create a team that would conquer all before them.

The way the kids' league was organised, initially it was 5v5. At that time we had seven teams. So for games we picked the seven kids who were the furthest ahead in their develop-ment, and split them across the seven teams, then the next seven, and so on. Then we got to age 11–12 and you play 7v7, then we had five teams. Again, for the games we picked the five best kids and put them on five separate teams. Then we get to 13, and we play 11v11. From then on we had two teams in the elite, and one and a half teams, one 11v11 and one 7v7 that were more recreational. So we had fourteen kids in each of the two elite teams, and those two teams were evenly balanced. In training all 40 were fully mixed. The first season when they were 13, our elite teams finished second and fourth in their league. When they were 14 they finished second and third in the league. So we had 28 play-ers who got to test themselves at a good level. But it was as important to us that both those teams had five players who all really stood out, and were able to shine much more than if they had just been one out of ten very good players on one elite team. And it gave them a bigger challenge.

Having a mixed group of players demands a lot of the coaches. Within the framework of the group, children of differing abilities need differ-ent challenges and types of feedback.

People would tell us that we had to spend more time with the most talented kids, but the point is that we did spend a lot of time with them as well. Differentiating also means that you give different feedback to different kids. But the aim with any training session wasn't that Erling or someone else should score a lot of nice goals, it was that at the end of a training session all 40 kids should have a feeling that it was good that they came. That was my most important job, to give them that feeling. Regardless of whether or not they strike the ball cleanly. It supersedes everything else. So if I'm speaking to number 39 or 40 and I say 'good to see you', but before I've finished my sentence I've turned around to watch Erling score a goal, kids will see through that straight away. You have to fully commit to it, and that can be a challenge.

'We could have put all the best ones into one team and travelled around showing them off,' Berntsen says.

Twice a year we were invited to elite tournaments against good academy teams from bigger clubs, where we would bring our strongest team. We went to eight of those tournaments and won seven. We won a tournament hosted by Stabæk, against Brann, Stabæk, a few others, and we were almost annoyed. Because we were playing against clubs that had tried to assemble all the best young players in their entire region, whereas we had a team of classmates from little Bryne. People forget what a small place Bryne is. If you gather the most promising kids in a region like Stavanger, with 150,000 people, you have to do a lot of things wrong at the same time for them not to be a good team.

Putting all the most promising kids in one team may have yielded even better results in the games, but it may actually have harmed their development. After all, if Bryne's best team of 14-year-olds won every game 7–0, their defenders wouldn't have learned much about defending. And Berntsen points out that there is an important social aspect to this as well:

Typically in the past you would start splitting up teams in the last year of primary school, when they're 13. And you know yourself how everything changes in secondary school. Totally different world, hormones, people can feel insecure even if they act tough on the outside. So that's when football can be the most important thing in your life. If you take that moment to break teams up according to ability, you get kids who are told they can no longer play with their mates, and you can end up ruining friendships that way. And so in that regard I think we have other considerations to bear in mind than just footballing ability. We kept them all together in training when they were 13 and 14, and the year they turned 15 they were allowed to choose for themselves. We ended up with 20 who wanted to play with the recreational team, which was two training sessions a week and games in a weaker league. And 20 who wanted to play with the elite teams, which meant four training sessions a week and games at a higher level. And we let them decide for themselves. But even then, when they were 15–16, the training session on Monday was with everyone together. The rest of the week they were separate, but on Mondays they'd all meet in the dressing room first and then have warm-ups together, before then playing and doing different exercises separately. But at that point they'd stayed together for those very formative years when they're 13 and 14 and they'd formed those very strong bonds.

This may all sound very theoretical, but it has real-world consequences. Erling Haaland is still close friends with a handful of old teammates from his youth team days, friendships that no doubt helped him create some kind of normality within the maelstrom of pressure and attention he now has to live in. But not all of those friends played in the elite team with him when they were young. If they had been separated and forced to train with different teams, as would have happened in other places or in years prior, would they still be friends today?

These days, Alf Ingve Berntsen is asked about Erling Haaland often. Very, very often. And he is keen to strike a balance between taking pride in his work and the successful outcome of the project, while making it clear that he isn't taking credit for Haaland's success.

> It's Erling who deserves credit for Erling. It's not us, it's not Bryne or anyone else. He had good genes, he grew up in a good place, but a lot of kids have those two things. He's the one who has done the hard work. But we were important, the team, the coaches, myself, we were important for him during formative years from when he was 8 to when he was 15–16. Those years really shape you as a person. And in a sense he was lucky that he was with us, because we were well educated and we knew what we were doing. But first and foremost it's about him, he has made the sacrifices and done the hard work.

The first time Erling Haaland trained with this group he was just five and a half years old. His father brought him along and asked if he could play with the boys that were a year older, and the coaches agreed. Little Erling immediately started scoring goals. For the next few years he mostly played with kids his own age, but gradually it became clear that he needed to train at a slightly higher level.

When he was moved up to us [it] was because he wasn't being pushed enough in his own age group. Erling could be a challenge, but the best ones are often challenging. I had to be strict with him, but it was done with heart and with warmth, and Erling understood this. If he had been somewhere else where maybe the adults had been afraid to intervene because his father [had] played in the Premier League – and that can be very difficult – then that could have been an issue. But it was good that he was in a group where there was discipline and where demands were made of him in terms of following the rules. And he wasn't a difficult kid, he wasn't a problem at all.

In fact, Berntsen describes Erling in almost the same words that Erling's former teacher, Andreas Vollsund, used: 'Totally normal kid, a bit restless.' And like Erling's former teacher, Berntsen couldn't help but notice that young Erling was unusually determined to reach his goals.

He didn't care about established truths. What do you think happened when Erling was 12 and started telling people he was going to be a footballer? What do you think they told him? 'Think about it. You're from Bryne. There are so many good players out there in Brazil and Argentina and Germany and Holland, you don't stand a chance.' But he didn't care, and to not care about that and to believe to the bottom of his soul … There's nothing unusual about 12-year-old boys who say that they want to become footballers, but you could see in his eyes that there was a conviction there. It wasn't just something he said, he believed in it totally, with every fibre of his being.

Jærhallen, the indoor venue built on the ashes of the old dance hall that had burned down in 2001, provided a perfect arena for young Erling to train and develop. Though Berntsen insists that some press reports about this contain a fair bit of embellishment. 'I've seen some people say that Erling was there every day, at all hours of the day, which is bullshit,' he scoffs.

Jærhallen is rented out from Monday morning to Friday evening, it's full. But it's never locked, so it's always available for use Saturday and Sunday. They built it between 2004 and 2005, when my kids were five and Erling was four. They started going there when they were 7–8 years old, and Jærhallen was still very new. During the weekends it was much better for them to have fun on their own than me interfering with sensible exercises. That's when you get the quantity of repetitions, and we bring the quality of the work in training during the week. We can show them and give advice. And then we played a lot of football at a high tempo from a young age, with offside.

Erling was quick at a young age, and he had an eye for goal. But he was still light and skinny, and against boys one year older he had to learn how to be clever.

Erling played against Tord Salte and Andreas Ueland, two defenders who both ended up as youth internationals for Norway. Erling wasn't small, he was normal height, but he was skinny. He was too good for his age group, so he started training with us. There he met Ueland and Salte, and when you're playing against good defenders, with normal rules, offside, high tempo, for him to even get chances in front of goal he had to develop a smartness. If we didn't use the offside rule he could have just stood 10 metres ahead of everyone else and waited for the ball, and that wouldn't have taught him anything.

The fact that he didn't have outstanding physical characteristics is often brought up as part of the secret to Erling Haaland's success. After all, if you learn to be sneaky, to find space in the box without any physical advantages, and you suddenly grow up and become both faster and stronger than almost everyone else, well, you become the complete package. But Berntsen insists that early physical development doesn't have to be a drawback either, it's all about the coaching.

You have kids who develop early, and if people bear that in mind with their coaching programme then that doesn't have to be a drawback. If Erling had been unusually big, strong and fast when he was 13, like he is now, and we had just used him as a striker to run in behind all the time, that would have been downright destructive for his development. It's not a problem to develop early, it's not a problem to be good early, but it can be a problem if you have coaches who don't plan accordingly.

Either way, Erling Haaland developed a unique instinct in the penalty box to go with his physical gifts. But his old coach is keen to remind us that no one is born with this kind of instinct:

He says he plays on instinct, but that instinct is not something he was born with. No one is a goal scorer at birth.

It's based on what he's been doing for many many years. When we say instinct, what we actually mean is that we're acting based on what we've experienced before. He is very good at varying his movements, which is important because if you make the same run all the time the defenders will figure you out. But if we had a situation in training where you have a cross coming in, maybe we'd stop the training and ask him 'when the ball is coming in from the left here, and there are two defenders, where is the best place for you to be?' We very rarely stopped, we very rarely gave specific instructions, but occasionally we might stop and ask 'when the defenders are where they are now, what is a good place for you to be?' And then explain that, for instance, if you're in a certain spot then the defender has to turn to see you, but the defender also has to follow the ball, so you make it more difficult for him.

On a laptop in his living room, Berntsen shows a video of a young Erling scoring a goal in training in Jærhallen, and then the next video is of a grown Erling scoring a goal for Dortmund in the Bundesliga. They are, movement for movement, the exact same goal. 'It's identical. Through ball, Haaland is lurking, the same finish. It's identical.'

But coaching Erling was not always easy. 'When you work with a group like this you have to find out not just how good each of the kids are at football, but also what kind of feedback they respond to,' Berntsen explains.

Erling didn't respond well to being told off. It was better to explain things to him. We had as a principle that the team is always the most important thing. You are allowed to dribble of course, and it's OK to lose the ball, but when you do you have to work hard to win it back. If Erling dribbled and lost the ball and just stopped, we'd sub him. We never told him off, but we asked him 'What had we agreed on here? That we're going to try to regain the ball straight away. Why? Because if not then your teammates have to spend extra energy just because you didn't. It's OK to make mistakes, but you have to contribute.' There would be little things like that, there always are, but you have to figure out what kind of feedback works for each person. With Erling, telling him off didn't work well.

As well as being unusually determined, young Erling also had an unusually strong will to win. The flipside of that was that when he didn't win, he would show his frustration more than other kids and more than what some Norwegian coaches might be used to seeing. 'People misunderstood his will to win and his attitude,' says Berntsen.

That people are angry when they lose, I think that's a good thing. But then we teach them how to behave. You still have to shake your opponent's hand afterwards. And if you're a youth coach you have to understand what young people are like, that a 13- and 14-year-old brain isn't the same as the brain of a 19-, 20- or 22-year-old. I think that's really important.

There's an old saying in Norway: *'Tap og vinn med samme sinn.'* It literally translates to 'lose and win with the same mind,' the idea being that you should try to regulate your mood, your reactions, that you should have the same attitude after a game whether you've won or lost. Berntsen acknowledges that even from a young age, that simply wouldn't work for Erling Haaland. He would show his frustration, but he would put it to good use. 'Someone like him will just use a defeat as motivation to work even harder. And to encourage this we have to make sure someone like him faces resistance and challenges in training and in games.'

Berntsen's approach to youth coaching – the idea that you be inclusive, yet at the same time differentiate your methods within the group to provide each child with the right level of challenge – hasn't been met with universal approval, even in Norway. That you can keep the youngsters together for such a long time, rather than split the ambitious kids from the more casual participants: 'People say it was a form of overkindness,' Berntsen says, slightly exasperated.

> But it's not being overkind to teach kids how to deal with different kinds of situations. Some say it doesn't make them tough enough to handle what awaits them if they actually become footballers. Well, Erling certainly seems tough enough. Even if he was taught how to behave, he can still be cynical. Because at his level, he has to be. You have to be incredibly tough mentally.

Berntsen spent years coaching a youngster who ended up becoming one of the best players on the planet, something most youth coaches can only dream of. And while he is happy to talk about his methodology, a way of working that he passionately believes in, he is reluctant to take any credit for Erling Haaland's ultimate success. He repeatedly stresses that 'Erling is responsible for Erling,' that his success is down to his unique physique, mentality and his desire to work hard. And he also points to the role of Erling's father, Alfie. 'He stayed away totally from training in the beginning,' Berntsen recalls.

But he came to watch matches, and I'm sure they had discussions among themselves. And when Erling started becoming very good, Alfie could prepare him for what was to come. What does it mean to be a professional footballer? When you move away to Molde and Salzburg, what do you have to do to get by and to be accepted? What are the dangers, what do you have to be wary of? So the advice he got from Alfie when he started getting good will have been extremely important. If training had been terrible I'm sure he would have gotten involved, but he could see that Erling was enjoying himself and improving, so there was no need to intervene.

But Berntsen does, almost reluctantly, accept that it wasn't a bad place for young Erling to learn how to play football.

I started being invited to hold lectures about our way of working in 2015, after the local newspaper had an article about us. That article focused more on how many kids were still playing and how few had quit, rather than how good some of them were. And when I was invited to various clubs to hold a lecture, I was often told that our way of working would sabotage the most talented kids. At least now I can say that we didn't exactly ruin Erling.

He is asked often, perhaps too often for his own liking, if he's proud of Erling's success. 'It doesn't matter to me if Erling plays for Manchester City or for Hognestad,' Berntsen insists.

My job with him was the same as with everyone else, to help him become a better footballer. But first and foremost we wanted to develop the human being. People ask me if I'm proud of Erling because he is scoring so many goals. I say no, I'm not proud that he's scoring so many goals. I'm happy for him that he is doing something he wants to do and is good at. But what will make me proud is if he behaves according to the values we had.

6

PROGRESS

Not a huge number of people will remember Erling Haaland's first few minutes of first-team football. He was subbed on for Bryne in the 69th minute of a 1–0 defeat away to Ranheim, in front of an attendance of just 549. It was 12 May 2016, and Erling Haaland was still just 15 years old. The manager who gave him his debut, Gaute Larsen, was sacked two days later. It was seven games into the season and Bryne had picked up just six points from them. Things were not well at the club. Alf Ingve Berntsen was put in charge of the first team, so for the next game, four days later, Erling Haaland started. Usually in the story of Erling Haaland, with a build-up like that, the payoff will be a goal or even a hat-trick. But this was very early in his career, he had yet to grow into himself, was far from the finished article, and he was playing for a deeply dysfunctional team. Bryne lost 1–0 again.

Author and football writer Nils Henrik Smith, a Bryne native and prolific contributor to the prestigious *Josimar* magazine, was in the stands when Haaland made his home debut against KFUM a few days later. 'I remember that I had heard of him already. I had heard that Alfie Haaland had a son who was a big prospect,' says Smith. 'But I did take it with a pinch of salt initially because, well, the rumour that Alfie Haaland had a son who was an outstanding striker, that didn't seem very feasible.' Alfie Haaland is many things, but a prolific goal scorer is not one of them. The *Guardian* once described Haaland senior as 'a workaday defender/midfielder with a face like pastry, little discernible skill and a huge heart', which is more than a little harsh. But certainly the idea that Alfie Haaland has somehow sired and reared a goal-scoring phenomenon initially seemed a bit strange. As if David Batty's son had become a swashbuckling number ten with perfect technique and vision, or Michael Dawson had fathered a fleet-footed winger with blinding skill. Either way, the rumours of young Erling's potential had preceded his full debut.

He was already known to people such as Smith in part because of a couple of games he'd played for the Norwegian U-15s the year before. In September 2015, the Norwegian U-15s were coached by the former Chelsea defender Erland Johnsen. Johnsen later revealed that they strongly considered leaving Haaland out of the squad for that camp. 'He was incredibly inconsistent. And players are, at that age,' he told TV2 in October 2020. Erling Haaland had started to grow taller, which in the short term can have a very detrimental effect on your footballing ability. 'Erling had suddenly grown 10 centimetres in eight or nine months, and then your technique will be all wrong, your coordination will be all wrong, all of it.' Johnsen remembered, 'We were really discussing if Erling should even be called up to the squad for the next camp, because some on the coaching staff felt he had just been hopeless. But we decided to give him another chance.' It was not a bad decision. As part of the training camp the Norwegian U-15 team was going to play a double-header against Sweden. In the first game

Norway lost 4–2, but Haaland played well and scored both goals. In the second game Sweden took the lead in the first half, but after the break young Erling went to work. After a quick conversation with his strike partner Erik Botheim, Botheim rolled the kick-off towards Haaland, who scored – direct from the centre circle. The Swedish goalkeeper was dawdling, and Erling saw his opportunity. 'He is totally insane,' Botheim later told TV2. 'Who thinks of shooting from there? That's why he's so good.' Haaland would add another goal, and Norway won 3–1. Haaland and Botheim ended up becoming close friends.

In fact, Botheim would become one of Erling Haaland's most recognisable friends, for a deeply strange reason. Just under a year after their kick-off goal heroics, Haaland and Botheim were again away on Norway duty. This time they were in Poland with the U-16s. On 30 August 2016 Haaland, Botheim and defender Erik Tobias Sandberg uploaded a somewhat baffling music track to YouTube under the name Flow Kingz. The track, titled 'Kygo jo', in reference to popular Norwegian DJ and music producer Kygo, shows the three displaying what one could politely call varying degrees of competence behind the microphone, with choreography to match. But this is exactly what makes the track so endearing. Young Erling in particular looks distinctly gawky and awkward, and it is to his eternal credit that even after becoming a global superstar he saw no particular need to have the video taken down. The track currently has 11 million views on YouTube. It remains the only video released on YouTube by the Flow Kingz account, but they have over 75,000 subscribers waiting patiently for more. On the day the video was uploaded, the Norwegian U-16s beat Latvia 3–0, with Botheim scoring a hat-trick and all three members of Flow Kingz playing 90 minutes.

Home at Bryne, 'Alfie's son' had been a familiar face around the clubhouse for years. Rógvi Baldvinsson, who was born in the Faroe

Islands but grew up not far from Bryne, remembers a then 13-year-old Erling Haaland making an impression all the way back in 2013. 'He has always been confident.' Baldvinsson laughs.

> Back in 2013, Bryne had their best season in the last ten years and we nearly got promoted. You had some real characters in the team, some good players like Marius Lode and Anders Kristiansen who ended up going further. But young Erling would just stroll around the clubhouse like it was his front room. Of course we knew who he was, he was Alfie's son. But he was always a very confident person. I remember, and this is from when he got older as well, that he would speak to everyone as if they were his friend. Whether that was Edith the cleaner, new people who had just arrived or the CEO of the club. He saw everyone and would speak to everyone in the same way, and only nice things. That's the way he's always been. For me it warms my heart to see people who are like this.

Baldvinsson moved clubs a few times before returning to Bryne, and wasn't part of the team when Haaland made his debut. But he does remember noticing in training that there was something unusual about the young striker.

> My first memory of Erling and training with him [was] out back here on the artificial turf … and he missed a big chance. And one of the older players in the squad really had a go at him, shouting something like 'for fuck's sake, Erling, what are you doing?!' Which of course is totally normal in football and in training. And Erling was disappointed. But

afterwards he immediately wanted the ball again. And he didn't keep it simple, he wanted the ball and tried to dribble someone. Just to have that mentality when you're 15–16 years old, and you're playing with grown men, you don't see that every day. It's something you notice. He doesn't talk back or anything, he's just in his own bubble and focused on doing better next time. And you see this now in England. He misses an open goal on his debut, is ridiculed, and then he goes on to set records in his first season. He has that mentality, he doesn't let things affect him.

Young Erling kept getting minutes for Bryne's first team over the summer of 2016, but the team kept struggling. For all his experience with youth coaching and coaching teams at a lower level, Berntsen was unable to steady the ship and won just one game in nine. Acknowledging that he hadn't been able to improve the team as he had hoped, Berntsen resigned. Between June and late August the team went ten games without a win. Being a 15-year-old striker in a team that's in free fall, getting most of your minutes off the bench, is not an easy job. Nils Henrik Smith remembers this period well.

He was quick and he made many smart runs, but he played for a team that wasn't functioning at all, and where all the passes came either at the wrong time or into the wrong space – which in a way is the same thing. He made a lot of runs but rarely got the ball, that's very much the story of the games he played for Bryne.

While young Erling was having a frustrating time when he got on the pitch for the first team, he was very productive indeed for Bryne's second team. Bryne 2 were playing in the fourth tier of Norwegian football at the time, not exactly the highest level, but 15-year-old Erling was still very much a skinny boy playing against grown men. A skinny and increasingly lanky boy who showed two qualities the world would become familiar with soon enough: his turn of pace and his eye for goal. In 2016 he was involved in 11 games for Bryne's second tier and scored no less than 16 goals. There are few secrets in football when it comes to talented young players, and if the son of a former national team and Premier League player starts putting up numbers like this, even for a reserve team, people quickly notice. Haaland's four goals and impressive performances in the two games against the Swedish U-15s the year before are unlikely to have gone unnoticed by the talent-scouting fraternity either. So while the Bryne first team continued to struggle and looked like they were heading for relegation to the third tier, things started moving in the background. A demotion from the second tier would be a disaster for the small but proud football club, but it would also mean that Erling Haaland would have to move on. He was developing fast, and having shown emphatically that the fourth tier was way too easy for him, it was unthinkable that he would stay and play for Bryne in the third tier for a full season. The question was: where to next?

It was the first huge career decision Erling had to make, along with his ever-present father. Already at this point he could have gone abroad, with German Bundesliga club Hoffenheim showing serious interest. FC Copenhagen, the biggest club in Scandinavia, was also interested. Ominous rumours of interest from Viking have never been officially confirmed, but it is hard to imagine the Haaland family going to Bryne's local rivals. The decision, in the end, was to move to Molde and play under Ole Gunnar Solskjær, and on 1 February 2017 Molde announced the signing of Erling Haaland. 'Erling is a versatile attacking player, but first and foremost a talented striker with many abilities in front of goal,' Ole Gunnar Solskjær said on the player's arrival. 'He visited us in the autumn and gave a very good impression. He is still young, he will make big strides with our many promising players, and he is a boy we hope we can develop into a top player.'

Erling himself was fairly candid in a brief interview with the local radio back in Bryne after the transfer, explaining that he and his father had been impressed by their visit to Molde:

> It was nice that Molde wanted me and that they wanted me to come and train with them, I agreed to do that. So me and my dad went up there to look at the facilities. I trained with them for a couple of days to see what that was like. We were impressed with the conditions there, we thought this could be good.

He also reiterated that his father's advice had been a big part of the decision.

> He thought it was a very professional set-up. He's helped me a lot and he pointed to Molde as something that could be very good for my development. There were a few other clubs who wanted me, but I felt in the end that Molde was the best fit … you can see that they put a lot of emphasis on developing young players.

Erling also said that he had a lot of belief in Molde's coaching staff. 'I think this could be good,' he concluded. He wasn't wrong.

7

TANTE

Idrettsgallaen is an annual awards ceremony hosted in early January by the Norwegian Olympic and Paralympic Committee and Confederation of Sports. There have been exceptions, but these awards tend to be the domain of skiers. Football may be a huge sport in Norway in terms of interest and participation, but Norway has produced few world champions and few footballers who can truly match the success the nation's skiers enjoy on the world stage. That said, the 'Name of the Year' award, the ceremony's most coveted, has in the past been won by boxer Cecilia Brækhus, chess champion Magnus Carlsen, the entire women's national handball team and cyclists like Thor Hushovd and Alexander Kristoff. The award has been handed out since 2001, but for over two decades no footballer had won the prize. Until, unsurprisingly, Erling Haaland claimed it in 2023. But this was not Erling Haaland's first appearance at the glitzy award ceremony; in January 2020 he appeared via video from Dortmund's mid-season training camp in Spain to accept an award for 'Breakthrough of the Year'. Haaland, still a bit media shy, thanked his former coach Ole Gunnar Solskjær at Molde, but then proceeded to puzzle a good number of viewers by thanking 'Tante' for cooking him good food, which he said caused him to grow *grævla godt*.

Grævla, first of all, is a word that requires some explanation. It's a local expletive from the southwest of Norway, and a word particularly favoured by Haaland. It is just a couple of letters away from *Jævla*, which is one of the more serious swear words in the Norwegian language. According to Inge Særheim, a linguist from the University of Stavanger, people from this part of the country are particularly prone to finding replacement words for more commonly used expletives and swear words. 'In the Rogaland region religion has a strong position. So swear words of a religious origin have more force here,' Særheim explained to *Stavanger Aftenblad* in 2012. And so the need arises for replacement expletives that can be used more liberally. *Grævla*, being phonetically very close to a very serious swear word, is excellently suited for this, and it is a word that Haaland often turns to in his strong Jæren dialect – a dialect he has proudly refused to water down over the years. In this case *grævla godt* means 'very well', though for the full meaning of the phrase you'd do well to replace the word 'very' with another four-letter word starting with an F.

With that being established, it is clear that this 'Tante' is being given credit for Haaland's remarkable physical transformation while at Molde. Haaland told *VG* in November 2017 that he had grown '11–12 centimetres' in 2016, so when he joined Molde in January that year he was already quite tall. But he was still very skinny. According to Solskjær, Haaland had put on 10–12 kilograms in just the first nine months of 2017. 'But it's all muscle and confidence, so the boy has had a fantastic development,' Solskjær added. And in addition to all that muscle, Haaland also added another 5 centimetres of height in

2017. All of which means that in just under two years he grew almost 20 centimetres and put on over 10 kilograms of muscle. When he came home to visit his hometown of Bryne, people were baffled and amazed at what they saw. As were his teammates at Molde. 'We call him the manchild! You think he's 27, the way he plays and the way he looks,' centre-back Ruben Gabrielsen told *VG* in November 2017. Haaland, at the time, was still just 17. So who is this 'Tante'? Well, *tante* means 'aunt', but Erling Haaland wasn't talking about a blood relative in his big acceptance speech a few years later. He was talking about Molde's club chef Torbjørg Haugen.

If you get in a car and drive inland from Bryne, you soon cross over into the neighbouring county of Gjesdal. Here you leave the lowland plain of Jæren behind and the terrain becomes hillier and dotted with huge numbers of sheep. Drivers must be wary, as there are long stretches of road where sheep can occasionally take to the asphalt. Beyond Ålgård the terrain gets steeper still, and if you continue on through a narrow valley, past the village of Oltedal, you eventually reach Dirdal. Here the landscape really does look like a Norwegian tourism advert. A narrow fjord snakes its way through the landscape, with steep mountains either side. From here, at sea level, it's only a 45-minute drive into the mountains and you are in Sirdal, 600 metres above the sea level you just left behind. Sirdal is a hugely popular winter sports destination for people from Norway's southwest. A large number of families from the Stavanger and Jæren regions either have cabins here or go on day trips during the winter. This is where Torbjørg Haugen grew up, and this is where she has returned to run a small cafe towards the end of an eventful career.

Haugen, now in her sixties, is a formidable woman who exudes both authority and empathy at the same time. Before cooking food for footballers at Molde, she had a long career cooking for the very best Norwegian skiers. And as anyone who has ever watched the winter olympics will know, the best Norwegian skiers are very, very good. She ended up working in football almost by accident. 'I was at Kvitfjell with the Norwegian cross-country team, the women's team,' Haugen recalls.

> And they had a physiotherapist who was married to a phys-iotherapist who worked with Molde FK. She told me 'I wish you'd go to Molde,' and I said 'Of course.' So I travelled to Molde, and this was before Ole Gunnar Solskjær had started working there. I spoke to them about what they should be doing, that they should maybe be making more food from scratch, use as many vegetables as they can, but it wasn't so easy for the people who were there. They maybe didn't have anyone at the club who really understood how important this stuff is. They weren't used to it. So this isn't a criticism of them, it was just that they weren't used to it. I had been working with this stuff for 15 years.

The initial visit didn't amount to much, but two years later Molde hired Ole Gunnar Solskjær as their manager. One of the areas where the former Manchester United man felt the club could improve was when it came to the players' eating habits, and he invited Haugen to come back. 'I went up to spend a week there, and when I'd been there for a day or two Ole Gunnar took me aside and said, "Listen, I want to hire you."' But for Haugen, the decision to accept the offer was difficult: 'I'd just started a new job, I felt like it wasn't something that I could do. And I felt like this would be a very demanding job, and I wasn't sure I'd be able to accomplish the things I wanted to.' When Haugen left Molde again she initially sat on a plane heading for Oslo, because the Norwegian team from the 2010 Vancouver Olympics had been invited to the Royal Palace. The king of Norway, Harald V, is a huge sports enthusiast, an accomplished competitive sailor and a Tottenham Hotspur fan. While on the plane to go see the king, Haugen had a change of heart. 'I thought, you know what, I'll say yes to Ole Gunnar. This job is too interesting to turn down.' A big draw of the offer was the ability to have a more regular job. Years of travelling to training camps with skiers had taken its toll. 'I had years where I'd be away from home for 230, 240 days. I was a bit tired of that.'

When she started working for Molde, she quickly realised that methods would have to change. But this also included her own methods. 'I was meant to start at the turn of the year, but I'd promised to go to Germany with the biathlon team, so in the end I went straight to Molde from Germany and the first week was a shock to me,' she says.

> They hardly trained, compared to what I was used to! I asked them, 'are you really not going to train more than this?' I was used to the athletes eating breakfast at seven in the morning and then being out training for four to five hours. Here they came in and had breakfast at half past eight, and then they were back for lunch before noon! But of course I understood quickly that they can't train like a cross-country skier, that's not what they're preparing their bodies for. So when I first got there I realised I had to change my recipes. I was accustomed to using a good amount of cream and things like this in the cooking, because with the skiers and the biathlon guys they needed the fat. Here I definitely had to use less of that. It's a totally different sport.

But working with elite skiers had also given her a vast amount of experience of working in a high-performance environment, and there were some areas where working for a football club was a lot more pleasant.

> It's a very different way of training, and a very different job. When skiers and biathlon people travel to training camps, it's full-on. And we could end up staying far from the nearest shop, for instance. We ended up in some pretty rundown apartments and cottages. I think the footballers would have been shocked if they'd seen some of the places we stayed. Because with the skiers, they need to train at altitude. So we didn't always have much of a choice, we had to take what was available. Sometimes there weren't hotels. They plan the camps by altitude, if the competition is at a certain altitude you have to plan your camps accordingly. So you wouldn't believe some of the places we stayed, sometimes it was just crazy. Sometimes I didn't have a kitchen at all! With football you had everything.

This, one would think, would be the most basic ingredient in preparing elite athletes to do their job, but with the skiers nothing could be taken for granted.

> There was one World Championships camp, Khanty-Mansiysk in Russia, three weeks, and when I arrived in the place where the athletes were staying and where we had to cook for them, there was just nothing there! There was one sink. Not even a stove. So the first thing I had to do was get in the car, drive to town and buy an entire cooker.

The cooker was easy enough to buy, but there also wasn't a fridge. But the rooms in this compound had mini-fridges, so I gathered some of those and put five on top of each other in the kitchen. We didn't really need a freezer, but because it was –25 degrees outside you could just leave stuff out on the balcony.

For what it's worth, at the Biathlon World Championships in Khanty-Mansiysk in 2011, athletes from Norway won gold at the men's 20-kilometre individual event, the men's relay event, the men's 15-kilometre mass start and the men and women's mixed relay. The food Haugen managed to cook was, evidentially, sufficient.

So that was totally different from football. I would often drive to a lot of these camps around Europe. You notice that there is more money in football, because you travel to nice hotels. I still had to work, but there is less to do. Things are much better prepared. There have been some places where we were worried about contamination and food poisoning and I had to get to work, but mostly it's been OK.

With decades of preparing food for world-class performers under occasionally trying circumstances behind her, Haugen got to work helping Ole Gunnar Solskjær and the team. 'Of course he had his background at Manchester United, and brought some ideas from there. So we tried to do things a bit similar to what they had done there. And it's very interesting to have been part of that process.'

One of the things that Haugen had learned from her career was that food isn't just fuel, and the place people eat together isn't just a petrol station for their bodies. 'It's about energy, it's about your mental well-being, it's about the boys feeling at home and feeling like they have a home to come to. This is important. I think the youngest boys need it more than anyone else.' Mealtimes can also be a place where a team builds togetherness and cohesion, a crucial element to any successful football team.

When Ole Gunnar brought Richard Hartis from Manchester United, I had noticed in the canteen that when they came in for breakfast, players were sitting in different smaller groups. And I felt that wasn't quite right. With the older players in one place, the other experienced players somewhere else, and maybe you get a new player coming in and he'll feel like he doesn't have a place. When that happened I felt really upset about it. But I wasn't quite sure what to do, and Richard came in and we discussed it for a bit and we had an idea: round tables. Perfect, I said, let's bring round tables. So we threw out all the square tables and brought in three big, round tables. That was the solution to that.

For Haaland, who was still so young and going through a spectacular growth spurt, food was very important. But he was also a teenager living alone for the first time in his life. In Torbjørg Haugen he found a friendly face, and someone whose nurturing instincts made her a perfect ally for a young boy far from home. 'He was such a small and innocent boy. I almost wanted to put him on my lap, but of course I couldn't do that.' Haugen laughs.

He was a wonderful boy when he walked through the doors. I didn't know his father but of course I knew who he was, and I had heard about Erling. The thing that was so unusual was that he started growing straight away. He became much bigger straight away. So they had to be careful with him in training, because he was growing so much. I spoke to Ole Gunnar about it, [and said] we have to get him as much good food as possible because he is growing so much. He had something special about him. But he had those things about him before he came to Molde. He knew he had to train the right way, he knew that he had to eat the right things to function.

Eating the right things can be easier said than done, especially for a young boy living on his own for the first time. At such times, it can be helpful to have a friend behind the counter at the club canteen.

Maybe the players need people around them, especially the younger ones. So you try to look after them a little bit. If I had a bit of food left over, for instance, I would make sure it was available to take home. Erling would often ask if I had some extra food that he could take with him. Because he already knew how important food was. But we saw that the boy was growing like crazy. He was growing all day and all night. So I just had to try to feed him as much as possible.

There is also the question of what eating the right things actually means. Because any number of experts on nutrition might give any number of different answers. A long career of preparing meals for elite athletes has taught Haugen to take a pragmatic approach.

I think food is a lot more important than people realise, and the correct food is more important than people realise ... it's important to add as much variation as possible. I always had good conversations with the boys, I asked them what they wanted. Because whatever you make, it's no good if the boys won't eat it. And if a new boy arrived at the club I'd speak to him: is there anything you can't eat? Do you know why we eat protein? And so on. Some will say that they have no idea! So I asked them about carbohydrates, and some will say we don't need them at all. So you see what kind of effect the media can have on some of them. But I would also ask them, 'What do you like? What should I cook for you the day before a match?'

Haugen is wary of overdoing the healthy element of cooking. Especially when cooking for athletes, some of whom are still teenagers, whose young bodies can still metabolise just about anything. While elite athletes tend to strive for perfection, it's easy to forget that they are still human beings. Eating is fundamentally about refuelling the body, but the act of eating has both a social and mental component. You can offer the players food that is nutritionally flawless, but if they don't like it then they will be less happy and eat less of it. A long career feeding world-class athletes has taught Tante the value of compromises. Simply put: a perfect meal isn't actually perfect if the players won't eat or enjoy it.

We had one coach who came to me and asked 'why don't you use wholegrain pasta, because it's healthier?' And I said sure, I can use wholegrain pasta, but then what will happen is something that I don't like. Normal pasta on a matchday, the boys will eat about 3.5 kilograms between them. If I make wholegrain pasta, they'll eat 1 kilogram. It might be healthier, but they'll eat a lot less. And that's something you have to see and experience to really understand. Healthy food isn't always better, if they eat that much less of it. They end up not having enough energy when they need it. And then variation becomes incredibly important. So we had lasagne the day before every match, but we also had other dishes available. The day before a match maybe we had five different dishes on offer. But there was always lasagne, and 90 per cent of them loved that. Even if I don't understand it.

Erling Haaland's pre-match lasagne became the stuff of legend after he credited his father's lasagne with helping him score three consecutive hat-tricks in the Premier League. Haugen is now thoroughly fed up of making it. 'This damned lasagna.' She exhales. 'I made 20 litres of lasagne, the day before the game, every game for 11 years … Let me tell you,' Haugen admits, 'it'll be a while until the next time I eat lasagne myself … But [the players] need the carbohydrates before a match, and it was an easy way for them to fill up.'

Getting the players ready for games is one thing, but one of the big changes Haugen made at Molde was stressing the importance of eating *after* games. 'When I arrived at Molde they didn't eat at all after matches,' she remembers. 'So I pushed for that to be introduced, because that's possibly the most important meal for an athlete.'

Sometimes it's just two days really for them to get ready for the next match, and after a match they're pretty empty so we have to refuel them. And then it's a question of what to feed them. They tried dinners, burgers, and we ended up with a lot of pizza. But then I started cooking *lapper*.

Lapper is a kind of Norwegian pancake, whose exact recipe will vary according to local traditions.

> It is a bit lower in fat, and I would use a massive amount of eggs, so you get more protein into the boys … Mostly the boys don't really want to eat, but it's very important that they eat something. If your body is empty, then it's empty. And the quicker you get food into you, the quicker you'll be ready to perform again … As long as you get something in you, it doesn't have to be much, but it makes a big difference.

There is a balance to be found, Haugen insists, between cooking food that has precisely the ideal content of nutrients, on the one hand, and just making sure the body has been fuelled in some way at the right time, on the other.

There is also a mental, emotional side to this. Humans are not machines and eating isn't just about refuelling. The players – especially young players – should not, Haugen insists, forsake everything they enjoy. 'I think it was important to do things, like, occasionally we'd make a cake.' Haugen heard about lots of other clubs where 'they don't eat dessert, they never have anything nice,' and coaches would tell certain players what they can and can't eat, but, she says firmly, 'I don't believe in that at all … if they want a small bit of cake that's not something that's going to hurt them – and for some of them it means a lot.'

For a club from a town of just some 32,000 people, Molde have an impressive record of both success on the field and success in developing players who go on to have a career outside of Norway. Rival supporters will argue that the financial support they've received from local billionaire Kjell Inge Røkke, one of Norway's wealthiest men, is a big part of that success. Molde's model has for a long time been to use some of that wealth to attract the most promising young players in the country and then create an environment in which they can develop themselves. And Haugen is convinced that a positive environment off the pitch is a part of why they've been successful. She brought that mindset from her time working at training camps with ski teams, where 'there was a very strong sense of togetherness.' She confesses, 'My job is to make the athletes better and to help them thrive. That's a very unusual job for a chef,' but 'it's a fantastic job and it's been a fantastic journey.'

And part of that journey was to feed a young boy who is now considered one of the best players in the world. 'I think Erling felt at home at Molde,' she says.

I don't know for sure, but maybe he felt some safety in that I was there in the kitchen. Molde became a place where he was happy to spend his time, and I think that means a lot, especially for the younger players. With Erling, he spent a lot of time on his own. He lived on his own. Because of that I think it was extra important that he had a place to go, that our canteen was always there for him in the daytime. Him mentioning me in that speech, it's just fantastic. That the boy remembers where he comes from. I think this is a great thing. And it really shows what kind of person Erling is.

8

MOLDE

Surrounded by hills, mountains and fjords, Molde is another Norwegian location where first-time visitors will feel more like they're walking around in a postcard than in a real place. Located 62 degrees north of the equator, Molde is technically as far north as Alaska or the southern tip of Greenland. But thanks to the warming effects of the Gulf Stream, the western coast of Norway is reasonably mild. Located on a south-facing shore of the Romsdal Peninsula, Molde enjoys more natural shelter than a lot of other places on the Norwegian west coast. This means that the place feels milder and is less prone to being battered by storms. On a clear day, if you look out over the Romsdalsfjord from any point in Molde you will be treated to a spectacular view of the sea and snow-capped mountains in the distance, with as many as 222 peaks said to be visible.

Because of its stunning scenery and comparatively gentle climate, Molde became a popular tourist destination in the late nineteenth century. For wealthy foreign visitors who wanted to explore the famed Norwegian fjords, Molde was an ideal place to stop along the way. It was also a perfect jumping-off point for British gentry looking to enjoy the many excellent opportunities for hunting and fishing in the region. At the time, the town was notable for its luscious parks and gardens, initially earning it the nickname 'the city of flowers' and then more specifically 'the city of roses'. The latter in particular was embraced by the locals, with hoteliers welcoming visiting tourist ships with bundles of roses.

Today, the first landmark to catch your eye as you approach Molde is Seilet, a 16-storey high-rise hotel that protrudes into the fjord and is designed to resemble a sail. The next landmark you'll notice, right next to the hotel, is the football stadium. The stadium was designed by the same architect as the hotel, and is eye-catching enough in itself. But its location gives it something extra: it's located right on the waterfront, meaning a stray shot or clearance would have a very real chance of ending up in the fjord. Built in 1998, the stadium was a gift to the club from local businessmen Bjørn Rune Gjelsten and Kjell Inge Røkke. The pair's generosity didn't end there. According to Norwegian business magazine *Kapital*, over the last three decades the two have supported the club to the tune of 1.1 billion kroner – about £80 million in the current exchange rate. The majority of that sum has come from Røkke, who grew up in Molde and is now one of the richest men in Norway.

Though Molde itself is a small place with a population of just 32,000, their football club has over the last couple of decades become one of the driving forces in Norwegian club football. The support from Røkke is a big part of that story, but it would also be misleading to suggest that the football club has used financial brute force to strong-arm its way to the top. Molde's strategy, especially in recent years, has been more about using its financial and sporting clout to attract some of the most promising young players in Norwegian football. In 2007 Molde started up the Aker Academy – Aker being the company where Røkke is the chairman and largest shareholder – with the aim of further improving the club's youth development. Molde, a small city with few distractions, is an ideal place for an ambitious young player to spend some formative footballing years. Because, as one seasoned observer of Norwegian football privately observed, 'There isn't much to do in Molde, aside from making money and becoming a better footballer.'

The list of players that have gone through Molde on their way to playing in a bigger league is not short and includes Premier League players like Mame Biram Diouf, Moi Elyounoussi and more recently Chelsea's David Datro Fofana. Benfica's Fredrik Aursnes played five and a half seasons for Molde before initially going abroad to Feyenoord. Full-back Martin Linnes left Molde to play for Galatasaray for five and a half seasons before coming back to Molde in 2021. Playmaker Magnus Wolff Eikrem left Molde for Dutch side Heerenveen in 2013 before joining Cardiff in the Premier League. Defenders Stian Gregersen and Ruben Gabrielsen were at Molde before they left for France, moving to Bordeaux and Toulouse respectively. Mats Møller Dæhli left Manchester United's academy to join Molde, moved to Cardiff and has eventually made a career for himself in Germany with second division sides St Pauli and 1. FC Nürnberg. Jo Inge Berget also went from Molde to Cardiff, and later played in the Champions League for Swedish champions Malmö FF. Fredrik Gulbrandsen left Molde to go to Red Bull Salzburg in 2016, and in 2019 signed with İstanbul Başakşehir, where he won the Turkish Süper Lig. The list goes on. No superstars perhaps, but the recurring theme is clear: for talented young players who are prepared to work hard, Molde is a proven finishing school on the path to a more lucrative career in a bigger league abroad.

Most people in footballing circles outside of Norway will likely associate Molde with Ole Gunnar Solskjær, but Solskjær is actually not from Molde. He was born and grew up in Kristiansund, some 40 miles to the northeast, and his first club was local team Clausenengen. He then spent one and a half very productive seasons up front for Molde in the mid-1990s before being sold to Manchester United. There, Solskjær played his part in one of the most successful eras of Manchester United's history, and scored the winning goal in the Champions League final in 1999. At the time, Norwegians were used to seeing their country represented in the Premier League, but having a goal-scoring hero in the best team in the land was something new. And Solskjær's popularity in Norway went beyond his goal-scoring exploits for United: his status as the loyal squad player, the substitute who never complained but was always ready to do his best, struck a particular chord with Norwegians.

It's impossible to understand Scandinavian society without being familiar with 'The Law of Jante'. The Law of Jante is a set of behavioural rules for society set forth by the Danish-Norwegian author Aksel Sandemose in his 1933 novel *A Fugitive Crosses His Tracks*. There are ten rules, which read as follows:

1. You're not to think *you* are anything special.
2. You're not to think *you* are as good as *we* are.
3. You're not to think *you* are smarter than *we* are.
4. You're not to imagine yourself better than *we* are.
5. You're not to think *you* know more than *we* do.
6. You're not to think *you* are more important than *we* are.
7. You're not to think *you* are good at anything.
8. You're not to laugh at *us*.

9. You're not to think anyone cares about *you*.
10. You're not to think *you* can teach *us* anything.

According to Sandemose, his novel illustrated 'human beings' inherent evil and ability to push each other down', and was intended to be a kind of satire, a skewering of the petty, small-mindedness of life in small-town Denmark at the time. But the ideas of the Law of Jante have come to represent the prevailing social attitudes in Scandinavian society. For selflessness, humility and modesty to be guiding principles of a society isn't necessarily a bad thing, but when taken to excess these values can also become oppressive. There is a fine line between embracing these values and discouraging achievement altogether. Pride may be a sin in many places in the world, but there are few places where it's considered quite as deadly as it is in Scandinavia. At times it can seem like being a humble failure is preferable to being confidently prosperous. In that vein, the Law of Jante has come to represent a certain resentment of ambition and achievement, and younger generations in particular see it as a sociocultural Achilles heel that must be confronted and overcome.

Either way, in Ole Gunnar Solskjær, the Norwegians had their perfect Jantean hero. Here was a player who excelled, who achieved at the highest level, yet remained unfailingly modest and humble. In some cultures, a talent like Solskjær may have been encouraged to move away from Manchester United. After all, he was frequently on the bench. But in staying loyal to his club rather than seeking a more important role elsewhere, Solskjær made himself the ultimate sporting role model for Norwegians. It also helps that he is a committed family man, who has eschewed the typical modern footballer lifestyle of glitz, glamour and fast cars. To Norwegians Solskjær wasn't just an inspirational sportsman, he represented a model of how their society's obsession with humility could in fact be combined with outstanding achievement. Not just a sporting role model, but a Norwegian ideal made flesh.

For Molde, which was aiming to create a centre of excellence in the middle of the fjords, what manager could be better suited to lead the team and guide the youngsters than the near-mythical figure of Ole Gunnar Solskjær? In January 2011, after one and a half seasons in charge of Manchester United's reserves, Solskjær was appointed manager of Molde. He led the team to Molde's first league title in their history in his first season, and won the title in his second season as well. 'He is such a warm and friendly person. He makes you feel part of the club,' Mattias Moström, one of the more experienced players in that squad, later told the *Guardian*.

> He goes out of his way to talk to everyone, from the people working in the canteen and the administrative staff to the players and the ball boys. He makes himself available to everyone at the club. And it's not only about football. He wants to make sure you know he is there for you, regardless of what you want to talk about.

Initially there was a suspicion in Norway that Solskjær might in fact be too nice to be a manager. His results did a pretty thorough job disproving that hypothesis. And Solskjær also has a side to him that the public rarely, if ever, sees. 'It's like his eyes change colour when he's angry, you wouldn't believe it,' Ruben Gabrielsen, one of the players who captained Molde under Solskjær, told the *Heia Fotball* podcast. 'He scared the shit out of me many times. But he's the best coach I've ever played under. Not just when it comes to football, but on a human level. He doesn't just want to create footballers, he wants to develop *men*.'

Developing players is something that Solskjær is passionate about. In an interview with *Josimar* back in 2012, he outlined his vision for Molde and their academy:

> The idea, at the end of the day, is that we should have one or two new players in the first team squad from the Aker Academy every season. That's what we're hoping for. We have a lot of promising young talent, and I'm certain we'll see more and more.

One of Solskjær's core beliefs for developing young talent is to empower them to take risks, to allow them to attempt the difficult things on the pitch. 'I see way too often with 10-, 12-, 14-year-olds,' explains Solskjær, 'that you have coaches on the sideline that shout "Stop dribbling, you're part of a team!"' But, Solskjær continues,

> If the boy is good at dribbling, and you want him to become very good at dribbling by the time he's 19, you have to let him dribble. Then, maybe, when he's 15–16 you teach him more about when and how to dribble. Once he's good at dribbling, it's easier to teach him more about when and how than it is to teach dribbling to an 18-year-old who has never been allowed to try.

Though often perceived from the outside as a model of humility and selflessness, Solskjær the coach wants his players to be bold and to take risks on the field. 'You're allowed to try, and you're not allowed to tell anyone off for trying. Yes, we're a team, but if you're going to improve you have to be allowed to try things.' Solskjær's status in Norwegian football gives him a kind of aura and gravitas that may not have fully translated to foreign dressing rooms when he later managed abroad. In Norway, if Solskjær walks into the room, people sit up and pay attention. And if you're a footballer who grew up watching him score goals for Manchester United, well, then you *really* listen.

Molde had been a competitive team in Norway for a long time before Solskjær became the club's manager. Molde won the Cup in 1994 and 2005 and finished league runners-up in 1974, 1987, 1995, 1998, 1999 and 2009. These near misses, particularly in the 1990s, were much to do with Rosenborg's remarkable stranglehold of Norwegian football. The team from Trondheim won the Norwegian league every season from 1992 to 2004. But even as Rosenborg started to lose its grip on the league in the 2000s, Molde still couldn't quite get across the line. But with Solskjær at the helm, Molde immediately won the league twice in a row. This added a degree of coaching credibility to Solskjær's already enormous status in Norwegian football, and so when he returned from a disappointing spell in charge of Cardiff, his reputation was undiminished. He was still a manager that Norwegian players were excited to play for and to learn from. And as Erling Haaland himself put it, Ole Gunnar Solskjær, combined with Molde's proven record of developing players, were the main reasons why he decided to stay in Norway rather than go abroad for his first big move.

9

TURNING POINT

In 2017, Erling Haaland's first season at Molde, he ended up playing fewer minutes for the first team than he had probably hoped. But the stark reality for Haaland was that he was still a boy. He had been a substitute for a team battling relegation in the second tier only a few months prior, and he had now joined a team with ambitions of winning the Norwegian top division. It was a significant step up and, besides, he was going through an extraordinary growth spurt. He had to be treated carefully. But he settled well into the team and the town, and became particularly close friends with midfielders Fredrik Aursnes and Eirik Hestad. Hestad's apartment in the centre of town became a bit of a social hub for the three. 'Me and him got off on the right foot and we spent a lot of time together,' Hestad later told *DW*.

As you see him on the pitch, he is quite the same when he's at home. He has a lot of energy and a lot of jokes in him. He spreads good vibes when you're around him. But also when you make him pissed he gets really pissed, as you can see on the pitch as well. But when you get him on the good side again he's back, you know.

On the physical side, Molde's coaches quickly noticed that Haaland was struggling with the demands at this higher level. 'Physically he was a big, young guy, but mostly skin and bones,' Molde's then fitness coach Børre Steenslid told Sky Sports in 2022. 'So we needed to do a screening of him and to make a long-term plan.' Perhaps surprisingly, given that Haaland is now so well known for his brute strength, building muscle was not a big part of this plan at all.

> Gaining some muscle was one of the factors, but we tried to make him even more explosive. Because he came as an explosive player. He was clearly athletic. So I didn't want to do too much of the classic strength sessions. We varied a lot in the gym, different kinds of gym sessions, and he was what we call a responder. He responded quickly to the gym work, and we saw big progress. Of course it helped that his work ethic was fantastic.

Already that summer Haaland's physical transformation was striking. Heading into a game against Sarpsborg in June 2017, Molde were missing eight players to injury, two to suspension and two more picked up injuries during the game. This meant that 16-year-old Haaland got his league debut, coming off the bench for the last 20 minutes of the match. Haaland was fired up, perhaps too fired up, and got booked after just 65 seconds. The injury-hit Molde team lost 1–0. (Haaland had actually had his official first-team debut for Molde a few months earlier, in April, against a team from the lower leagues in the first round of the Norwegian Cup. Molde beat Volda

TI 3–2, and Haaland had scored the opening goal. But now, in June, he was starting to get minutes in the league.) After coming on for 19 minutes against Sarpsborg, he got 12 minutes off the bench against Tromsø in the next game. He had two more brief appearances off the bench that summer, before scoring his first goal in the Norwegian top division in August.

Molde were playing Tromsø away, which meant that they were well inside the Arctic Circle. Tromsø IL are the northernmost professional football team in the world. In the winter, from late November to mid-January, the sun never climbs above the horizon in the daytime. Conversely, in the summer the sun never sets. Tromsø had recently appointed Simo Valakari, the Finnish former Motherwell and Derby County player, as their manager, and their players were keen to impress the new boss. They took the lead in the 19th minute and had the better of the first half, but Sander Svendsen grabbed an equaliser for Molde with a neat finish. Still, Tromsø kept coming and had chances to go ahead again. In the 71st minute of the game, Ole Gunnar Solskjær brought on Erling Haaland. His instructions were simple: 'Go out there and win us the game.' After just a few minutes Haaland had his first chance. He dribbled his way through a packed Tromsø box but, by the time he got his shot off, the angle was tight and the ball went wide. Molde kept pushing, and just 30 seconds later Eirik Hestad lofted a high cross into the box, which Haaland charged at and powered past the goalkeeper: 2–1, and three very handy points away from home. 'He's asked for extra training on his heading, because he didn't think he was good enough at it,' Solskjær beamed after the game. 'He's been doing that for three to four weeks now, and then he goes and wins us the game!' Privately Haaland had perhaps been hoping for more minutes that season, but his manager had no doubts about his potential even then. 'The incredible thing about him is the development he's had since he came to the club,' Solskjær said. 'He's a boy with positivity and energy around him. He's unpleasant to play against. He's going to become a very, very good footballer.' Haaland himself, as would become his custom, was straight to the point and used no more words than necessary in his post-match interview: 'It felt really great to get my first goal in Eliteserien. It was great. That's what I came on to do.'

Haaland's next goal for Molde, about a month later, was another match-winner. And this was one that Haaland took particular delight in. From his days with the Bryne youth teams, Haaland had taken great pleasure in scoring against Viking, Bryne's rivals from the nearby city of Stavanger. In truth, attitudes have softened over the years and children of Erling Haaland's generation don't seem to possess the same antipathy towards the city-dwellers of Stavanger as some of the older generations did. But still, a rivalry is a rivalry, and Haaland has never been one to shirk a big occasion. If anything, the bigger the occasion the more fired up young Erling seemed to be. So when Molde headed south to face Viking in Stavanger, the match will have meant a little bit more to him than just about any other league game.

The year 2017 was a disastrous one for Viking. The team had problems, and the club had no money with which to fix them. The bright but inexperienced Englishman Ian Burchnall had been put in charge of the team in November 2016 after having been the assistant manager the previous season. Viking was bottom of the league, but had picked up a few points over the summer. But fighting a wounded, cornered animal can be a dangerous thing. Just two minutes into the game Viking took the lead from a set piece. Molde's season, too, had so far not gone to plan. The team had dropped too many points in the spring, and Rosenborg was running away with the title yet again. However, this Molde side was determined to finish the season strongly. Ending the season in second or third place would mean qualifying for the Europa League, and those places were well within reach. It was the middle of September, there were nine games to go, and Molde was fourth. Beating rock-bottom, crisis-stricken Viking should have been a straightforward task. But there the players were, two minutes in, a goal down from a set piece and there were opponents fighting for their lives.

But Viking was bottom of the league for a reason. After just 13 minutes Molde winger Fredrik Brustad was clumsily brought down in the box by Viking's Jose Manuel Cruz, which meant a penalty for Molde and a red card for the Spanish defender. Icelandic forward Björn Bergmann Sigurðarson made it 1–1 from the spot, leaving Molde with plenty of time to get the winner against ten men. In the 33rd minute Martin Ellingsen made it 2–1 to Molde. But in the second half the Viking players refused to lie down and accept their fate. Erling Haaland came on in the 64th minute and missed a couple of huge chances to score against his archrivals. Instead, ten-man Viking equalised, through a certain Tommy Høiland.

Høiland is himself a former Bryne youth prodigy. Like Haaland, he grew up in Bryne and was a third-generation Bryne player, with both his father and grandfather having played for the club. He scored on his debut for Bryne shortly after turning 16, had a trial with Spurs in the Premier League before that, and played a number of games for Norway at various age groups. But at 17, just as he was looking to establish himself in the first team, Høiland was hit by a car on his way to training and suffered a badly broken ankle, which kept him out of football for over a year. He came back, but his development had taken a hit. Determined to make a career for himself, he did the unthinkable and moved from Bryne to Viking. Høiland eventually carved out a career for himself as something of a journeyman striker in the Norwegian league, even playing for Molde for a couple of seasons. He won the Cup with Molde and scored a panenka penalty away to Fenerbahçe in the Europa League. But he also earned himself a reputation for being a nasty player, prone to both diving and putting in dangerous tackles on opponents. This, combined with an aggressive, high-energy playing style, made Høiland a prodigiously annoying opponent. In 2017 he was back at Viking, now aged 28, hoping to drag them out of the relegation mire. For the moment, at least, it looked like he had earned Viking a point against the mighty Molde. For Erling Haaland, it was miserable. Missing huge chances and watching Tommy bloody Høiland steal two points away from Molde is not what he would have had in mind for this game.

But the game wasn't over. Høiland had equalised in the 77th minute, so there was still time for a winning goal. And just two minutes later, with Høiland barely back up from his knee slide, a long ball out from the Molde defence found Aursnes. Aursnes had made a well-timed run in behind the Viking defence, looked up, and with his first touch squared the ball towards his young friend Haaland, who calmly finished past the Viking goalkeeper, sending his old rivals another step closer to relegation. Haaland immediately went to celebrate right in front of Viking's supporters' club, 'Vikinghordene' (the Viking Hordes). A delighted Haaland cupped his ear and pointed to the opposing fans. 'Of course I was a bit fired up, a bit extra fired up,' Haaland said after the game. 'I'm from Bryne, it was against Viking, there has always been a rivalry, so it does fire you up a bit extra.'

'It hurts for me as a Viking player, who knows that our supporters have had many bad experiences this season,' Høiland said. 'We played ten against eleven for eighty minutes, so then I think him celebrating like that was totally unnecessary. He should show a better attitude.' But Solskjær was altogether more relaxed about it all.

He's a 17-year-old boy. You have to be allowed to show some emotion. It meant a lot to him. I'm sure Tommy Høiland was annoyed, but Tommy is no angel himself. We need guys like Tommy and Erling in Norwegian football. Yes, there is something un-Norwegian about them, but that's how it should be.

Solskjær was more concerned with another aspect of Haaland's game: 'I told him good job, but then we went through the chances he missed. He's a boy who is eager to learn.' Solskjær, like Haaland's youth coach Alf Ingve Berntsen, realised that Erling's occasional emotional excesses were simply part of his character, and that they stemmed from his immense desire to succeed. Norwegian society may preach humility and to 'win and lose with the same mind', but Erling Haaland simply cannot do this – nor should he be encouraged to. He will be furious with himself when he fails; he may briefly go overboard in celebration when he succeeds. But there is a straight line between these volcanic emotions on the pitch and his remarkable drive and determination to work and improve off it. And though Norwegians may have seen Solskjær as an icon of modesty and humility, Solskjær himself understood that this was a side of Haaland that he shouldn't try to curtail. Instead, he backed his player. Over and over.

Haaland was still very much an unpolished gem for Molde, and the winning goals against Tromsø and Viking were the only ones he scored in the league that season. But he continued to impress for the Norwegian national youth teams. In early September he scored as the Norway U-18s beat Sweden 4–2, with his former teammates at Bryne, Tord Salte and Andreas Ueland, playing in defence for Norway. He added more goals in October, as he played for Norway in their bid to qualify for the European Under-19 Championship. Qualifying consisted of two group stages, and in their first group Norway faced Ukraine, Montenegro and Albania. Haaland scored one against both Ukraine and Montenegro, and two against Albania. Norway won all three games. This meant that they qualified for the second group stage, to be played in March the next year. There they were drawn against Germany, Scotland and the Netherlands – a far more daunting task. In their first game, against the Netherlands, Norway were thumped 6–1. But the young Norwegians rallied, and in their next game they beat Germany 5–2, with Haaland setting the standard by scoring twice in the first half-hour. This meant that their third game, against Scotland, would be the decider. It was a wild game that went into injury time with the score 4–4, Haaland having scored two of Norway's goals. In injury time, Norway got a corner kick. In a massive tangle in the box the referee spotted a foul and gave Norway a penalty. Up stepped Haaland, who kept his cool and made it 5–4. Norway became one of just eight countries to qualify for the European Under-19 Championship.

In that tournament, played in Finland during the summer of 2018, Norway first lost to a talented Portuguese team, beat host nation Finland and then drew 1–1 against Italy. Haaland's only goal in the group was an equalising penalty against the Italians. This was enough for Norway to finish only third in their group. Group winners and runners-up qualified automatically for the prestigious Under-20 World Cup, to be played the next summer. The two third-placed teams would face each other in a play-off for a last spot in that tournament. On 26 July, at the Seinäjoki Stadium – home to both Finnish top-division team SJK and the local American football team the Seinäjoki Crocodiles – Norway beat England 3–0 to qualify for the Under-20 World Cup, though Haaland missed out on the game after being recalled to Molde because the club had a Europa League qualifier coming up. At this point, Haaland had established himself as an important first-team player with his club. In fact, it was at the start of July 2018 that Haaland reached a bit of a turning point in his career.

'I think he believed in it himself. I didn't believe. He believed in it, not me,' laughed Ruben Gabrielsen on the *Heia Fotball* podcast when asked if he thought Erling Haaland would become a superstar. Gabrielsen was the captain of Molde when Haaland was at the club. 'Not one person in that dressing room can say "I knew all along that he would become this good",' Gabrielsen insists. 'He arrived as a thin, young boy. He was OK in training, but nothing special.' But the big turning point for Haaland at Molde came in the summer of 2018. He had been getting more minutes in the first half of that season, even becoming a regular starter, but he had only scored twice in 12 appearances. His best moments had been at youth level, for Bryne's second team and for Norway's youth teams. There were still questions. There were still doubters. In September 2017, a Norwegian Twitter-user named Andreas Bryhn infamously declared: 'Erling Håland. Will be playing up front for Sandnes Ulf when he's 23. At best.' Sandnes, an unglamorous city between Stavanger and Bryne, has a team in the Norwegian second tier and would not be considered a particularly glorious place for Haaland to end up. In the summer of 2023, after turning 23, Erling Haaland was asked about the tweet. He chuckled and said, with the typical understatement of someone who grew up in Jæren: 'Yes, that was a good one. I've read that one a few times, and I have to say he maybe got that one a little bit wrong.'

So in the spring of 2018 Haaland was getting minutes for Molde, but he had yet to start scoring goals. He was tall, had started to bulk up and fill out, and was quick for a player of his size. But he could look clumsy and be wasteful in front of goal. With the benefit of hindsight one would now say that this was a boy who had yet to fully come to terms with his new physique, who had yet to perfect his finishing and who simply needed time and faith. But this wasn't obvious at the time. He had also had a disrupted preseason, spending two weeks in hospital with a bad case of pneumonia. Torbjørg Haugen, 'Tante', quickly noticed that 'the boy' hadn't come in for his regular meals, texted him to find out what was wrong and upon learning that he was in hospital immediately offered to bring him food. Haaland gratefully accepted. But while he still had doubters outside of Molde, one person whose belief was unshakable was his manager: 'He's very good. I am totally convinced that he's a potential national team player, as long as he stays clear of injuries,' Solskjær told *VG* in June, before joking that Haaland being forced to lay still in a hospital bed for a while probably just made him grow another centimetre. 'That he's recovered so well, and was even able to play three games for the Norway under-19s in the international break, it's impressive. The boy is just a bundle of energy.'

But Haaland had yet to fully repay Solskjær's faith in him on the pitch, and Molde had endured a mixed start to the season. As the team prepared for a big game against SK Brann, the team that was top of the league at the time, Gabrielsen recalls that there had been nothing in training to suggest that Haaland was about to do anything useful for the team. 'We were playing Brann next. Haaland isn't scoring a single goal in training, not a single ball touches the net. It's a disaster. Penalties. Everything. Nothing works,' Gabrielsen continues:

I saw him standing on the training ground the day before the match, on the verge of tears, and Ole Gunnar is talking to him. The ball isn't going in, no matter what he tried. Then Ole Gunnar comes to me and says 'I'm considering starting

Haaland tomorrow.' And I say 'no, you can't do that.' Ole Gunnar says 'I have a good feeling.' I say 'no, you can't start Haaland.' So then we're sat in the dressing room at Brann Stadium, looking over at Haaland, and we're thinking this is going to be a difficult game.

SK Brann is a club based in Bergen, a city located just under 100 miles north of Stavanger along the Norwegian west coast. The city was founded 900 years ago, and in the 1300s it grew into one of the most important trading ports in Northern Europe. By 1600 it was the biggest city in the Nordic region. But stagnation, along with the growth of Oslo, eventually saw it lose its primacy as Norway's most significant city. Though don't try telling that to the people of Bergen today. A strong degree of local pride is a common thing all over Norway, though few are quite so overtly delighted with their home town as the people of Bergen. And they may have a point.

Situated between seven mountains, Bergen is big enough to be interesting, small enough to be cosy, and on a clear day stunningly beautiful. Though 'on a clear day' is an important caveat here: it's a city squeezed between the mountains and the sea, and every year Bergen is subjected to a spectacular amount of rain. As the local saying goes: 'When God created Bergen, he was so pleased with his work that he decided to wash it every day.' The city averages well over 200 rainy days a year – the amount of annual rainfall is about three times as much as in Manchester. Whatever you say about the people of Bergen, they know a thing or two about rain. But on a clear day the tree-clad hills surrounding the city seem to radiate a kind of luminous green, forming a resplendent backdrop to the picturesque buildings of downtown Bergen. The pride so readily expressed by the locals is, one has to admit, not entirely unjustified.

Another thing that the people of Bergen are proud of is their football team – at least occasionally, that is. Brann and their fans have a reputation for getting carried away when things go well, but also for letting even minor setbacks quickly develop into full-blown crises. With the club's tendency to lurch wildly between progress and disaster, its fans have developed a healthy dose of gallows humour. One fan account on Twitter is simply named 'Is it any wonder we drink?' But there are few more excitable and exciting football towns in Norway than Bergen when Brann is doing well. And in the summer of 2018 the team was doing very, very well.

When Molde came to town in July 2018, Bergen was not only enjoying one of its hottest and sunniest summers on record, but Brann was top of the league. The city was buzzing. The locals, used to watching a wildly inconsistent team while being rained on, were revelling in the success and the sunshine. The team was undefeated in their first 13 games of the season. Their manager, Lars Arne Nilsen, had made them a well-organised and rugged outfit. In those first 13 games they had conceded just five goals. A central defensive partnership of the tough Costa Rican international Bismar Acosta and the uncompromising former Dutch U-21 international Vito Wormgoor had proved an impenetrable wall for most opponents in the Norwegian league. Molde, on the other hand, was languishing in sixth place after an uneven start to the season. For Solskjær to start with the 17-year-old Haaland, who had been a mess in training, against the brutish partnership of Acosta and Wormgoor seemed like a downright eccentric decision. The other players were, according to captain Gabrielsen, puzzled and not feeling particularly optimistic about the game. But the Molde players dutifully filed out in front of a raucous and confident home crowd, with the highest of Bergen's seven mountains looming over the stadium. As the game kicked off the home team was confident, the sun was beaming and the Brann fans were expecting another win. But only 20 minutes later, Molde was winning 4–0, and Erling Haaland had scored all four goals.

'We were standing there wondering what was going on,' Gabrielsen said, laughing, many years later. The Brann fans were stunned. Even the surrounding mountains, who have seen a lot of odd things in this football stadium, must have been rumbled. The first goal was what would later become a typical Haaland goal: a ball in behind the defence, a clever run by Haaland and a brilliant first touch to take the ball past an onrushing goalkeeper. The through-ball was not an immaculate pass, it was more a hopeful header by Haaland's friend in midfield, Fredrik Aursnes. But Haaland spotted the opportunity just a little bit quicker than the defenders spotted the danger, and once he got moving he had them comfortably beaten for pace. The first touch, taking a bouncing ball in his stride with the underside of his boot and poking it perfectly past the goalkeeper, was a deceptively difficult piece of skill executed to perfection. The second goal came from a long diagonal ball by Haaland's other midfield mate, Eirik Hestad, who found him isolated one-on-one against Brann's left-back Ruben Kristiansen. Ordinarily a diligent defender, Kristiansen was rushing to get back and never found his balance as Haaland breezed past him with ease and finished confidently past the goalkeeper. For the third goal, Brann's holding midfielder tried to clear a hopeful ball up the field but missed it entirely, succeeding only in bamboozling his own defender. Suddenly Haaland was away again. He deftly took the ball past the onrushing goalkeeper, before finishing neatly in the near corner. For the fourth goal, more confusion in the Brann defence ended with their goalkeeper giving away a clumsy penalty. 'What is happening to the Brann defence?' the television commentator asked, bewildered. 'Are they having a heat stroke?!' Erling Haaland stepped up, sent the goalkeeper one way and the ball the other. None of the goals were stunners, as such, but it was a complete and comprehensive showcase of the qualities the world would become familiar with soon enough: Haaland's extraordinary physical ability, his alertness and his capacity to make the right runs at the right time. And though he'd been missing chances in training all week, here he showed a remarkable deftness of touch and gave a masterclass in calm, accurate finishing.

It was also a brilliant piece of management by Solskjær. Haaland would later give his version of the week leading up to the game, in the documentary *Haaland: The Big Decision*. 'I was so fucking bad in training that week,' Haaland admitted, using the full Norwegian swear world *jævla* rather than his oft-favoured replacement word *grævla*. He smiled ruefully.

> Every passing drill I'd play a bouncing pass. In possession I lost the ball every time. Just ask Ole Gunnar. Then suddenly two days before the match he said, 'Erling, I think this is a good game for you, you're going to start.' And I thought what the fuck, what's wrong with him? Now I really have to deliver.

Perhaps Solskjær had anticipated that Brann would play a high line with two defenders who were stronger than they were quick, but more likely he just had a lot of faith in the boy. Solskjær, after all, had been steadfast in his belief that Haaland had a big future. The game became a turning point for Haaland in a Molde shirt. 'After that, everything in training went in. He was a totally different person,' Gabrielsen said. Before the Brann game Haaland had scored two in twelve. Having added four in one afternoon, he then notched up three goals and three assists in his next three league games.

Haaland also got his first taste of European football that summer, as Molde made their way through the early qualifying rounds of the Europa League. He started when Molde put in a curiously tepid performance away to Northern Irish club Glenavon FC and lost 2–1, but they smashed the same opponent 5–1 in the return leg. In the next round Haaland started the home leg against Albanian team KF Laçi and scored the first goal from the penalty spot as Molde won 3–0. In mid-August, when Molde hosted Hibernian, Haaland started and scored twice. And in the final qualification round before the group stage, Haaland started both games as Molde faced Zenit St Petersburg. The team lost 3–1 in Russia, which made their task in the return leg difficult. Haaland scored yet another goal when Zenit came to Norway, but Molde could only manage a 2–1 win and so lost on aggregate. By the time the games against Zenit came along, it had already been decided that Haaland would be moving on after the end of the Norwegian season. It was clear, already, that he had outgrown Molde.

10

INTO THE UNKNOWN

The game against Brann was the day most Norwegians realised that this Erling Haaland kid could be a bit special, but within football he already had a number of prestigious admirers. In fact, on that sunny afternoon in Bergen a Manchester United scout, the late Tommy Møller Nielsen, was there in the stands to have a look. BRAUT HAALAND (17) THRASHED BRANN WITH A MANCHESTER UNITED SCOUT IN THE STANDS was the headline after the game in Norway's leading newspaper *VG*. 'There's a lot of interest. There have been offers from good clubs earlier this year, but we've turned those down,' Solskjær said. 'This isn't something he should be thinking about, because speculation is something he's going to have to deal with for the rest of his life.' Haaland himself was, as usual, a young man of few words after the game. 'It was cool to score four goals. I can't say anything about my future other than the fact that I'm a Molde player. But of course it's fun that there is interest,' he told *VG*. Solskjær joked that 'with a father who has played for Leeds and Manchester City, I'm not sure he's that tempted by United,' but when asked about it a cheerful Haaland insisted that this would have no bearing on his future. 'I have nothing against that club, so that has nothing to do with it,' he said. 'I just want to go to a club that will take good care of me. That's the most important thing.'

One of the big clubs keeping a close eye on Haaland was Juventus. At one point he was invited to Italy to visit the club, but on his way to Italy he had to make a stop back in Jæren. 'That was all a bit dubious,' Alf Ingve Berntsen says, laughing.

> He had forgotten his passport, so he had to go to Bryne to fetch it, and he learned that his mates on the recreational team were training that night so he turned up and played with them. A few hours after training with Molde and he was flying to Juventus the next day. From a sporting perspective, a terrible idea. In terms of proper restitution, it was indefensible … He was definitely not supposed to do that.

Erling Haaland may have been a budding teenage superstar invited to come visit serial Italian champions Juventus, but if his childhood friends were having a kickabout in Jærhallen he wasn't going to stay home on the sofa. 'It was all wrong. But it also shows you the kind of guy he was,' Berntsen says.

Juventus had been following Haaland for some time, and in early 2018 they came close to an agreement. 'One of my biggest regrets was a deal for Haaland,' the then Juventus CEO Giuseppe Marotta said at *La Gazzetta dello Sport*'s Festival Dello Sport in Trento in 2021. 'I was CEO at Juventus and we had the opportunity to sign him for €2 million from Molde. We were close.' Speaking to the Italian newspaper *Tuttosport* in 2021, Juve director Federico Cherubini also admitted that missing out on Haaland is something the club still regrets.

> It would be stupid to say something different. However, things must be put into context. Young players can be scared about going out on loan, we were at the beginning of our U23 project and perhaps the perspective we offered wasn't too exciting. Maybe the idea of going out on loan wasn't ideal for a player like him.

Juventus had launched an U-23s team, effectively a B-team to play in the third tier of Italian football, Serie C. The idea of playing with a B-team did not seem like the best solution for Haaland. 'I was of course flattered by the interest from Juventus,' he told *VG* in January 2019. 'But I felt it was wrong to go there so early in my career.'

Solskjær would also later reveal that in the summer of 2018, six months before he himself became Manchester United manager, he got in touch with his former club suggesting they sign Haaland. 'I got in contact with United because we had this talented striker who they should have had,' Solskjær said. 'But they didn't listen, unfortunately. Four million, I asked for. But they never signed him. Four million!' Steve Walsh, then director of football at Everton, also told *The Athletic* in November 2019 that he believed he could have brought Haaland to the Premier League. 'I had him and his dad at the club with a deal done for €4 million. The club wouldn't back me,' he said. Duncan Ferguson has also said that Everton had a chance to sign him at an even earlier stage, before he went to Molde. Every successful footballer has their fair share of these stories, moves that supposedly could have happened and the different routes they could have taken. In the case of Haaland, a lot of the stories seem to ignore a crucial aspect: what the Haalands, both Erling and Alfie, felt was the right move at the time. In rejecting Hoffenheim and FC Copenhagen to sign for Molde, and later rejecting Juventus, they made it clear that the biggest league or the biggest contract was not Erling Haaland's priority. As he said himself, 'I just want to go to a club that will take good care of me.' This, is particularly important for a teenager about to move abroad for the first time in his life. And so to help them find the right club, make the right decision and, of course, secure favourable terms with the buying club, the Haalands enlisted the help of the experienced, notorious 'super-agent' Mino Raiola.

Raiola was one of a kind. Erling Haaland would later describe him as 'the best agent in the world'. *La Gazzetta dello Sport* called him 'the most powerful, the best, the most discussed' agent in the world. Sir Alex Ferguson called him 'a shitbag'. Raiola was direct, brusque, unconventional and uncompromising. Unlike a lot of other agents, Raiola would happily torch his relationships with influential club directors and managers if that's what it took to get his client the best deal. He would also make sure he did well out of those deals himself, leading to accusations of greed and self-interest from clubs and fans alike. But his clients loved him. And that wasn't just because of the way he would fight their corner, but because he would push them to improve themselves as well. Zlatan Ibrahimović's autobiography, *I Am Zlatan* (2021), revealed a fascinating relationship between the Swedish superstar and his agent. Rarely does a career-long relationship between agent and superstar start with the agent telling the star to 'go fuck himself', but that was the first instruction Zlatan got from Raiola back when Zlatan's teammate and friend Maxwell tried to set up a meeting between the two. When they eventually did meet, Raiola's message to Zlatan was clear: 'Sell your cars, your watches, and start training three times as hard. Because your stats are rubbish.'

Raiola later mused that 'Zlatan decided to sign with me because I was the first, and maybe the only one, to tell him he was an asshole. Everyone else was just telling him nice things, but I told him the truth, to make him better.' Zlatan appreciated Raiola's direct, honest and confrontational approach, and has repeatedly given Raiola credit for helping him reach his potential.

Ibrahimović and Haaland don't have much in common. No one needed to tell Erling Haaland to work harder. But it won't have escaped Haaland's notice that the last truly world-class striker from Scandinavia received expert guidance and mentoring from Raiola throughout his career. The family could use the advice of someone who knew the European transfer market better than most. And of course, when it comes to getting the best deal for a player, there have been few better than Raiola. It was actually Raiola who approached the Haalands, and Alfie had a number of meetings with him in Monaco, where Raiola was based. They ended up agreeing to work together. Alfie's reasoning was simple: 'He's one of the best, and I wanted to use the best,' he told *VG*. And Raiola's explanation for why Haaland turned down the mighty Juventus was simple enough: 'Why didn't Haaland move to Juventus? They would have put him in the Under-23 squad,' he told *la Repubblica* in May 2020.

With Raiola on board and a number of exciting potential destinations for Haaland to choose from that summer, the rumour mill went into overdrive. And the questions from the press about Haaland's future were constant. When asked about it after scoring twice against Hibernian, Erling Haaland replied, 'I think I've said a million times now that this is a question I won't answer. So that's the answer you get.' He was doing his best, and mostly succeeding, in keeping his tone polite. At this point his destination was widely known, if not yet confirmed. A few days earlier the Norwegian press had reported that Haaland was close to a transfer to Red Bull Salzburg. He had been to Austria to have his medical and for his team to discuss personal terms. 'We have a positive dialogue going, but nothing has been signed. We've been there to negotiate, but there are quite a few things left,' Alfie said. One of the points Molde and Salzburg had to reach an agreement on was what Haaland would do in the second half of 2018. Molde were one step away from qualifying for the Europa League group stage and they did not want to lose their attacking prodigy in the middle of the season. On 18 August the announcement came: Erling Haaland had signed a five-year contract with Red Bull Salzburg, but he would finish the Norwegian season with Molde and become a Salzburg player in January 2019. Reports in the Norwegian press at the time put the transfer fee at an initial 60 million kroner (around €6 million in 2018), rising to 100 million kroner (€10 million) with add-ons. Molde also reportedly secured a sell-on clause of 15 per cent of Haaland's next transfer fee. The deal was lucrative for Bryne as well, with a reported 15 million kroner finding its way to Jæren as a result of Bryne securing a sell-on clause when he moved to Molde. A potential transfer fee of €10 million was a significant sum for RB Salzburg to pay for a player who had only just turned 18, but the Austrians were confident that in Haaland they had a future star. And RB Salzburg have shown over the years that when it comes to identifying young talent they get it right more often than most.

From its inception, Red Bull Salzburg has been a controversial project. Technically the club was founded in 1933, but in any sense that matters the club as it exists today was founded in 2005. The club it used to be, SV Austria Salzburg, was founded in 1933 and had a golden age in the 1990s. The club became Austrian champions three times and even reached the final of the UEFA Cup in 1994.

But towards the turn of the millennium Austria Salzburg fell back into mid-table and started having financial problems. In 2005 the Austrian billionaire Dietrich Mateschitz and his company Red Bull bought the club and rebranded it entirely.

'Initially, there was plenty of positivity given Red Bull were a Salzburg company and Dietrich Mateschitz was a Salzburg-native, but that turned sour quickly,' Karan Tejwani, author of *Wings of Change: How the World's Biggest Energy Drink Manufacturer Made a Mark in Football*, explains.

> It wasn't uncommon in Austria for professional football clubs to be transformed by major companies, but the scale Red Bull went to had never been seen before. Not only did they want to change the name of the club, they wanted an overall rebrand, changing colours, kits, stadium name and more. This caused plenty of outrage and a large group of Austria Salzburg fans who had supported the club for years decided they couldn't do so anymore. A year after Red Bull's takeover in 2005, they formed their own phoenix club which still runs to this day and retained the Austria Salzburg name and colours. Red Bull did offer to retain the original Austria Salzburg colours, but only on the socks of their goalkeeper kit, which was seen as a massive insult to the many years of history and support by the fans. What was supposed to be a great story of a company from the city taking over the operations of its local football club and making them successful turned out to be something divisive and many fans felt discarded.

Red Bull Salzburg, with 'Der Kaiser' Franz Beckenbauer on board as an advisor, initially used some of that energy drink money to sign recognisable but ageing names from the German Bundesliga, including Thomas Linke, Niko Kovač, Alexander Zickler and Vratislav Lokvenc. The club also threw its financial weight around domestically by signing the then Austria captain, 22-year-old play-maker Andreas Ivanschitz, from title rivals Rapid Vienna. With the help of Beckenbauer's connections, Red Bull also appointed the legendary Italian manager Giovanni Trapattoni and brought in Lothar Matthäus to be his assistant manager. These recruits were successful, at least in the sense that the club was winning domestic trophies. But Mateschitz had bigger targets in mind than just turning Red Bull's Salzburg team into a domestic force in Austria. In the German state of Saxony the company had created RB Leipzig by purchasing the playing licence of SSV Markranstädt in the fifth tier of the German football pyramid and rebranding the club completely. Because the German Football Association (DFB) doesn't permit clubs to have the title of a corporation in their name, Red Bull called the club RasenBallsport Leipzig. 'RasenBallsport' literally translates as 'Lawn Ball Sports', and it gave the company the abbreviation they wanted: RB Leipzig. But getting a team from the fifth tier to the Bundesliga can be a challenge, even if you have money, and in 2012 RB Leipzig made a decision that would have big knock-on effects for Red Bull Salzburg as well.

'The strategy changed in 2012 after Ralf Rangnick's arrival at the club,' Tejwani explains.

It could be said that it would not have happened had their cousins in Germany, RB Leipzig, not been struggling. They were in the third division at the time … and were struggling to go up. That's when they turned to Rangnick to streamline their transfer and scouting policy, given that previous years had also seen them sign older and more expensive players. Rangnick now saw the opportunity to merge all the Red Bull clubs into one family, making Salzburg the de-facto developmental roster before [players] could move to Germany to play in the Bundesliga. Rangnick wanted a uniform style of football and coaching across all RB clubs so that players and coaches could easily transition between them. When they were signed, many players first moved to Salzburg to get a hint of the type of football they would be playing and if they made the grade, they would be signed by Leipzig.

The model worked, at least in the sense that a large number of players and coaches have moved from Salzburg to Leipzig over the years. RB Leipzig has become a serious force in the German Bundesliga, and Red Bull Salzburg has combined domestic success in Austria with earning a reputation for being a world-class incubator of footballing talent. Rangnick was initially seen as a bit of a maverick in German football who struggled to implement his ideas at other clubs, partially because the leaders at those clubs had been stuck in their old ways. At other clubs, if Rangnick wanted to bring in a sports psychologist, he might be told that this isn't something the club has had before and thus not something they needed now. But within the Red Bull footballing empire Rangnick was given a free hand to modernise and innovate. In his role as sporting director for Red Bull Salzburg Rangnick also hired ambitious young coaches for the first team, and he recruited them for their ability and footballing philosophy rather than how famous their surnames were. While footballing purists will probably never fully forgive Red Bull the company for its rebranding antics and highly commercialised approach to football, Red Bull Salzburg has gradually won a lot of people over.

'Many have accepted RBS' place in Austrian football,' Tejwani explains.

> They've been vastly successful, winning almost all the league titles and cups in the last decade, as well as making the knock-out rounds of the Champions League, which has boosted Austria's UEFA coefficient ranking. They've also vastly helped improve the Austrian national team, and Rangnick is now leading the national team which includes players he helped develop. Many of the purists still despise their place in the country and the fact that it's almost impossible to compete with them given their financial advantage, but I do feel fans are less resentful than they were when it first happened.

Turning down Juventus to move to the Austrian league might, on the surface of things, sound like a strange thing to do. But for the Haalands the decision made perfect sense. Moving to the Italian giants would have meant being unceremoniously dumped in the U-23 squad or sent out on loan to a club that would have no stake in his development. Moreover, a move to a Premier League club at this time would likely have meant the same thing: reserve-team football or a loan. In Red Bull Salzburg, Haaland was moving to a club that had been shaped and designed primarily with a view to developing young players – a club that could offer first-team football, modern facilities, modern methods and coaches who knew that developing youngsters is one of the most important parts of their job. Crucially, Red Bull Salzburg also had a proven track record when it came to developing players and selling them on. A decision that might seem strange on the surface actually made perfect sense on closer inspection. The transfer fee that Red Bull Salzburg paid for

Haaland also tells a story. It was one of the biggest transfer fees the club had ever paid for a player, which in itself is a form of guarantee. It signals the club's faith in the player, and its commitment to helping him develop. This total package convinced Alfie Haaland that Red Bull Salzburg was the best place for his son to continue his development: 'What excites me the most is their strategy of developing players so they can make the next step in European football,' he told *VG* after the move had been sealed. 'This is meant to be a springboard for Erling, but he understands that he has to perform. If he thinks about the next step already then he'll get nowhere. He has to deliver here first.'

'Haaland is one of the biggest talents in European football,' Red Bull Salzburg's sporting director Christoph Freund said when the signing was announced. 'He has decided to continue his promising career with Red Bull Salzburg. That he is coming to us, in spite of offers from many big clubs, makes us proud and shows that we have a good name in Europe.' A few years later, Freund revealed more about the process leading up to Haaland signing for the club. 'It was a very long process for Erling,' he told *Goal*.

> We first noticed him in 2016 at a game for the Norwegian U16 national team. Because it was difficult to get recordings of his games, we had it filmed. He convinced us right from the start, so the scout contacted him and his father. It is a great advantage to be in personal contact with a talent and their guardians before any other potentially interested club.

When asked what the club told the player at that early stage, Freund said that the answer was twofold: 'On the one hand, that he will get the chance to play international games very early on. And on the other hand, that he can still develop really well without much pressure due to the calm environment in Salzburg.' Freund added that when he first spoke to Haaland himself, in 2018, he got a very good impression. 'He seemed very focused, intelligent and confident to me. He knew exactly what he wanted.' Salzburg is not a club that will just hand a player a contract and leave them to their own devices: 'First of all, we organise a suitable apartment with the player, provide him with a German teacher if necessary and see that he can settle in well in Salzburg,' Freund said of how Red Bull Salzburg welcomes its new players.

> We have our own integration team consisting of three or four employees for this. They accompany our talents not only in football, but also in private life: show them the city, do things with them. We only sign so many foreign talents that we can look after them all very intensively and in a family manner.

For Erling Haaland, Red Bull Salzburg was a perfect destination in theory. And it would prove, in time, to be the perfect destination in practice as well.

11

SALZBURG

Having made the decision to join Red Bull Salzburg, Haaland initially had to be patient. Salzburg could offer a much clearer pathway to the first team than a giant club like Juventus could, but that didn't mean that the pathway was entirely without obstacles. Salzburg already had strikers, most notably the Israeli forward Munas Dabbur, who had scored 22 goals in the Austrian Bundesliga the season before Haaland arrived and was on track for another 20-goal season now. The squad also included the speedy Zambian striker Patson Daka, as well as another former Molde forward in Fredrik Gulbrandsen. Haaland, still only 18 years old and still an unpolished gem, had to bide his time. After all, things had progressed pretty rapidly for him. It had only been about six months since his big breakthrough game for Molde against Brann, and already he had been the subject of a tug-of-war between big European clubs. Not that Haaland himself would necessarily agree that it had all happened exceptionally quickly: 'If you compare me with another 18-year-old who is playing in the fourth tier in Norway, then it's been fast,' he told *VG* in an interview a few weeks after moving to Salzburg. 'But if you compare me with Mbappé, who is two years older than me, then it's going very slowly.' He had yet to make his official debut for Salzburg, yet here he was matter-of-factly comparing himself to French superstar Kylian Mbappé. This kind of confidence and ambition is not typically encouraged in young Norwegians. Remember the first Law of Jante: you're not to think *you* are anything special. Well, Erling Haaland had no time for that.

Before Christmas 2018, Haaland was awarded Young Player of the Year by the Norwegian online newspaper *Nettavisen*. He declared, 'From an early age I've told myself that I'm going to become the best footballer in the world,' which is not a very Norwegian thing to say. But what has always marked Erling Haaland out is that his ambition has been matched by an iron-clad determination and willingness to put the work in, to do whatever it takes. 'I'm very critical of myself. I have a long road ahead of me footballing-wise, but I've always tried to be a bit special, to stand out in different ways. To have an X-factor, so people will notice me,' he told *Nettavisen* in late November 2018.

> It's no use being afraid when you're going onto a football pitch. The worst thing that can happen is that you fail, and that's nothing to be afraid of. I have a bit of bravery and I'm not afraid to stand out on the pitch. Confidence is an important factor, to believe in yourself. You have to know that you're good enough, but at the same time be humble and work hard.

When talking about doing what it takes to succeed, people often speak about what they're willing to do, how hard they're willing to work, the hours they're prepared to put in. What is less often talked about, and probably should be a bigger part of the conversation, is what you're prepared to *not* do. 'I've not lived like a normal youth, who goes to school and parties on the weekend. I've enjoyed myself, but I've sacrificed a lot to get to where I am today,' Haaland explained. Those sentiments are echoed by his father:

> He's always been very conscientious. He's a regular kid, don't get me wrong, but he's always been dedicated and understands that you have to give up quite a lot of things if you want to become good. He's been willing to accept the consequences of what it takes. That's what's impressed me the most.

Alfie, in his interview with *Nettavisen*, said he knows talent alone isn't enough to succeed. According to him, Erling

> always had talent, but a lot of kids have talent. When it's been tough with school, homework and training, he's always had that drive to go out and play sports for fun as well. It's never been a chore. He's kept training and had that inner drive. That's what made me realise that he really wanted this.

Erling himself credited his old youth coach Alf Ingve Berntsen with helping him get to where he was, being named Young Player of the Year and on his way to Salzburg.

> He was like a father to me. He has been incredibly important to me, both on the pitch and off. He was strict with me, but he gave me a lot of advice and helped me stay motivated. He told me to focus on the football, and then my physique would come in time.

Haaland said he didn't mind at all that his growth spurt came a bit late, and is happy that he wasn't a strong player growing up: 'I was playing with the older kids … bigger and stronger players. I had to be smarter and find other ways of being good. To use my technique and my reading of the game.' He also talked up Solskjær's influence: 'He's been a big part of me getting to where I am today, and I'm still learning from him. I hope that one day I'll be as good a finisher as he was. Then I'll score bucket-loads of goals all around the world.' When asked about his temper, and the suggestions that as a child he was prone to being sulky when he didn't succeed, the then 18-year-old Haaland insisted that this could be a strength. 'The worst thing I know is losing. Even now I get angry just thinking about it … but it's about finding a balance and not losing your focus.' He admitted, 'I was a bit sulky when I was younger, yes, I'm not going to lie. And I'm still the same player, and I'm working on improving that.' The other thing he said he was starting to work on more at the time was his body.

> I enjoy learning more things about my body, to optimise my health and to biohack a bit. I'm becoming more and more wise and I understand my body better, and I'm taking on more knowledge. I have to find the perfect body that I can have, which will enable me to perform as well as I can.

So while Erling Haaland comparing himself to Kylian Mbappé may sound like bravado, delusion even, this was not a teenager with his head in the clouds. Far from it. The young Erling Haaland was, if anything, unusually self-aware, not only of his strengths but of what he could and had to do to improve. He was simply willing to set himself a target that others may have considered unreasonable. And for all the talk of hard work, sacrifice and 'biohacking', Haaland underpins it all with one important thing: having fun. 'If it's not fun,' Haaland says, 'you might as well retire.' Beyond having fun, though, at the same time you need to 'have a big goal of becoming as good as you possibly can. Then have fun, and have smaller goals along the way.' This was the mindset of the young man who came to Austria comparing himself to Mbappé. And as he himself had acknowledged, he had a long road ahead of him.

He got his first minutes for Red Bull Salzburg in February, coming on as a substitute for 19 minutes as the team beat Wiener Neustadt in the Austrian Cup. He then played his first minutes in the league a week later, this time coming on for the last 13 minutes as the team suffered a surprise 2–0 defeat to Rapid Vienna. It was the first time that Salzburg had lost in the league that season. Haaland was kept out of Salzburg's matchday squad for the next couple of months, but played 45 minutes in the Cup as they beat Grazer AK 6–0. But he wasn't at his best and didn't score. His adaptation to football outside of Norway was not instantaneous. He did get his first start for Salzburg in May, playing up front next to his compatriot Fredrik Gulbrandsen. After 13 minutes, a clipped ball over the top of the LASK defence found Haaland all alone, in acres of space, and he finished calmly past the goalkeeper for his first goal for Red Bull Salzburg. But that was his only goal and his only start in the league for Salzburg that spring. For Haaland, these months were about finding his feet in Austria, working hard in training and being patient. That summer Munas Dabbur was sold to Sevilla for €17 million and Gulbrandsen departed for İstanbul Başakşehir, clearing the way for Haaland to start the next season as a first-team regular.

Another change at Red Bull Salzburg that summer was the manager. Marco Rose moved on to manage Borussia Mönchengladbach in the German Bundesliga, and his replacement was the Wisconsin-born Princeton graduate Jesse Marsch. With 15 games for DC United, 200 for the Chicago Fire and 106 for Chivas USA, Jesse Marsch was until 2005 the record appearance maker in Major League Soccer (MLS). After his playing career he worked as an assistant manager to Bob Bradley with the US men's national team before taking on the always difficult job of being the first manager of a so-called 'expansion franchise', the Montréal Impact (now CF Montréal), which he led in their first ever season in MLS. Montréal finished seventh out of ten teams in the Eastern Conference of MLS, and Marsch left the club after one season. The *Montreal Gazette* reported that 'team management had been emphatic at a season-ending news conference this week they were satisfied with Marsch's work,' and Marsch had left the club because of 'philosophical' differences about how the team should be run. 'This is not a dismissal or a resignation,' said the team president Joey Saputo, confusing matters further. Marsch was back in management in MLS two years later, taking charge of the New York Red Bulls. He led the team to the Supporters' Shield, which is the award handed out to the team that takes the most points in the regular season. In Europe it would just be called winning the league, but in MLS there are play-offs, in which the New York Red Bulls were eventually stopped by the Columbus Crew. Still, Marsch was named 'MLS Coach of the Year'. He left the club in 2018, having finished in the play-offs in all three of his completed seasons with the club and top of the Eastern Conference in two of them.

He moved to Germany to work as an assistant manager under Ralf Rangnick, the man who had been the primary sporting architect of the entire Red Bull football project and was now the manager of RB Leipzig. After a year of working under Rangnick, Marsch took charge of Red Bull Salzburg. Again, on the surface of things it might seem strange for the super-ambitious RB Leipzig to put a man from

Wisconsin in charge of the team, but in reality this was more a kind of internal promotion. Marsch had impressed with the New York Red Bulls, had won Rangnick's approval at Leipzig and was then put in charge of Red Bull's Salzburg-based talent factory. Marsch, who had become the first ever member of RB Leipzig's coaching staff who was not a native German speaker, later explained how working under Rangnick taught him a lot. 'The first thing I learned was how specific and detailed the Germans are in the way they think and talk about football,' he told *The Athletic* in spring 2022.

> They're lasered-in on the smallest of details. It's a qual-
> ity of Germans, I think. They're very detail oriented and
> specific. I thought I was detail oriented about football until
> I met Rangnick. Then I knew I wasn't. This was a guy who
> worked through a system, a vocabulary and a methodology
> that I never even thought was possible. I called it an explo-
> sion in my head, because it was a new way of thinking.
> From there, I was learning more and more and detailing
> things more and more.

After a frustrating first half-season at Salzburg, it was clear that Jesse Marsch was the right manager at the right time for Erling. Marsch had a positive approach to management, both on the pitch and in his man management. He combined an enthusiasm and determination to win, which one might crudely describe as typical of the American sporting mentality, with experience of working within the renowned Red Bull system. Haaland himself would later tell *CBS* that Marsch was 'an amazing manager for me', and that 'I am lucky to have gotten to know him as a coach, but also as a person. He was very good with me.' Haaland was not the finished article when he arrived in Salzburg. According to a 2020 piece by Phil Hay, Raphael Honigstein and Tom Worville for *The Athletic*, 'one Salzburg player jokingly referred to him as "a cow" because of his huge frame and less than assured touch.' His first manager at Salzburg, Marco Rose, would later admit to German sports magazine *Kicker* that 'the first six months weren't easy for him.' Still growing into and coming to terms with his massive frame, Erling Haaland was prone to moments of clumsiness. But he was gradually becoming stronger, more confident and more assured. In the summer of 2019 he had made global headlines for the first time when he put a staggering nine goals past Honduras during the FIFA U-20 World Cup. He came back to Salzburg with renewed confidence and now with an enthusiastic new manager who was keen to work with him. At the start of the new season Marsch put Haaland in the team, and Haaland never looked back. In fact, for all of Red Bull Salzburg's experience with developing young talent, they'd never seen anything quite like this.

12

LIFT-OFF

The first official game of Red Bull Salzburg's 2019/20 season was the first round of the Austrian Cup, where they faced SC/ESV Parndorf from the fourth tier of the Austrian league system. The newly minted Salzburg manager Jesse Marsch started with Patson Daka and Erling Haaland up front, and Dominik Szoboszlai and Takumi Minamino on either flank. Against a team from the fourth tier it was a total, total mismatch. Minamino put Salzburg in the lead after just five minutes, before Haaland scored his first goal under Marsch, from a penalty in the 35th minute. The goalkeeper went the right way and nearly saved the penalty, and Haaland looked sheepish, almost unhappy with his effort, while being congratulated by his teammates. Salzburg then surged ahead, with full-back Patrick Farkas scoring twice and Patson Daka getting on the scoresheet. With the score 5–1 to Salzburg, Haaland added two more goals in the last 20 minutes of the game. First, he finished a rebound off the back post after a set piece, then he pounced on a defensive error to make it 7–1 in the 89th minute. A penalty, a tap-in and a defensive goof by a hopelessly outmatched opponent: as far as hat-tricks go, they don't come much uglier. But a hat-trick in your first game of the season is still a hat-trick in your first game of the season.

Jesse Marsch liked what he saw, and went into the start of the Austrian Bundesliga with Haaland as his first choice up front. He was rewarded with seven wins in their first seven games in the league, and a goal difference of 34 goals scored and six conceded. That's a frankly ridiculous average of 4.8 goals scored per game. And Haaland had done his part, chalking up eleven goals and five assists in seven games. Yikes. He didn't actually score in the first league game of the season, a 2–0 win against Rapid Vienna, but he did score in the second game against Mattersburg. He then secured his second hat-trick of the season, against Wolfsberger, scored twice against St Pölten, scored a goal against both Admira Wacker and WSG Tirol and netted another hat-trick against TSV Hartberg. Yes, this Salzburg team was way too good for the Austrian league. Yes, some of the defending Haaland was coming up against was questionable. But still. Three hat-tricks? Eleven league goals in seven starts? This was not normal, even at Salzburg. But there were bigger tests on the horizon for this high-flying squad. The time had come for Red Bull Salzburg to test themselves in the Champions League.

The Red Bull Salzburg project had long been a huge domestic success in Austria, but participation in the group stage of the Champions League had so far eluded them. The club had repeatedly lost in the play-off rounds, often by excruciatingly thin margins. But by putting in good work in the Europa League the club had helped improve Austria's UEFA coefficient to the point where the domestic champions went straight into the group stage. No more play-off agony for Salzburg. They'd been drawn in a group with Liverpool, Napoli and Genk, and after their glorious start to the season everyone involved with the club was excited to prove that they could do more than just trounce hapless Austrians in their domestic league. And no one was more excited than Erling Haaland. He had always dreamt of playing in the Champions League, and here was his chance. Salzburg's first group game was against the Belgian champions, Genk. The night before the game, Salzburg's captain Andreas Ulmer was out walking his daughter. A car pulled up next to them, the window came down. It was Erling Haaland, and he was driving around listening to the Champions League anthem. The boy was hyped. He was ready to go.

One of his opponents on the Genk team the next day was Sander Berge, who knew Haaland well from international camps with Norway. 'I'd been talking him down in our dressing room before the game,' Berge later told Viaplay.

This guy couldn't keep the ball in the rondo at international training earlier that autumn. OK, he scores in the Austrian league but I thought that was a bit of a bad league, since they were winning 5 and 6–0. I saw that he was direct, but I didn't think he'd score against us in the Champions League.

Before the game, Berge had seen Haaland looking crazed and manic in the tunnel. 'I laughed a little, but all my teammates thought this guy looks like he's going to go out and tear us to shreds.' They weren't far wrong.

On his Champions League debut it took Haaland less than two minutes to get his first goal. A ball was played into Minamino just outside the edge of the penalty area, and the Japanese international showed some very clever feet to sneak the ball into Haaland's path. Haaland found himself with the ball at his mercy, well within the 18-yard box, and finished with ease. He wheeled away, arms spread wide, shouting into the evening air, with his whole face and body looking like it was about to rupture from sheer emotion. In the 34th minute the South Korean international Hwang Hee-Chan was able to control a hopeful punt up the field, and he played it into Haaland – who was already on the move. Again Haaland was free and clear, and again he put it past the Genk goalkeeper. Hwang added a third goal himself just two minutes later. Genk then got one back, but with 44 minutes and 12 seconds on the clock Haaland poked in a low cross to make it 4–1. He had to wait for confirmation as the video assistant referee (VAR) investigated his positioning ahead of the goal. Haaland looked worried, thinking he had been offside, and was reluctant to accept congratulations from his teammates. But after a minute's deliberation the decision was announced. Haaland had scored a first-half hat-trick on his Champions League debut. 'When you run around with your celebrations, I understand why the players on the other teams get annoyed,' Genk midfielder Berge said to Haaland much later. 'It's not a mild celebration, you make a huge deal of it. Which suits you very well. But it was annoying at the time. And when you scored the third you were standing on the advertising hoardings.' But Haaland couldn't help himself. This wasn't against a Norwegian team, or some bewildered Hondurans or some profoundly outmatched Austrians. This was the Champions League, and he had scored a first-half hat-trick on his debut. This was just something else. In the end, Salzburg won the game 6–2.

'Erling is quite simply a good guy and a good person. Everyone in the team loves him and he is always smiling. We really enjoy having him around,' Marsch said after the game. 'I think everyone saw that what he did today was special,' Salzburg defender Maximilian Wöber told *VG*. 'It's not normal for a 19-year-old to play his first Champions League game in this way. His attitude, his mentality, his speed is just unique I think.' *VG* reporter Joachim Baardsen succeeded in tracking down a jubilant Haaland after the game and simply asked him, 'What is happening?' A grinning Haaland replied, 'We continue to do what we've done all season, really. And then this is what happens.' 'But what about you?' the reporter asked. 'Well, I had a good start and so I kept going.' Haaland's words were understated, as is so often the case, but here his face was beaming and his smile was as wide as it's ever been. 'How did it feel to score after just two minutes?' the reporter asks. 'It's the sickest thing I've experienced in my entire life,' Haaland grins. 'I was enjoying myself, put it that way.' When asked about the fact that only two other players had scored a hat-trick in the Champions League at his age, Raul and Wayne Rooney, Haaland's smile widens further and he nods. 'It's an achievement to manage that. But now the next game is in five days, against LASK. So we've got to keep working, we've got to continue,' he said. And when asked about what was going on with his mobile phone, Haaland answered, 'it's exploding, so I'm going to have to put it on flight mode for the next half-hour.' He was then asked, jokingly, about reports that he was spotted driving around listening to the Champions League anthem the night before the game, and again Haaland's grin threatened to exceed the capabilities of his facial muscles. 'My whole life I've watched the Champions League and listened to this damned beautiful song, so it's big. It hasn't really sunk in yet. We'll see if I manage to digest it now during the night.' Haaland showed off the match ball and said simply 'nice to have this one', then walked off into the night. A hat-trick in his first 45 minutes of Champions League football and 17 goals in his first nine games of the season. None of this is normal.

In the next game, against LASK, Haaland started on the bench and Salzburg drew 2–2, their first dropped points of the campaign. Then Haaland fell ill. He had to miss out on Salzburg's game against Rapid Vienna, and the next Champions League game, against Liverpool at Anfield, was in doubt. The Premier League is the most famous and popular league in the world, but for Norwegians its popularity goes beyond that. For Erling Haaland, playing an English team in England would mean something extra, not just because his father played in England but because for Norwegians the Premier League is something akin to a national obsession. This was not a good time for him to fall ill. He tried his best but was only fit enough for a place on the bench at Anfield. Before the match, Haaland told Salzburg's in-house media team about his excitement for the game ahead. 'They've won the Champions League, the best team in the world, very good fans, stadium, atmosphere, everything.' And with a wide, boyish grin, he added: 'It's a dream coming true, to play here.' In his last team meeting before the match Jesse Marsch stressed the importance of being brave. 'Guys, hold on to your self-esteem, no matter what the result,' he told his players, in more than passable German.

> Don't think about the result. What should be in your heads is our mentality, our attitude, our team spirit, our concentration as a team. Our team solidarity. Luck favours the bold. No matter what happens, we will be fucking brave. Let's be bold! Let's be bold!

The first half was not good for Salzburg. Liverpool, who had won the previous season's Champions League only a few months earlier, were rampant. Salzburg, used to overpowering weaker sides in Austria's domestic league, were cut apart by the brilliance of Liverpool's forwards. The first goal was classic Liverpool: Sadio Mané, himself a former Salzburg player, cut inside from the right flank, went past an opponent, played a one-two with Roberto Firmino and scored. The second goal came through some slick one-touch football from Liverpool, with Mohamed Salah playing a ball back to Jordan Henderson, who played it first time out to Trent Alexander-Arnold. With his first touch, the right-back played a cross into the box, where left-back Andy Robertson, of all people, put the ball in the net. In the 36th minute Salah pounced on a rebound from Salzburg's goalkeeper to make it 3–0. It was all too easy. Salzburg had yet to lose a match so far that season, but this situation looked unsalvageable. A few minutes later, however, Hwang Hee-chan gave them hope with some neat footwork in the box and a fine finish.

At half-time, Jesse Marsch was upset. He asked his players how many fouls they'd conceded, with the answer being two or three. *'Das ist nicht ein fucking Freundschaftsspiel!'* he exclaimed. This is not a friendly. 'It's a fucking Champions League game, we must give everything on the pitch and get fucking stuck in,' he continued, mostly in German. 'Come on, guys, you're showing too much respect. Are they good? Yes, they are. But we can't just play nicely, with a bit of pressure here and there. We need a really good tackle or a fight!' The footage of his speech was published after the game and went viral. With his passion, earnestness and his commitment to speaking German, Marsch came across as an inspirational and likeable figure. Ten minutes into the second half, Hwang played a fine cross from the left and the retreating Liverpool defenders failed to pick up Minamino, who scored to make it 3–2. In the 56th minute, a not entirely fit Haaland was substituted on for Patson Daka. Just a few minutes later Minamino was released in the box and squared the ball in front of goal. Haaland, of course, was lurking: 3–3. Haaland, excited to be playing against Liverpool at Anfield, had invited friends from Bryne to England to watch the game. When he scored, he knew roughly where they were in the stands and went over to point to them. Marsch sprinted down the touchline to celebrate with the players. When asked by the Norwegian press after the game about what Marsch had said to him during the celebrations, Haaland simply replied, 'I was focused on finding the boys from Bryne in the stands,' and confirmed that he did in fact find them. But Salzburg couldn't quite hold on. Salah made it 4–3 in the 69th minute, and Liverpool managed to hang on to the salvaged win until the final whistle. No points to the Austrian side, but a point had been made all the same. Not too many teams come back to equalise after going down 3–0 at Anfield. 'The biggest takeaway was that we can play, we can play with the best teams,' said Marsch after the game. 'I think our fans can go home and be proud.' 'It was nicely done by Minamino, so I could celebrate before the ball even went in,' Haaland said about his goal after the game. His Champions League stats now read one start plus 34 minutes off the bench, and four goals.

What was less widely reported in the international press at the time was how close Haaland came to missing out on the game altogether. Like at Molde some 18 months earlier, he had been ill and had trouble with his lungs. 'You can imagine a 19-year-old from Bryne who has problems with his lungs the week before a game against Liverpool at Anfield,' he told the Norwegian press after the game. 'You can imagine what's going on in his head. You want to go out and train, but you're not allowed. I've been in bed and thought a lot, put it that way,' he said. Considering he had been in the hospital two days before the game, he was 'pretty happy', to put it mildly, 'when the doctors said I could play for 30 minutes. You have no idea how happy I was that I could even be on the bench.' Haaland missed out on Salzburg's next game, against SCR Altach, but was back on the pitch when his team drew 1–1 against Sturm Graz later in October. And he was ready when it was time to play in the Champions League again, this time at home against Napoli.

The Salzburg fans, excited to see more Champions League action in their home stadium after the 6–2 thrashing of Genk, saw visitors Napoli take the lead in the 17th minute through Dries Mertens. But the lively Hwang Hee-chan was fouled in the box shortly before half-time, and as soon as the referee blew his whistle Haaland was running towards the loose ball. He made no mistake from the spot: 1–1. The goal meant he became only the second ever teenager to score in his first three Champions League games. He celebrated by assuming the lotus position, in reference to his enthusiasm for meditation – and perhaps also his determination to stay calm and relaxed amid the increasing hype and noise surrounding him. But Napoli proved a formidable opponent, with Mertens scoring again to make it 2–1 in the 64th minute. Less than ten minutes later, Haaland was left unmarked in the box as Zlatko Junuzović put a fine cross in, and the score was 2–2. Unfortunately for Salzburg the visitors struck again immediately afterwards, with Lorenzo Insigne making it 3–2 from a deflected shot. But Haaland had made an impact again, and this made it six goals in his first three Champions League appearances.

Around this time, the world was really starting to sit up and take notice of Haaland. If you score six goals in your first three games in the Champions League, it changes your life. It became increasingly important to shield Haaland from all the attention and the media. But just after the Napoli game, Haaland granted a big interview to a reporter from *Stavanger Aftenblad*, the regional newspaper from back home in the southwest of Norway. The journalist, Egil Ø. Nærland, had covered his father's career back in the day and was practically a friend of the family. 'It's going well, I'm playing for a good team, a big team. It's a shame we lost to Napoli. It's just details and better defending, from the whole team, that keeps us from being right at the top,' Haaland said. When asked about his six goals in just three games in the Champions League, Haaland was philosophical. 'It's big, it's great, but to be honest, it's almost a bit normal to score. That's why I'm a striker,' he said matter-of-factly. As much as football is in Haaland's genes, he could never have been a defender like his father. 'My dad was a defender, but that's boring. I've always been a striker, because that's where it happens.' Haaland was keen, as always, to give credit to the people who have helped him along the way.

> I've been lucky, I've had good people around me my entire life. In Bryne, in Molde and here in Salzburg. I've had coaches who understand me. Alf Ingve Berntsen has meant a lot. Ole Gunnar Solskjær at Molde, and the one I have now, Jesse Marsch. He's a great guy. We have a great time, we understand each other.

In terms of his family heritage, his genetics, Haaland has a lot to be grateful for. 'My speed I have from my mother and grandmother, and the football I have from my father and from Børahodl. They're good and active families on both sides,' he says. Børahodl is the farm belonging to Haaland's great-uncle, Gabriel Høyland, 'Mr Bryne', who played 596 games for his club and got 23 caps for his country.

Haaland's life in Salzburg was, as he described it, calm. 'We go out for dinner sometimes, mostly the Danish guy and Dominik Szoboszlai from Hungary and me.' (The 'Danish guy' in question was full-back Rasmus Kristensen.) Haaland insisted that he didn't have time for a girlfriend, and didn't make time to go to the cinema.

His days were split between training and rest. In fact, his life revolved fully around looking after his body. After every single game Haaland would use the ice bath and jacuzzi facilities that Salzburg had at their disposal. After an evening game in the Champions League that could mean hitting the ice bath well after midnight. 'It's been great for me to come here to Red Bull Salzburg,' Haaland said. 'I knew I'd get to play in the Champions League and to fulfil that part of my dream. You can't buy experience. You have to be on the pitch. That's what the club is giving me.' But with his sensational goal return in autumn 2019, both in the Austrian Bundesliga and the Champions League, it became inescapable that Haaland would not stay in Salzburg forever. Speaking in late October, Haaland was relaxed about it all: 'You can see for yourself that I'm enjoying myself. I'm enjoying every moment in the city and at the club.' But, on the clear speculation about his future, he said, 'You never know what will happen in football. The Premier League is the biggest thing in Norway, but if a big Spanish club knocks on the door then that's big as well.' He then added, 'Maybe Germany would suit me. There are a lot of good teams there now, and they play a bit like us, with a lot of pace in attack.'

Inevitably, players who do well for Red Bull Salzburg will be mentioned as potential transfer targets for RB Leipzig. That is, after all, a big part of why the Salzburg club is run the way it is. But in the case of Haaland, his team had an ace up their sleeve. Mino Raiola had ensured that Erling Haaland had a release clause in his contract. This meant that Salzburg would have to accept offers of a certain number, whether the owners wanted to or not. Without such a clause Salzburg could, hypothetically, have steered Haaland towards the mothership RB Leipzig by rejecting offers from other clubs. Indeed, the club could have complicated matters for Haaland by rejecting offers from clubs he wanted to move to. The release clause gave Haaland agency over his own future and, as long as his suitors were prepared to meet the asking price stipulated in the contract, it would be up to him and no one else where he moved next.

There were three more Champions League games for Salzburg in 2019, and Haaland scored two more goals. In the league he added another hat-trick against Wolfsberger on 10 November, meaning he had scored two league hat-tricks against the same club in just over three months. Fans of Wolfsberger AC, or to give them their full name, Riegler & Zechmeister Pellets Wolfsberger Athletik Club, were presumably keen for Erling Haaland to leave Austria as soon as possible. As for Haaland, he was enjoying life playing under Jesse Marsch, who he felt he had a real connection with. Marsch too was enjoying working with Haaland. 'The first thing that comes to mind about Erling Haaland: he is a professional! It's fun to work with him. He comes to training every day with a lot of energy. I like guys like that,' he told *Goal* in 2020. 'The positive effect he gave to our whole group was massive. If he needs a little help, we are always there for him. But he also has his family, his father, a really solid foundation to understand how to deal with these moments.' Haaland's teammate at Salzburg, Maximilian Wöber, was also a fan. 'He is an absolute top professional,' he also told *Goal* in 2020.

While we are playing cards on trips away, you can only see him reading some scientific articles on how he can improve his sleep or diet. He is always looking for the smallest details that he can improve to take another step forward. He is the same guy I met in the summer, before his eight Champions League goals. He's crazy insane, but that's what makes him so good.

So good, in fact, that keeping him in Austria for much longer was going to be very difficult for Red Bull Salzburg. Haaland's release clause was set at €22.5 million, and there was no shortage of big clubs who would gladly pay that sum for a 19-year-old who had scored eight goals in his first six games in the Champions League. Yet again, less than 18 months after deciding to move to his current club, Erling Haaland and his team had to find the best possible answer to a very difficult question: where next?

13

ALL FOR NORWAY

On a late summer day in the year 1000, somewhere in the western Baltic Sea, King Olaf Tryggvason of Norway witnessed his fleet come under attack. He had sailed into an ambush set by Svein Tjugeskjegg, the king of Denmark and Olaf's brother-in-law, in alliance with Olof Skötkonung, the king of Sweden, and one of Olaf's Norwegian rivals Eiríkr Hákonarson. According to legend, Olaf's fleet consisted of just 11 ships and the opposing force numbered at least 70. A savage battle erupted, in which arrows and spears rained down on Olaf's men in such quantities that they could hardly keep their shields up. But they initially held their own, so the story goes, in large part due to the skill and power of Olaf's peerless royal archer, Einar Tambarskjelve. But then calamity struck: Tambarskjelve's mighty bow was hit by an arrow and broke. King Olaf heard the sound and asked, 'What was that, that broke with such a noise?' 'Norway, king, from thine hands,' Einar replied. As the battle turned decisively against him, King Olaf jumped into the sea and was never seen again. 'This,' Per Joar Hansen chuckles, 'is how I see Erling Haaland for the Norwegian national team. Like Einar Tambarskjelve and his bow. With him we have a chance against anyone. Without him, well, that chance becomes much, much smaller.'

Per Joar Hansen was the assistant manager to Lars Lagerbäck when Haaland got his debut for the Norwegian national team. He visited the player in Salzburg just after Haaland had moved there, 'just to get to know him better'. 'That was the first time I met him, really,' Hansen remembers. 'My impression then was that he was a guy who, even though he was still young, knew what he wanted and had a clear plan for his career.' Since Haaland was born in Leeds, he was eligible to play for England – but, before anyone gets too excited, there was never any real prospect of this happening. With Haaland having represented Norway at U-15, U-16, U-17, U-18, U-19, U-20 and U-21 level, it's fair to say that the Norwegian FA was well on top of the situation. The first time that Haaland had made international headlines was with the Norwegian U-20s during the FIFA U-20 World Cup, played in Poland during the summer of 2019. The Norwegian youngsters had been ecstatic to qualify for the tournament by beating England the summer before, but the tournament didn't start well for the team. They lost 3–1 to Uruguay, with Darwin Núñez scoring one of Uruguay's goals. And while there is no shame in losing to Uruguay, the next game was a huge disappointment. Norway lost 2–0 to New Zealand. 'We went down to Poland and watched a game, against New Zealand, and you have to say neither Haaland nor anyone else on the team looked ready for the senior squad in that game,' says Hansen with a laugh. 'Then we went back home, and in the next game he scored nine goals.'

'He came to the World Cup unsure of himself, I think,' the Norwegian U-20s manager Pål Arne 'Paco' Johansen later told *The*

Athletic in April 2021. It had been a very long season for Haaland, in effect a season and a half. In early 2018 his preseason with Molde had been marred by illness, he had then gradually established himself with the team, had his big breakthrough moment against Brann, played in the U-19 Euros during the summer, gone back to Molde and finalised a transfer to Salzburg in August. Then he stayed with Molde until the end of the Norwegian season in late November, moved to Salzburg, and spent the first half of 2019 getting used to living abroad but also not really playing for the first team. In one sense it had been relentless, but in another he was also lacking match fitness. In Norway's first two games, against Uruguay and New Zealand, Haaland was not the best version of himself.

It had not been a good tournament for Honduras either. The Central American nation is not without footballing pedigree – they have qualified for three World Cups (1982, 2010 and 2014) and often give a good account of themselves in the CONCACAF Gold Cup. But here they started the tournament with a disappointing 5–0 defeat to New Zealand. In the next game they kept it respectable against Uruguay and lost 2–0, but this left the game against Norway as the nation's last chance to salvage something from the group stage. They didn't. Norway were 5–0 up at half-time, with Haaland scoring four. 'He was in a place where I was aware he didn't need to be pushed with more feedback about why he wasn't scoring. From the first kick of the ball, you see he's there,' Håkon Wibe-Lund, on the Norwegian coaching staff that day, also told *The Athletic*. 'I sensed it before the Honduras game because I'd seen it before.' Wibe-Lund didn't expect nine goals, of course, but could tell that Haaland was going to try something special: 'He's very easy to read. You know when he's going to perform at his best. My thought was: good luck to the opposition.'

Haaland put Norway ahead after just six minutes, and thought he'd scored another just two minutes later, only for VAR to spot a soft foul in the build-up. But he got his second in the 20th minute, and then Norway's captain, Leo Skiri Østigård, powered in a header from a corner. Haaland added two more before half-time, and the game was no longer a contest. The young Honduran players had given up. Heads had dropped, their spirits sapped, any kind of focus was gone. But Norway, and Haaland in particular, were not about to let up. Haaland just isn't built that way, and this was a team that liked to attack. After all, they had beaten Germany 5–2 and Scotland 5–4 not that long ago. And because they had lost their first two games, Norway could only finish third in the group, and in this tournament the four best third-place finishers from the six groups would progress. Goal difference could become a factor. So in the second half, against a demoralised and disorganised Honduras, Norway kept going. The final score was 12–0, with Haaland scoring a scarcely believable nine goals. A triple hat-trick. 'It is the first time I have scored nine goals in a game. That's a milestone for me,' he said after the game. 'It's hard to put into words. It's fun. There's no point saying much. You know this is fun for me.' But, Haaland being Haaland, he wasn't fully satisfied with his efforts. 'I wanted to get into double figures for myself, I can't deny it, but in the end it was nine and I'm happy with that,' he told NRK.

The result raised eyebrows around the footballing world, but it also raised some suspicions. Norwegian TV pundit and former player Jesper Mathisen tweeted in the first half that 'Honduras must have bet on Norway. This is going to go into double figures if they behave like this for the rest of the game.' The rest of the game did little to change his mind, and he told TV2 after the match,

While it's impressive that Norway won by this much, I have to question what Honduras were doing during this game. To me it looked like they wanted to lose. It looked suspiciously like match-fixing. Honduras are not the greatest country in the world when it comes to football, but they looked totally disinterested during the entire game. They didn't do much to stop the Norwegian players, even inside their own box.

'I think the boys were nervous, and there was a lack of coordination,' president of the Honduran FA, Jorge Salomón, said in the aftermath of the game. 'I hope to God that this was the reason, for the boys' sake.' FIFA investigated, but concluded later that summer that they had found no evidence of foul play. Norway's manager Paco Johansen told *Nettavisen*:

> As I said after the game, my view is that Honduras first and foremost looked like themselves in a footballing sense. I rarely see two games of football that are as similar as Honduras's game against New Zealand and their game against us.

New Zealand, of course, didn't have an angry Erling Haaland who was out to prove a point.

That autumn, as Haaland started getting more minutes on the pitch for Salzburg and inevitably started scoring goals, it became obvious that the time had come for his senior debut for Norway. He made his debut in a Euro 2020 qualifier win against Malta on 5 September 2019 and then came off the bench a few days later against Sweden. 'The impression I had then was that he had grown already during his time at Salzburg,' says Hansen. When Haaland was called up to the senior squad he immediately made a positive impression.

He was smart socially, I would say. He didn't come barging in, trying to be something he wasn't. You saw that this was a boy who had his feet on the ground. He had done very well for his club side and he knew that, so he had no need to come in there and show off and be one of these cocky young guys.

His debut was a game where Norway struggled to create as many chances as you'd expect at home, but the team eventually won 2–0. 'I'm proud, I'm proud,' said Haaland after the game, adding that walking out with the team and hearing the anthem gave him goosebumps.

For the next game, against Sweden, Per Joar Hansen had an idea. He found an old clip of Norway beating Sweden 2–1 in a 1977 European qualifier and showed it to Haaland. The grainy old footage showed a Norwegian player with the number seven on his back receive a high ball some 25 yards away from goal. He controlled it with his instep, let it bounce once and then let fly with a flawless, dipping half-volley that arced perfectly into the top corner. The Swedish goalkeeper never moved, and indeed any attempt at saving the shot would have been a waste of calories. The video cuts to the post-match interview with the goal scorer, and Haaland suddenly exclaimed, 'Hey, wow, that's my electronics teacher!' The goal scorer was Rune Ottesen, who had moved to Bryne in the late 1970s to play for the football team and became a teacher at the local upper secondary school after retiring. 'I don't know if he knew about this goal because it's 40 years ago,' Hansen laughs. 'It was very funny!' The game against Sweden was Haaland's first really big game with the national team and Hansen figured he would show him that players from Bryne had tormented the Swedes in the past. 'I joked with him later, when he was banging in goals in Dortmund, that if you score a few more goals now you'll be almost as famous as Gabriel

Høyland and Rune Ottesen. Though I think we can say that he's moved beyond that now.'

Haaland started on the bench against Sweden. In their history, Norway had played seven qualifiers against Sweden away from home, but never managed to win one. Here they took the lead in the first half after a mistake by the Swedish defence. It was 1–0 at half-time, and Norway was looking the better team. But in the second half the players became passive, and Swedish attacker Emil Forsberg scored an equaliser. Haaland was only brought on with 15 minutes to go, but Norway couldn't find a winner. The draw was not a bad result in isolation, but Norway had dropped too many points earlier in the group. It left them needing to get a point against Spain and then beat Romania later that autumn. Haaland missed those games due to injury and, while Norway held Spain, the team was unable to beat Romania. Wins against Malta and the Faroe Islands in the last two games of the group, also with Haaland absent through injury, weren't enough. Norway finished third in their group.

But Norway had one last chance to get to Euro 2020: a play-off, secured through results in the Nations League. First the Norwegians would face Serbia, and the winner of that match would come up against either Scotland or Israel. These games were due to be played in March the next year, but were moved to October and November due to the outbreak of the COVID-19 pandemic. By the time the game against Serbia came around, Haaland was a superstar. He had made the move to Dortmund, and he was scoring for fun in the Bundesliga. With Haaland up front and Martin Ødegaard in midfield, the Norwegians had reasons to feel optimistic, but the game was a monumental disappointment.

Alexander Sørloth was coming off a remarkable campaign in the Turkish league for Trabzonspor, where he was on loan from Premier

League club Crystal Palace and had scored 24 goals in 34 games. In a Nations League game against Northern Ireland in September 2020 the Norway manager Lars Lagerbäck had deployed Sørloth and Haaland together up front to great effect. With Sørloth being 6 foot 5 and Haaland 6 foot 4, the two would form an unusual 'large and large' partnership up front, and against Northern Ireland they scored two each. But fitting them both in the starting 11 meant shunting Martin Ødegaard out wide into a notional left midfield role, which reduced his ability to affect the game. Against an aggressive, technically proficient Serbia team, this system malfunctioned badly. The Norway players were never able to get a hold of the midfield and created next to nothing for the rest of the match. Having two tall goal scorers up front does very little for you if you can't get the ball to them. Serbia took a deserved lead in the 80th minute, and Norway were fortunate in that a lively Mathias Normann scored an equaliser out of nothing in the 87th minute. In extra time Serbia continued to be much the better team, and Sergej Milinković-Savić scored the winner with a delicate chip from a tight angle. 'I'm not going to swear, but it's very painful. We had a good opportunity to get to the Euros, but we just weren't good enough. They deserved to win,' a downcast Haaland told TV2 after the game.

For Haaland, the game had been particularly frustrating. His only real chance was a header from a corner in the first half. Service wasn't just bad, it was non-existent. Haaland kept running, and passes kept being misplaced. But while Haaland was at times visibly frustrated, he never appeared to criticise or complain to his teammates. Because a reality that Haaland has to accept when playing for Norway is that some of his teammates are of a very different standard to the players he is used to playing with for his club sides. For instance, one of the other starters in the crucial game against Serbia, left-back Haitam

Aleesami, was without a club at the time. It's not a great sign for any national team when you head into a game with tournament qualification at stake and one of your starters is temporarily unemployed.

'I think this is a scenario that Erling has worked through with himself,' says Hansen.

> He understands that his teammates for the Norwegian national team are not of the same quality as the ones he's playing with at his club. He knows this. He knows that with Norway, maybe he'll get two fantastic passes that can set him up for a chance every game, but at his club he might get seven or eight. He's intelligent enough to be aware of this ... which is very mature for a young guy who is in that position. He could be shaking his head or showing his frustration in other ways when he doesn't get the passes he wants, but you just never see that.

In his first 25 games for the Norwegian national team Erling Haaland scored 24 goals. No one can accuse him of not playing his part. 'He's a leader when it comes to hard work,' says Hansen.

> He never shirks his duties when it comes to pressing, when it comes to tracking back, when it comes to his assignments on defensive set pieces. He is a player who commands respect in the dressing room because there is no vanity. Everyone in the squad understands that they're sitting in a dressing room with a global superstar. He could have decided to behave in a very different way, and he could have gotten away with it. But that's just not him. He's been raised well, he has solid values, at least as far as I've experienced.

Haaland's club career has been defined by constant progress, leading to near-unprecedented success, but with Norway there have been setbacks. The Serbia game was one, and more would follow. But Erling is not one to point the finger. 'I've met a lot of footballers in my time who loved talking about themselves, and if we're evaluating a game after a defeat they don't see their own part in that, they just see the rest of the team,' says Hansen.

> I've never experienced Erling to be like that at all. He never blames others, he blames himself. If he had a bad touch or missed a chance in the game, he'll focus on doing that better next time – rather than whatever the other players did in the game. That's one of the reasons he's so well liked by his teammates. The players who play with him, they can see this, that he is someone who takes responsibility for his own performances and that he's part of the group – even if some of the other players come from a very different level. I think that's why he ends up being so well liked.

'I've never known him, in any setting, to have *stjernenykker*,' Hansen continues. *Stjernenykker* is a Norwegian word that's not easily translated, but it means little habits or behaviours that stars with big egos might start to indulge – and be indulged – in. To have the tendencies of a diva, to be a prima donna, essentially.

> You see him in team meetings, he's always focused. He's always on time. In warm-ups, the little things, everything he does is 100 per cent professional. There's never been any case of him overlooking details or doing anything half-way. I would call him just a super professional. Probably the most

professional player I've ever come across, along with Martin Ødegaard. Both when it comes to details, about understanding the game, and about doing what it takes to succeed.

But Norway, as a team, did not succeed. In December 2020 Lars Lagerbäck was relieved of his duties and replaced with Ståle Solbakken. As a player, Solbakken won 58 caps for Norway and was a significant contributor to the team's success in the 1990s. He was part of the Norway squad both for the 1998 World Cup and Euro 2000. In one sense, Solbakken's first tactical decision as Norway boss came not after he was put in charge of the team in 2020, but in the summer of 1998. Norway were playing Brazil in their last World Cup group-stage game and needed a win to progress. It was the second half, it was 0–0, and the manager, Egil 'Drillo' Olsen, wanted to bring on Egil Østenstad. Then things took a turn for the worse, as Brazil took the lead. 'I didn't say it to Drillo, I said it to Nils Johan Semb: if there is any point to having Jostein Flo in this squad, this right here is it. We should use him,' Solbakken told the *Heia Fotball* podcast. Jostein Flo was 33 years old and not in the best physical shape of his career. But he was 6 foot 4, strong and possessed a mighty leap. In his youth, he had been a promising high jumper, with a personal record of clearing a very respectable 206 centimetres. One of Egil Olsen's successful stratagems with Norway in the 1990s was putting Flo out wide and playing high diagonal balls in his general direction. Full-backs, more accustomed to defending against tricky wingers, were terrified. Many a Norwegian triumph was built on knock-downs out wide, as the brutish Flo left a string of traumatised full-backs in his massive wake. Østenstad was a fine player in his own right, but Solbakken had identified that if Norway were to unsettle the Brazilians then the mountainous presence of Flo made more sense. He told Semb, the assistant manager, and the message was passed up to Olsen. Østenstad, who had warmed up and was ready to come on, was told to sit down, while Flo had to scramble to locate his shirt. With the added aerial threat of Flo on the pitch, Norway succeeded in building more attacks against the Brazilians. His younger brother, the then Chelsea forward Tore Andre Flo, grabbed an equaliser for Norway and won a penalty, which Kjetil Rekdal converted. Beating Brazil at the World Cup to progress from the group is regarded by many Norwegians as the greatest moment in the country's sporting history. And though he was on the bench, Ståle Solbakken had played a minor but significant part.

In 2001, while a player with FC Copenhagen, Solbakken suffered a cardiac arrest in training. He was clinically dead for seven minutes, before the club doctor and ambulance personnel succeeded in restarting his heart. He was fitted with a pacemaker, and on the doctors' advice retired from the game. He had always been a leader and captained several clubs in his career, so going into management was an obvious next step. A successful stint with Hamarkameratene in Norway earned him a chance to manage FC Copenhagen, whom he led to four league titles in five seasons. He also took them to the group stage of the Champions League, where they memorably beat Manchester United 1–0. In November 2009 he agreed to take charge of the Norwegian national team with an unspecified start date. It was an unorthodox arrangement. The Norwegian FA wanted Solbakken, but they also didn't want to fire the boss at the time, Egil Olsen. Olsen had been the mastermind behind the Norwegian team's success in the 1990s, but at 67 years of age he was unlikely to be the long-term solution for Norway. Solbakken was the coming man. But Solbakken still had a contract with FC Copenhagen, so the idea was to let him finish his contract there and let Olsen finish the qualifying campaign with Norway. Solbakken would take charge either in January 2012 or after Euro 2012, if Norway were to qualify for the tournament. They didn't, and while waiting to take charge of his country Solbakken was instead offered a chance to manage 1. FC Köln in the Bundesliga. Keen to further test himself at club level, Solbakken opted for the Bundesliga rather than the Norwegian national team. At Köln he lasted less than a season. 'Jesus and José Mourinho would have struggled together at that club this year,' he said later, adding that the club had been 'killed' by in-fighting. After an unhappy half-season in charge of Wolverhampton Wanderers in the Championship, Solbakken headed back to FC Copenhagen and started winning titles again. He eventually left the club in 2020, and when the Norway job became available that December he was an obvious candidate. His success with FC Copenhagen, especially in taking them to the Champions League, where they often held their own against financially superior opponents, had established him as the most qualified Norwegian manager for the job.

After taking over, Solbakken was clear that his target was to lead Norway to their first international tournament since Euro 2000. The first set of qualifiers facing Norway were for the 2022 World Cup in Qatar, and Norway had been drawn in a group with the Netherlands, Turkey, Montenegro, Latvia and Gibraltar. The top team would qualify, the runner-up would go into a play-off. 'Percentage wise the World Cup will be a lot more difficult to qualify for than the Euros,' he told *VG* in December 2020.

> We will do everything we can during the World Cup qualifiers, we won't stand there cap in hand, anything can happen in football. But for the Euros there are more countries that qualify, and there is so much potential in our team that as long as we don't hit a bonanza of long-term injuries to our

most important players I think we have good chances to succeed with the Euros.

When it came to Haaland, Solbakken was also clear: 'His nose for goal, and how he's a constant threat with his runs, both in behind and with his movement in the box, I have to maximise these threats,' he said, before warning that Haaland won't always have an easy job. 'There may be one or two games where he has to bite the bullet and do other jobs than the things he's best at. That's life.'

When the qualifiers for the World Cup kicked off, the football calendar was still severely affected by the COVID-19 pandemic. Norway had to play three games in a week, with Solbakken having very limited time with his players to prepare. Gibraltar were beaten 3–0 as a matter of course, but in their second game Norway faced Turkey. This was supposedly Norway's home game against Turkey, a key match in the group, but because of the pandemic it had to be played in an empty stadium in Spain. Solbakken set his team up in a 4-4-2 formation, still with both Sørloth and Haaland up front, but now with an unfamiliar diamond shape in midfield. It didn't work at all. Turkey played through Norway with ease and won 3–0. 'I picked the wrong team for that game,' Solbakken later conceded, adding that he had made too many changes too quickly and that the players were uncomfortable with the set-up. 'It would have been better to play more like before, that one's on me,' he told *VG* in November 2021. Having lost to Turkey, Norway found themselves on the back foot in their group. In September, Haaland scored as Norway managed a creditable 1–1 draw against the Netherlands at home, scored again as they beat Latvia 2–0 and scored a hat-trick as they beat Gibraltar 5–1. But then, disaster struck for Norway: Haaland missed the remaining four qualifiers in the group with injuries. The king's archer had broken his bow. Without him, and missing several other regular starters, Norway got a respectable draw away to Turkey and beat Montenegro, but they then drew 0–0 with Latvia before losing 2–0 against the Netherlands. Norway finished third in the group. No play-off spot. No World Cup for Erling Haaland.

'I'm totally confident that we will make Euro 2024 in Germany if we continue the way we've started. The players feel secure, comfortable and are playing with confidence. They did that today as well, even if we didn't succeed with everything we tried,' Solbakken insisted after the defeat to the Netherlands. 'There's great optimism and belief in the team.' Norway may still make Euro 2024 but, in spite of becoming a global superstar, Erling Haaland has so far had to watch two major tournaments from the sofa. It's been a combination of bad timing, unfortunate injuries and the team around him being just not quite good enough. And this unlucky combination of factors appeared to continue in the beginning of Norway's campaign to qualify for Euro 2024. This time around, Norway were drawn in a group with Spain, Scotland, Georgia and Cyprus, and both the winner and runner-up would automatically qualify for the tournament. In March 2023 Haaland had to leave the Norway camp ahead of their first two qualifiers, against Spain and Georgia, because of a muscle injury. Suggestions that Haaland was saving himself for Manchester City's title charge in the Premier League were vehemently rejected by Solbakken. 'He was very upset in the hotel last night. He was dismayed and very frustrated. He's done everything he could,' Solbakken insisted. Without Haaland, Norway lost 3–0 to Spain and then could only draw 1–1 against Georgia. With Scotland claiming a surprise victory against Spain, Norway again start a qualifying campaign on the back foot. There is a real danger that Euro 2024 will be the third international tournament Erling Haaland has to watch from afar.

14

THE DECISION, PART ONE

In the first half of the 2019/20 season Erling Haaland played 22 games for Red Bull Salzburg and scored 28 goals. The fact that he had a release clause in his contract was widely known, and ahead of the January transfer window he was one of the hottest names in the entire global transfer market. Haaland may have had some exciting offers to choose from when he left Molde, but now it seemed like pretty much every major football club in the world was taking an interest. When Red Bull Salzburg hosted Liverpool in their last game of the Champions League group stage that season, scouts from a total of 40 European clubs were reported to be in attendance. Clubs that were linked with a move for Haaland included, but were not limited to, Real Madrid, Barcelona, Bayern Munich, Chelsea, Manchester City, Atletico Madrid, Juventus, RB Leipzig, Manchester United and Dortmund. And the last four were of particular interest.

Juventus had, of course, been after Haaland for a long time. They thought they were close to a deal two years before and, according to the Italian press, the club was making another big push to bring him to Italy. Manchester United, on the other hand, was now managed by Haaland's old boss, Ole Gunnar Solskjær, who had been a very important figure in Haaland's career. He put a lot of faith in Haaland at a very young age, at a time when Haaland was very far from the finished article. Haaland himself said that he received a lot of valuable advice from Solskjær. 'We've had a kind of father–son relationship, he's meant an awful lot to me,' Haaland said just before he left Molde. Manchester United needed a striker; Solskjær had a close relationship with the player and had a general idea of bringing young players to the club. According to *VG*, Solskjær flew to Salzburg on 13 December to speak to Haaland and his team. A lot of things seemed to add up, and both Sky Sports and the *Telegraph* had declared that Manchester United were favourites to sign Haaland in the January transfer window. But just a few days before Solskjær's visit to Austria, Haaland had taken a trip of his own. He had been to Germany.

In some ways RB Leipzig seems like the most obvious destination, given that the club is the mothership of the Red Bull footballing empire and the unofficial 'parent club' of Red Bull Salzburg. But Borussia Dortmund was a club that held an obvious appeal to Haaland. The second biggest club in Germany, Dortmund has a proven record of putting faith in younger players. On Wednesday, 11 December 2019, the Austrian newspaper *Heute*, along with a few other outlets, spotted that a private jet with the registration code D-CARO had flown a particularly interesting route. The jet had left its base in the German city of Hanover at 8.24am, flying south to Nice, the closest airport to Mino Raiola's home in Monaco. It left Nice and headed for Salzburg, where it landed at 12.08pm. Just 21 minutes later it left Salzburg, heading for Leipzig. The plane stayed in Leipzig for about two and a half hours, before departing in the direction of Dortmund. It landed in Dortmund at 3.53pm, stayed there for another couple of hours, then headed back down to Salzburg. It left Salzburg at 8.06pm, heading to Nice, where it landed at 9.17pm. Now, it was never officially confirmed that Mino Raiola and Erling, or Alfie, were on the flight. In a realm of infinite possibilities, it is theoretically possible that some other member of the European financial elite felt a pressing need to fly from Nice, stop in Salzburg, then fly to the eastern German city of Leipzig before moving on and making a stop in Germany's former industrial heartland of the Ruhr valley, before then returning to Salzburg and then back to Nice, for reasons that were not at all related to elite-level football. It's theoretically possible but, let's face it, it's not very probable. When Jesse Marsch was asked by the Norwegian press if Salzburg knew about Haaland's German sojourn the American assured them that 'we are communicating well with Erling and Alfie, and are involved in everything that happens.'

Given that Red Bull Salzburg's role in Ralf Rangnick's grand vision for Red Bull's football project was to be a kind of proving ground, and an incubator of talent that would ultimately benefit RB Leipzig, it would stand to reason that Erling Haaland would be pushed in that direction. After all, he had said publicly himself that Germany could be a league that would suit him. With his explosive pace and his ability to time his runs, the open, sometimes chaotic football of the Bundesliga should suit him perfectly. But there were drawbacks to a potential move to RB Leipzig. Later, in the Viaplay documentary *Haaland: The Big Decision*, Alfie Haaland said that the Red Bull mothership was actually not that keen. 'RB Leipzig were not that interested. Because they had Timo Werner, they had Poulsen, they had many good players,' he said. In hindsight this might sound silly, given that Timo Werner had such a difficult time in the Premier

Erling Haaland's determination and desire to score goals stood out to his coaches at Bryne's youth teams from a very young age.

As a young player Haaland had yet to develop his trademark physique, so he had to learn how to hold his own against bigger, stronger defenders.

Haaland joined Molde in February 2017. He and his father were convinced it was the best place for him to start his career away from Bryne. They weren't wrong.

Some of Haaland's biggest early successes came with the Norwegian youth international teams. Here he is with a towering header against Germany in a U19 European Championship qualifier on 24 March 2018.

Molde manager Ole Gunnar Solskjær, himself one of Norway's greatest ever goal scorers, proved the perfect mentor for young Haaland.

30 May 2019 was the day Haaland made global headlines for the first time, scoring an incredible nine goals for Norway, beating Honduras 12–0 in the FIFA U19 World Cup.

Haaland celebrating his first goal in the Champions League on 17 September 2019.

Jesse Marsch proved to be the right boss at the right time for Haaland.

In October 2019 Haaland came on and scored against Liverpool at Anfield, even though he had struggled with illness leading up to the game.

Patson Daka and Zlatko Junuzovic celebrate with Haaland after he scored against Napoli in the Champions League on 23 October 2019. He later became the first ever teenager to score in five consecutive games in that tournament.

In his first ever game for Dortmund Haaland came off the bench to score a hat-trick in just 34 minutes on the pitch.

Dortmund had a lot of creative players but needed a goal scorer up front. Haaland was happy to fill the vacancy. Here he celebrates his hat-trick goal on his debut against Augsburg.

Haaland is congratulated after scoring against Paris Saint-Germain in February 2020. The goals against PSG left no doubt that the football world had a new superstar.

On 13 May 2021 Haaland lifted his first major trophy when Dortmund beat RB Leipzig in the final of the German cup, the DFK-Pokal.

When joining Manchester City Haaland said he was looking forward to playing Manchester United. He then helped himself to a hat-trick in his first Manchester derby.

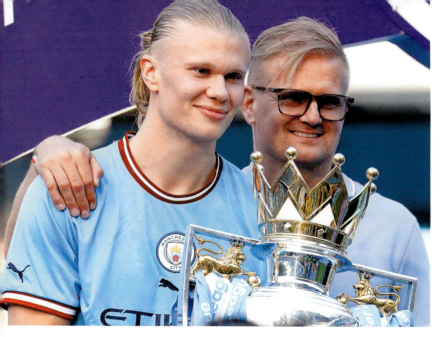

Haaland celebrating winning the Premier League with his father, Alfie Haaland. Manchester City today are a very different club to the one Alfie played for in the 2000/01 season.

In his first season in the Premier League Haaland was the top scorer in the division by some margin, securing himself the Castrol Golden Boot.

Not everyone was convinced that Haaland would be suited to Pep Guardiola's playing style, but they both have a tendency to make their doubters look foolish. A golden boot and a treble was a pretty solid answer to the questions.

City won the FA cup on 3 June 2023. But celebrations were brief: there was one more game to be played.

In Manchester City's Champions League round of 16 game against RB Leipzig Haaland ran wild and scored five goals.

The Champions League final was a difficult game for Manchester City, but defensive midfielder Rodri came up with the goal that secured the trophy.

Manchester City had won everything except the Champions League, and Haaland was brought in to do something about that. Together he and the club succeeded in his first season.

'A boy from Bryne wins the treble. It's not so bad in the first season in the Premier League', Haaland told Norwegian TV2 after the Champions League final. Not so bad indeed.

League with Chelsea, but in December 2019 he was half-way through a 28-goal season in the Bundesliga. Yussuf Poulsen may not be a superstar, but the powerful Danish international striker was an established player at RB Leipzig who had been at the club since they were in the third tier of German football. It may have been tempting to stay within the Red Bull footballing umbrella, since Haaland had been such a hit at Salzburg, but at RB Leipzig there would be no guarantees of playing time.

Dortmund was a different matter. They did have the Spanish forward Paco Alcácer, who had been scoring goals the season before, but he had picked up an injury in October and at 5 foot 9 he wasn't an obvious focal point in attack. Manager Lucien Favre had taken to playing various attacking midfielders up front as false nines, with mixed results. Dortmund was a team that had an abundance of creative talent in midfield but lacked a predator in the box to convert the chances. It couldn't have been set up any better for Erling Haaland to come in. 'They were desperately looking for a number nine. And they were very clear that he was going to play from day one,' Alfie Haaland told the filmmakers. 'So Dortmund was the choice.'

Borussia Dortmund, of course, had more to offer Erling Haaland than just a vacant spot on the team sheet. Author and journalist Uli Hesse, a Dortmund native and a Dortmund season-ticket holder, explains why the club has become such a popular destination for elite-level talent. Dortmund is, says Hesse, the 'perfect club for players like Haaland'.

> You come here, you're not exactly joining a small and poor club, you're going to make good money. But at the same time, you know that you're going to get playing time at the highest level. You'll get to play in the Champions League.

And you get to play in front of 80,000 people. So that's very attractive to young players.

Dortmund is a big club, with a huge stadium and a passionate following, and the club has made signing the brightest talents in the game a key part of its strategy. 'You get the playing time, you're guaranteed to play and to play in the Champions League, no one is going to cut your head off if you make a mistake. Everyone knows that this is the model, the fans know this.'

Dortmund was the last club not named Bayern Munich to win the Bundesliga, and during the last decade of Bayern dominance Dortmund has been the club that has come closest to besting the serial champions from Bavaria. However, Dortmund is a very different club from Bayern. 'Whereas for instance Bayern Munich has always been a nationwide, even international club, Dortmund has struggled for a long time to stay close to their working-class roots,' says Hesse.

To be a Dortmund-based club, maybe a Ruhr area club, and still have a broader appeal to people. It's a bit harder for Dortmund than for a club like Bayern, which has always been a more cosmopolitan club, more modern. Most people today think Bayern and Dortmund have always been these huge rivals, but for people at my age, for many decades of our lives as match-going football fans, Bayern were just light-years ahead of us. It was more about Schalke for us, really. But ever since the 1990s, it's really become a big rivalry. And the near bankruptcy is a big example.

The near bankruptcy in question happened in 2005, when years of overspending finally came back to bite Dortmund. At one point, in

March of that year, a group of more than 400 small-stake investors in the club had to be convinced to accept payment deferrals, or the club would be declared bankrupt. This was less than three years after the club had won the Bundesliga. 'What happened was that Dortmund tried to compete with Bayern by doing it the Bayern way,' Uli Hesse explains. This meant spending big in the transfer market and paying huge wages, but 'this had spiralled out of control and the club began losing money'. According to Hesse, what's interesting is that 'for all the talk of the club's working-class roots, that it's owned by the fans … we're one of only two publicly listed clubs in Germany.' At the turn of the millennium, Dortmund had told its fans it was going to go public,

> and it was going to raise a lot of money. Some would be spent on the stadium and some on players. What we didn't know at the time was that the club had to go public to stave off bankruptcy, it needed all this money to keep going. So it was just a question of time until the house of cards collapsed.

Dortmund went public in October 2000, becoming the first publicly traded football club in Germany. All seemed to be well as the club won the Bundesliga in the 2001/2 season. But, as Hesse said, the spending had been reckless, the debts were mounting, and as soon as results took a turn for the worse and the club missed out on European competitions the sums simply didn't add up any longer. Most football fans think finishing lower in the table than expected is a disaster. Dortmund fans saw their club go to the brink of disappearing altogether.

In the wake of this near calamity, it was obvious that things had to be different. The club had to be more careful with its money. And how do you compete with the best without paying for established stars? Well, one way is to try to find the stars of tomorrow. 'The current chairman [Hans-Joachim Watzke], when he came into power, said that the number one plan for Dortmund is to never go into debt again,' says Hesse. 'We have learned that we can't compete with Bayern by doing Bayern things. So we have to do something else. And [that is] attracting young players and then at one point selling them at a profit.' Dortmund was initially reborn under the leadership of Jürgen Klopp. The club won consecutive Bundesliga titles between 2010 and 2012, playing some of the most exciting high-tempo football that Germany and the rest of Europe had ever seen. Is it too much of a stretch to suggest that a young, football-mad Erling Haaland watched Klopp's Borussia Dortmund on TV and thought that this would be a fun team to play for?

Either way, for Haaland the Dortmund of late 2019 presented an irresistible prospect. There was an obvious place for him in the team. Haaland, the ruthless finisher, would have a formidable phalanx of creative players behind him. Haaland would also learn what it means to play for a big club, both the excitement and the responsibility that comes with playing in front of 80,000 fans every home game. But it is also a club where everyone understands and accepts that young-sters can have an off day, so there is marginally less pressure than at the absolute elite clubs of world football. And Dortmund, while it cannot match the sheer financial might of Bayern Munich, is no pauper. Haaland and his team would do well out of a move there. Mino Raiola would make sure of it. Whereas some clubs, particularly German ones, find Raiola difficult to work with, Uli Hesse explains that the Dortmund CEO Hans-Joachim 'Aki' Watzke has no such qualms. 'He once said that he deeply respects Mino Raiola. He said that they would always get into a shouting match, but they do respect each other. He's trying to do his job and I'm trying to do mine.'

One club that had a fraught relationship with Mino Raiola was Manchester United. But this animosity is unlikely to have had any serious impact on Haaland's decision. After the transfer had been concluded, Raiola was his typically bullish self when speaking to Sky Sports News.

At this moment [Haaland] had the best feeling of signing for Dortmund, and that this will be the right move for his career. So I don't understand all the fuss, everybody is speaking about Manchester United but there were 12 clubs interested in him and we had serious talks with every one of them. In the end it's the player that has to have the best feeling and makes the ultimate decision. I don't understand why in England there is such a fuss about the player having chosen Borussia Dortmund. He's a young player and he has all the time to come to the Premier League, and we hope there will be a time. He didn't feel it was the time at this point to move to the Premier League. Borussia Dortmund is a fantastic club and I think the best move for his development at this point.

Both when moving from Bryne to Molde and when moving from Molde to Salzburg, Erling Haaland could have received a larger contract and moved to a bigger club if he had wanted to. But in both instances he and his father decided his destination based on what they thought was the best thing for his development. There is no compelling reason to think otherwise about this move. True, Manchester United was managed at the time by his former mentor, but Haaland said later that he's never chosen a club based solely on the manager. 'It's even better if the club wants you than if the manager does, I would say,' he told Viaplay.

At the end of the day you're signing for the club. Then the manager will usually be a positive thing, but I've never moved to a club because of a manager. The manager can get fired three weeks later. Then I'm sat there thinking, what now? So I've never gone to a club because of the manager.

And he would later insist that his 'gut feeling' played a big part. 'If I sit here and I imagine wearing the shirt, that I score a goal and celebrate. How does that feel? Does it feel good? Or not? Does it feel very good?' Once the formalities had been completed, the documents signed and the player presented, it wouldn't take him very long at all before he felt very, very good while wearing a Dortmund shirt.

15

BIG IN GERMANY

In the spring of 2019 Borussia Dortmund had managed to push Bayern Munich all the way. The league was competitive up until the final game of the season, with Bayern eventually lifting the trophy with a winning margin of just two points. Bayern had thrashed Dortmund 5–0 in a presumed title decider in early April, but then dropped enough points in the remaining games that Dortmund were gifted a chance to win the league. That is, if Dortmund themselves hadn't also messed up. First with an inexplicable 4–2 defeat to local rivals Schalke in late April, and then by throwing away a 2–0 lead against Werder Bremen the week after. And so Bayern Munich won the Bundesliga. Again. Dortmund were left feeling not that they'd been outclassed by a financially superior rival, but that this had been a huge opportunity missed. The club had been top of the table for much of the season. Dortmund's squad was talented, packed with clever, technical players. But what the team lacked was defensive solidity. The players had conceded 44 goals that season to Bayern's 32 and RB Leipzig's 29. And, importantly, Dortmund had dropped points in games where they really shouldn't have. Getting trounced by Bayern, well, it can happen, but that season Dortmund also lost away to Fortuna Düsseldorf and FC Augsburg. They dropped points against Nürnberg and Hannover, and twice against Hoffenheim. They actually beat Bayern at home at the Signal Iduna Park, and they won home and away against RB Leipzig, Bayer Leverkusen and Borussia Mönchengladbach – the three teams that finished third, fourth and fifth, respectively. The collapse against Bayern at the Allianz in April had been spectacular, but the bitter truth was that Dortmund had lost the league by tripping over themselves against weaker opposition.

The club, knowing that it had been close and sensing that a Niko Kovač-led Bayern would still be vulnerable next season, decided to show some ambition in the transfer window. They brought Mats Hummels back to the club from rivals Bayern, hoping his leadership and experience at the back would fix their reliably unreliable defence. Thorgan Hazard was signed on the back of a very productive season for Gladbach. German internationals Julian Brandt and Nico Schulz were recruited from Leverkusen and Hoffenheim. All in all, Dortmund looked like a club that meant business, and the team won their first two games of the season. But then the team proceeded to win just two of their next seven. In November, after being trounced away to Bayern yet again, Dortmund only managed a 3–3 draw against newly promoted Paderborn. It was 12 games into the season and Dortmund was in sixth place. The club won a handful of games after that and climbed to fourth in the table, but in December conceded a late equaliser against RB Leipzig, and then foolishly threw away a 1–0 lead against Hoffenheim by conceding another two late goals. 'For a side attempting to win the title, this is not good enough,' Raphael Honigstein concluded in *The Athletic*, citing 'chronic problems at the back' and an 'unnervingly slow, intricate build-up game'. This was a far cry from the direct, hard-running, all-action Dortmund team of the past. Paco Alcácer, the only recognised striker in the squad, had struggled for form and fitness, which led manager Lucien Favre to experiment with playing attacking midfielders Marco Reus and Mario Götze up front. It hadn't really worked and, according to Honigstein, confidence in Favre was starting to run low. The only good news for Dortmund was the fact that Bayern had bungled the first half of the season as well. Struggling, and leading Dortmund by only three points in the table, the Bavarians had taken action, sacking manager Niko Kovač in early November and putting Hansi Flick in charge. There had already been clear improvements.

Dortmund's response to all of this was Erling Haaland. 'Despite receiving numerous offers from some of the biggest clubs in Europe, Erling Haaland has decided that the best option for his career is to come and join our project here at BVB. Our persistence has paid off,' said the Dortmund CEO Hans-Joachim Watzke when the move was announced. 'We can all look forward to having an ambitious, athletic and physically imposing centre-forward here at the club,' said sporting director Michael Zorc.

> Haaland boasts a real eye for goal and impressive speed, and we are confident that we can develop him even further here in Dortmund. At just 19 years of age, he is at the very start of what promises to be an incredible career!

Haaland himself said that he'd had 'several intense conversations' with the leadership of the club ahead of the move. 'Right from the very start, I knew I wanted to move here. I can't wait to get started and play in front of over 80,000 fans in the incredible Dortmund atmosphere.'

Because German football has a winter break, Haaland had just a couple of days in Dortmund before heading off to Spain with the team for a training camp. The camp meant that he missed the glitzy Norwegian awards ceremony Idrettsgallaen, where he won Breakthrough of the Year and used his speech to thank Torbjørg 'Tante' Haugen for all the good food. And Tante wasn't the only person from Haaland's youth who got name-checked by the young star on primetime television. 'I'm sad that I couldn't be there but I had to go to a training camp with my new club,' Haaland explained via video link. 'Thanks for this excellent award,' he continued, holding it up to the camera. 'It looks *grævla* good.' He went on to say that it had been a very good year, that he was glad to have had a manager and a club in Salzburg that believed in him, and that he was happy to have scored 'a *grævla* lot of goals'. 'I had my breakthrough this year, but of course there's a lot of training and preparations behind it,' he said.

> So I want to thank my former teammates, coaches and staff at Bryne, Molde and the Norway youth teams. I want to especially thank Reidar Omdal, who was the man behind the indoor pitch in Bryne, that's where I laid the foundation. Alfie Berntsen and his team at Bryne, Ole Gunnar and his team at Molde, Tante who made the good food which made me grow *grævla* well. And finally I want to congratulate the other nominees. My dad said I had no chance against them, but I'm very glad that I won. So once again thank you very much, enjoy the party!

It might seem obvious that Erling Haaland would win this kind of award in Norway that year, but he wasn't entirely without competition: one of the other nominees was the tennis player Casper Ruud, who would later be ranked as high as second in the world.

. . .

On 4 January Erling Haaland and his teammates boarded a plane in Dortmund and ascended into the grey clouds above the Ruhr valley. A few hours later they landed in altogether balmier conditions in Malaga. Shortly thereafter they checked into the Hotel Gran Melia Don Pepe in Marbella, a five-star hotel right on the seafront. Not a bad place to get to know your new teammates. On his second day in Spain, Haaland sat down with Dortmund's in-house media for his first interview since joining the club.

> They just went direct and said yeah, we need you up front, and we like your playing style and want to have you here. I liked how they spoke to me then and that's what triggered me. I just felt that me and Dortmund were a good match.

For a team that in the first half of the season was accused of being too slow in build-up play and of lacking a proper striker, Haaland would certainly add something different. 'I'm a quite direct player,' he said.

> If I could choose, I would go straight to the goal and score. That's the best thing that I can do. But I'm a guy who works hard, who loves scoring goals and loves to play football. And I also want people to see what kind of player I am, and not speak too much.

In his interview Haaland was quite stoic, a manner that almost mirrors his playing style: no unnecessary embellishments, straight to the point. But behind-the-scenes footage also released by Dortmund shows Haaland joking with the camera crew, smiling and laughing, and struggling to keep a straight face when recording. This would become a running theme with Haaland. His teammates, coaches and acquaintances describe him as a humorous, funny, likeable and approachable guy. But he adopts a far more careful stance in the media. Fans only really catch glimpses of the more light-hearted side of Haaland in rare, unguarded moments. But as Erling Haaland put it himself, he wants the fans to see what kind of player he is on the pitch, rather than hear him speak too much.

• • •

Back in Germany, Haaland's first few fixtures for Dortmund looked favourable. Augsburg away, Cologne at home, Union Berlin at home and then Werder Bremen away in the DFB-Pokal, the German Cup competition. But this was just it, Dortmund was a team that struggled to consistently take care of these supposedly winnable games. It was a problem that had cost the club the title the season before, and in this season the team had already lost to newly promoted Union Berlin and dropped points against the likes of Paderborn and Werder Bremen. But with Erling Haaland on board the fans were confident. In fact, according to author and Dortmund season ticket holder Uli Hesse, the fans were *very* confident. 'The strange thing about this transfer is that most people, and I'm totally serious about this, most people thought that he would be the kind of player that he turned out to be,' he says.

It was bizarre, I've never seen that before. Because usually with a transfer like that there will be some people saying he's not that good, or he's too young or whatever. But when this transfer was announced everyone felt like, OK, he's going to be a star. Before he actually played for us! I don't know where that came from, but everyone was convinced that he would be good for us.

Perhaps the fit was obvious. Dortmund had excellent wingers and attacking midfielders, but no forward. Jadon Sancho was having a brilliant season and had racked up nine goals and ten assists before Christmas. The gifted Julian Brandt could link midfield and attack, but suffered from the fact that there wasn't really an attack to link with. Then there was the captain, Marco Reus, who was a fine technician and would always deliver to a high standard as long as he could stay fit. The stage was perfectly set for a fast, physical striker to give them an outlet up front. It couldn't have been more perfect for Erling Haaland.

'I still remember this game, playing away at Augsburg,' says Hesse.

That's always very difficult, for some reason we just don't like playing Augsburg. And Dortmund went 3–1 down, and I was watching the game and checking social media, and there were all these Dortmund fans saying, 'Well 3–1 is OK, because we will bring on Haaland and he will score a hat-trick.' So as long as we're two goals down it's fine. Of course it was almost a joke, but only half-jokingly.

Football fans can sometimes expect too much or be overly optimistic on their team's behalf. But this, as it turned out, was not one of those times. Erling Haaland was subbed on in the 56th minute, and about 180 seconds later he was slipped through by Jadon Sancho. And Haaland, with his first shot in the Bundesliga, struck an inch-perfect drive with his left foot into the bottom right corner of the goal: 3–2. Haaland grabbed the ball and headed back towards the centre circle. Just two minutes later Jadon Sancho controlled a long ball over the Augsburg defence, took it past the goalkeeper and made it 3–3. In the 70th minute another ball in behind the Augsburg defence saw two Dortmund players escape the offside trap. Thorgan Hazard this time took it past the goalkeeper, but he was slightly off balance and there was a defender on the line, so he poked the ball to Haaland, who made it 4–3. The linesman flagged for offside, understandably puzzled as to how Hazard and Haaland had found themselves quite so alone deep within the Augsburg half, but VAR corrected the error and the goal stood. Nine minutes later Haaland made a textbook curved run and his movement was spotted by Marco Reus. The Dortmund captain played a perfectly timed through ball and Haaland was away again. The pass had taken him slightly wide of the goal, but his speed had bought him a few precious moments in which to move the ball more centrally before the panicking defenders could catch up with him. He finished neatly with his left foot. All it took was 20 minutes for Haaland to score a hat-trick on his Dortmund debut. The team had been 3–1 down when he came on, but the final score was 5–3 to Dortmund.

'He is crazy, but in a good way,' said Dortmund's sporting director Michael Zorc after the game. 'He helps us a lot and inspires his teammates this way.' Manager Lucien Favre, who had started to come under some pressure after the underwhelming first half of the season, was happy with his new forward.

Erling is a very good guy. He has a top mentality, he always gives everything. Naturally he can learn a lot, but that's normal. You saw his strengths immediately. His runs between the defenders. It's necessary and it helps the team. We play left, right, here and there, but now we can also play forward.

Dortmund had been accused of being too slow in their build-up play – but having a giant, crazy Norwegian constantly making runs in behind the opposing defence, well, that certainly gave them a very different option. If in doubt, look for Haaland. 'I came here to score goals and yeah, it's a good debut for me,' Haaland said matter-of-factly in his post-match interview. The interview was conducted pitchside, and in the background you could still hear the Dortmund fans in the away end making an almighty racket. Haaland cracked a smile and looked towards them. 'If you look at this support, you can see why it's amazing to play in front of [them]. It just gives you more joy to play football in front of such passionate fans.' When the Norwegian press tracked him down in the bowels of Augsburg's stadium Haaland was more relaxed. His boyish grin kept threatening to break out, and young Erling couldn't quite keep it in check. 'It's nice, isn't it? A nice debut,' he said when asked to sum it all up. Understated, as befits a son of Jæren, but with a smile that said more than his words. 'You said after the hat-trick in the Champions League for Salzburg that it was the sickest thing you'd experienced in your life, but how highly do you rate this?' the reporter asked. Haaland had to suppress a laugh, and smiled. 'No, this is up there as well, if I'm being honest, this is pretty sick as well.' By now, Haaland's joke about the match balls from his hat-tricks coming home with him and being his 'girlfriends' had become a bit of a meme, and the official Dortmund Twitter account had already posted a picture of Haaland with the match ball and the caption 'In Dortmund for only three weeks and this guy already found a new girlfriend'. But when asked by the Norwegians about it, Haaland said he had other plans. 'I'll be giving this one to my father.'

Dortmund's next game was at home against Cologne, which meant Erling was in line to make his debut in front of the famous 'Yellow Wall' and the 80,000 fans who fill the Signal Iduna Park for every home game. But Dortmund and Lucien Favre wanted to introduce him carefully into the team. Haaland had been injured for much of December, and his new club had to manage his physical load very carefully during their training camp in Marbella. On Friday, 24 January 2020 Dortmund faced Cologne in an evening match under the floodlights at their mighty stadium, and tens of thousands of fans were excited to see their new star. Favre made them wait, starting Haaland on the bench. But while they didn't get to witness Haaland play from kick-off, this was still a fun night to be a Dortmund fan. The home team took the lead after just 52 seconds, with Raphaël Guerreiro turning home a Jadon Sancho cross. In the 29th minute a long ball from Hummels found Reus all alone behind the Cologne defence, and the captain made it 2–0. The linesman initially flagged for offside, but VAR concluded that the goal was legitimate. After half-time Jadon Sancho made it 3–0 with some clever footwork in the box and a fine finish. Dortmund were in party mode but, just as Haaland was getting ready to come on, Cologne made it 3–1 through Mark Uth. When Haaland was subbed on, it took him just ten minutes to score his first goal in front of Dortmund's home fans. Guerreiro had fired a shot straight at the Cologne goalkeeper and Haaland was there to score the rebound. A tap-in, perhaps, but on closer inspection it was not a coincidence that Haaland was there to take advantage. He had started moving towards the goalkeeper as soon as Guerreiro took his shot. It's one of football's eternal truths that a striker should never wait for a rebound, instead he should treat all shots from his team-mates as rebounds-in-waiting and make runs accordingly. Haaland certainly subscribes to this. In the box he is always on the hunt.

Shortly before full-time Haaland was played through behind the Cologne defence and took the ball past the goalkeeper. The angle was tight, the goalkeeper was lunging back to make a block, but with serene calm and poise Haaland set himself for the finish and slipped the ball into the net. It ended 5–1 to Dortmund, and two goals for Haaland, which made it five goals in the Bundesliga in 59 minutes of football. This is not normal.

After the game Dortmund decided it was time to shield young Erling from the hype that was exploding all around him. 'We've agreed with Erling that he doesn't have to do interviews after every game,' a club spokesman told *VG*. 'We have to take it easy.' The next weekend Erling Haaland got his first start at the Signal Iduna Park, which did very little to calm the hype. The visiting side was Union Berlin, a team that had beaten Dortmund earlier in the season, but there was little chance of that happening here. Jadon Sancho made it 1–0 in the 13th minute, a goal that made him the first teenager to ever score 25 goals in the Bundesliga. In the 18th minute it was time for Haaland. Julian Brandt played a perfect cross in from the right and Haaland timed his run well for an easy finish. Half-way through the second half, Jadon Sancho played in Haaland, who was fouled by the goalkeeper when trying to take the ball past him. It was a clear penalty, which Marco Reus neatly dispatched. In the 70th minute Sancho set up Axel Witsel for Dortmund's fourth goal, and in the 76th minute Erling Haaland did it again. This time a clever back-heel from Brandt bamboozled the Union defence and left Haaland with a chance to hit it with his fearsome left foot. The Union goalkeeper, Rafal Gikiewicz, couldn't get down fast enough, and the score was 5–0. Favre, keen to manage Haaland's physical load, promptly took him off. No chance for another hat-trick, then, but after his third appearance for Dortmund Haaland had scored seven goals in 136 minutes of football. Asked after the game about the incredible start to his Dortmund career, Haaland replied, 'I think it's a combination of hard work and the teammates I have around me. They're so good. They make it easy for me.' He then made an announcement that must have sounded ominous for Bundesliga defenders across the country: 'There is much more to come.'

The three consecutive wins meant Dortmund were back in the hunt for the Bundesliga title. The club was now suddenly just three points off the top of the league. But a pair of setbacks quickly followed. Though Haaland scored again, Dortmund suffered a surprise 3–2 defeat to Werder Bremen in early February, in the German Cup. In their next game in the Bundesliga they lost 4–3 to Bayer Leverkusen – it was the first time that Haaland had played for Dortmund without scoring a goal, and it was a game where Dortmund were actually leading until the 80th minute, before conceding twice in two minutes. These were reminders for Dortmund that not all problems are solved by adding a goal-scoring sensation up front. And for Haaland, the experience was an unwelcome introduction to Dortmund's infuriating tendency to shoot themselves in the foot. On Friday, a week later, Haaland scored again as Dortmund claimed a routine win against Frankfurt. After that, all eyes were on the following Tuesday. Because Dortmund were taking on Paris Saint-Germain in the Champions League.

16

PARIS

'Coming from the Ruhr Area with its rich industrial history, the former working-class club BVB stands for ambitious and honest hard work whilst staying fair and humble. BVB prides itself on being a people's club and No. 1 challenger of the establishment,' Dortmund announce on their website. With one foot in its working-class roots and one foot in the global football elite, Dortmund are constantly attempting to straddle two extremes of the modern football industry. Paris Saint-Germain have taken a rather different approach. In 2011 they were bought by QSI, a Qatari sports investment firm established by Sheikh Tamim bin Hamad Al Thani, now Emir of Qatar, as a subsidiary of the QIA, the country's sovereign wealth fund. Since then only one club on the planet has had a higher net spend on transfers than PSG. In the 2018/19 season, PSG had a wage bill of €371 million, well over twice as much as the second biggest spenders in the French domestic league. In fact, there were 12 clubs in Ligue 1 that together had a combined wage bill of less than PSG's. Unsurprisingly,

PSG usually win the league, comfortably. The wild spending on the pitch has been matched with turbo-charged brand-building off of it. This has included a collaboration with Nike's Air Jordan brand, the French fashion designer Christelle Kocher and iconic English band The Rolling Stones. Over the years the TV cameras have spotted a remarkable array of celebrities at PSG's home games, though those celebrities have frequently looked nonplussed about the sport happening in front of them.

In football terms, PSG has found itself in a strange kind of purgatory. Its sheer financial might has rendered the French domestic league a non-contest, where if any team other than PSG wins the title, it is considered a profound embarrassment to the Paris giants – though PSG has managed to not win it a couple of times in the past decade. The Champions League, then, has become the only competition where the sporting success or failure for this team can rationally be measured, and the Champions League has been a struggle. As of February 2020, PSG had yet to progress further than the quarter-finals in the competition. The club's defeats have included some classic collapses, like throwing away a 4–0 aggregate lead against Barcelona in 2017 and a 2–0 aggregate lead against Manchester United in 2019 – the latter by losing 3–1 in a return leg where United only managed five shots. Fashion collaborations and bewildered celebrities can't help you when your team is badly unbalanced and filled with sulky stars who bristle at the mere concept of adversity. At times, the PSG squad has looked more like *Succession* character Kendall Roy's birthday party than a football club.

But every year is a chance to do better, and for all the club's flaws Paris Saint-Germain possesses a pretty staggering array of attacking talent. Kylian Mbappé being the most obvious one. As time started catching up with the duopoly of Lionel Messi and Cristiano Ronaldo and their shared throne was being vacated, Mbappé emerged as the most obvious contender to the crown and as the defining talent of the next generation. Mbappé's speed, technique, balletic grace and near-flawless finishing make him a player that on his day is pretty much unstoppable. And he has a lot of those days. It's also a sign of PSG's opulence that in a supporting role to Mbappé the squad includes Neymar, who himself was long seen as a potential heir to the label of 'best player in the world'. Indeed, Pelé himself insisted that Neymar was better than Messi, though you might struggle to find a person without a Brazilian passport who shares that view. Still, Mbappé and Neymar were a gruesome twosome for any defence to come up against. They could also be challenging players to manage. In February 2020, with PSG's tie against Dortmund drawing near, Neymar had irritated his manager, German coach Thomas Tuchel, by hosting a lavish birthday party just 24 hours after a league game and just 48 hours before the next. 'I always protect my players, and I really love my team,' Tuchel said.

> With this party, I accept that it is a bit difficult to protect the players, but the context is not simply black or white. Is it the best way to prepare for a match? No, clearly not. Is it the worst thing in the world? No.

Neymar's birthday party wasn't the only thing that Tuchel was wrestling with at the time. In the game before the party, a grumpy Mbappé had a minor altercation with his manager after being subbed off in the second half. 'There is nothing personal between him and me. These things happen,' Tuchel insisted. 'It was between a player who does not want to come off, and a coach who had his reasons for doing something and who wanted to give a game to players who deserved it.' Being the manager of PSG is often more about juggling egos than coaching and tactics.

With such a huge cultural dichotomy between PSG and Dortmund, there was more than enough spice for the occasion. The presence of Tuchel on the PSG bench added even more. Thomas Tuchel had been Jürgen Klopp's successor at Dortmund back in 2015. Initially, he was a success. In his first season the team finished second, and with 78 points they were the best runners-up in Bundesliga history. Almost any other year, a tally like that would have been enough to lift the trophy. The next season, Tuchel led the club to the German Cup. But while Tuchel's Dortmund team was successful on the field, the manager had a troubled relationship with the club hierarchy. At the end of his second season in charge, Tuchel was fired. In an open letter to the fans, Watzke suggested that there had been a breakdown in 'trust, respect, the ability to communicate and work as a team, authenticity and identification'. Watzke also wrote, 'We no longer believed the current coaching arrangement offered us a foundation for a successful future collaboration based on trust.'

These are strong words for a club CEO to use in public about an outgoing head coach. Losing to a former manager is never fun, but being knocked out of the Champions League by Tuchel would be particularly unpleasant for the Dortmund hierarchy. In short, there were a lot of things going on ahead of this game, a lot of conflict lines and narratives simmering underneath the surface. And then there was the more obvious point that the winner over two legs would progress to the Champions League quarter-finals, whereas the loser would not.

Not that Erling Haaland would have been particularly worried about any of this. He lined up for the pre-match ceremonies alongside his teammates with a smile on his face. As his beloved Champions

League anthem rung out while he stood beneath the floodlights, the camera passed him. It looked like Haaland was having to suppress a fit of the giggles. The weight of the occasion simply didn't register. Erling was just excited to play, and to play in front of a big audience. In the first half Haaland was aggressive and on the front foot. As one of his former coaches with the Norwegian youth teams once observed, Erling Haaland's body language is not subtle. He was fired up for this game, anyone could tell. He was on the hunt for goals and making runs. There were, however, a few instances of him not being fully attuned to his teammates. The timing wasn't quite perfect yet. Things weren't fully clicking. But after 68 minutes Haaland was alert to a rebound and scored, making it 1–0. Not for the first time, he celebrated by assuming the lotus position. But in the 74th minute the two most expensive players in the history of the sport combined to make it 1–1. Mbappé floated past a cluster of Dortmund defenders as if they weren't there, before squaring the ball for a Neymar tap-in. Whether they like a party or not, talent is talent, and the PSG attack had a lot of it. But Haaland wasn't finished. At this point Dortmund's attacking trident was fully made in England: Erling Haaland, born in Leeds; Giovanni Reyna, born in Sunderland; and Jadon Sancho, born in Camberwell. In the 76th minute Reyna collected a pass out from the back from Hummels, before he turned and ran at the PSG defence. To his right Jadon Sancho had half the Ruhr valley at his disposal, but Reyna was only looking for Haaland. He centred the ball and Haaland took a touch, but it ran across him – and the only thing he could really do was take a shot. The strike was pure, clean, immaculate, and hit home with a velocity the net could barely contain. Haaland wheeled away, attempted another lotus but instead fell to the ground and was quickly buried under a pile of his team-mates. Dortmund won the first leg 2–1.

'*Æg tenke bare å dryla te for å vær heilt ærlege,*' Haaland told Viaplay after the game, which roughly translates as 'I just figured I'd wallop it, to be honest.' And so he did. It was a goal that announced him on the world stage, elevated him from a prospect to an emerging global superstar. 'This boy is an animal,' Tuchel told Sky Germany after the game. 'He looks like Marco van Basten has eaten Lebron James for breakfast,' wrote *L'Equipe*. Back in Norway there wasn't much to do aside from cheer, applaud and even laugh. 'He couldn't even have dreamt it. It's so huge. It's not luck. It's not a coincidence. He's just good,' said Rune Bratseth, who won the Bundesliga twice with Werder Bremen and got 60 caps for Norway. Though, Haaland being Haaland, one suspects that he may in fact have dreamt of this exact thing. For Dortmund and their fans it was a moment of sheer euphoria. The club's gamble on youth had paid off, Dortmund had bested the bottomless pockets of PSG. At least for the moment. There was, of course, the small matter of the return leg. Before that, Dortmund had Bundesliga games against Werder Bremen, Freiburg and Gladbach. Dortmund won all three, though Haaland scored just one goal. Meanwhile, in the world outside of football, news of a coronavirus outbreak was starting to spread.

Two days after the defeat to Dortmund the PSG players yet again decided to have a big party, and a video of some of the players having a great time was posted to social media. Thomas Tuchel looked intensely unimpressed when asked about it at a press conference ahead of PSG's next league match. 'I was really surprised yesterday afternoon to see that video. Really surprised,' the Teutonic tactician growled.

You can be sure we spoke about it within the club and it's better if it stays within. I would rather not talk about it here.

It was a day off, yes. It was private life, yes. But we are not happy with this party image. I was very surprised.

Perhaps the PSG players were wise to get their partying done while they could, as people's lives were about to change. As more and more cases of COVID-19 were being reported around the globe, national governments and industry leaders tried to get their heads around how to deal with the coming crisis. For European football, in the immediate term, it meant that some return legs of the Champions League round of 16 were played without fans pitchside, while at others fans were permitted. The French authorities decided that the return leg between PSG and Dortmund would be played behind closed doors.

The game was a strange affair. Played in an empty Parc des Princes, PSG's stadium, thousands of PSG fans nevertheless assembled outside of it, trying to make their voices heard. Kylian Mbappé had been ill that week with a fever and a sore throat, and only made the bench. In the 17th minute the rapid Achraf Hakimi, then on loan at Dortmund from Real Madrid, was unleashed down the right-hand side. His cross was nearly met by Haaland, but the Norwegian striker couldn't quite get there. In the 24th minute the PSG players showed their class, as Ángel Di María received a ball on the turn and slipped Edinson Cavani through on goal. The Uruguayan struck with power, but Dortmund's goalkeeper Roman Bürki spread his legs and deflected the shot wide. A few minutes later PSG had a corner. Di María curled in a brilliant delivery, which Dortmund failed to clear. Neymar was more alert than his marker, Hakimi, and the Brazilian superstar made it 1–0. In extra time of the first half PSG went on the attack again, Di María spread the ball wide to Pablo Sarabia, who put it straight into the box. The retreating Dortmund defenders couldn't stop it. The ball reached PSG left-back Juan Bernat, who had come all the way up the pitch and into the opposition box. He got a touch on the ball and made it 2–0. Dortmund's aggregate lead had been wiped out. Dortmund had the entire second half to come back, but struggled to create clear-cut chances. They managed just one finish from inside the box in the second half. In the 87th minute Emre Can got himself sent off. The final whistle went and Dortmund were out. Erling Haaland hadn't even had a shot. 'We only had ourselves to blame,' manager Lucien Favre later told *France Football.* 'We had not managed to reproduce the same performance at the Parc des Princes as the first leg in Dortmund.' Erling Haaland was frustrated. 'It was terrible to play without fans, simple as that,' he said after the game. 'We could tell something was missing. We're used to 80,000, now it was zero, and it was awful. It's awful, but that's the situation. It sucks.'

That wasn't the whole story, though. The game had been ill-tempered, erupting in the late brawl that saw Dortmund's Can get sent off and Ángel Di María, Neymar, Marquinhos and Kylian Mbappé receive bookings. The Spanish newspaper *Marca* claimed to have identified Di María saying to his teammates, 'We have to score six, seven … All the goals we can. We are going to humiliate them, we are going to humiliate these sons of bitches,' as PSG scored their second goal. Why were the PSG players so upset? Well, the first leg had been a physical affair, where Dortmund had appeared to target a not fully fit Neymar with some rough treatment. And after their win Dortmund had been a bit giddy on social media. One post from the official Dortmund Twitter account showed a picture of Erling Haaland and Gio Reyna, noting Haaland's two goals and Reyna's assist, captioned with the following quote from former Dortmund player and current member of the coaching staff Lars Ricken: 'We don't buy superstars, we make them.' The dig at PSG's money was not very subtle, though it is perhaps worth noting that in the case of Haaland they had in fact bought him just two months before. On the eve of the return leg, a fake post that showed Erling Haaland, the word 'Paris' and the caption 'My city, not yours' did the rounds on social media. Any kind of rudimentary check would have revealed that the post was fake, but it seems PSG players fell for it. Neymar, after scoring the first goal, ran and celebrated by assuming the lotus position. At full-time, Neymar posted a photo of himself in the lotus position on his Instagram account with the caption 'Paris our city, not yours'. After the game, the PSG squad took a team photo with most of the players in a lotus position, and Kylian Mbappé posted a video on Instagram of him assuming the lotus position during post-match celebrations in the dressing room. It was quite the reaction. Since the takeover by Qatar Sports Investments, PSG had repeatedly failed to make headway in the Champions League. In spite of spending more money than almost every other club on the planet, the win against Dortmund represented one of PSG's first significant triumphs in European football during the Qatari era. And the players' first and only instinct was to troll a 19-year-old who had been playing in Austria just a couple of months earlier? It's hard to imagine a bigger compliment for Haaland. Paris Saint-Germain were well and truly rattled.

But Dortmund were well and truly out of the Champions League, and football was well and truly on pause. As world leaders scrambled to figure out what the COVID-19 pandemic meant and how best to combat it, it was clear that football couldn't continue in any kind of recognisable form. Gathering together up to 80,000 people in the same venue … it just wasn't a very sensible thing to do under the circumstances. And so, for a brief period, everything stopped.

17

GHOST GAMES

In the spring of 2020 the COVID-19 pandemic swept the globe, and football was put on hold. In mid-March, the Belarusian league was the only European league still active, leading to the Belarusian FA signing broadcasting agreements with ten countries. 'This is an unprecedented situation,' a spokesman from the Belarusian FA told *Reuters*, which was true in so many ways. On 9 May the Faroese league started their season, as the puffin-rich archipelago had been very successful at keeping the virus away. Starved for any kind of content, Norwegian TV2 picked up the rights – a deal that was brokered by none other than Bryne-defender Rogvi Baldvinsson. TV2 even launched a fantasy league for the Faroese Islands, hoping it could become a kind of cult hit. Mostly it was about bringing any kind of football to the people, people who were stuck at home with very little else to do. But Faroese aspirations of Norse dominance were dealt a heavy blow in mid-May: the Bundesliga was back. Having made some progress towards slowing the epidemic's spread, or 'flattening the curve', as was the terminology of the day, German politicians had given the DFL (Deutsche Fußball Liga) and the Bundesliga the green light to play games again under a very strict set of rules.

This was not a universally popular decision at the time. A survey conducted by the German public broadcaster ARD found that 56 per cent of people polled were against the Bundesliga restarting. Fanszenen Deutschlands, a national organisation representing various German ultras groups, called it 'an insult to society, and in particular to those fighting Covid-19 on a daily basis'. Christian Seifert, the head of the DFL, warned that it was 'the only way to keep the Bundesliga and the 2 Bundesliga alive'. Bayern CEO Karl-Heinz Rummenigge, on the other hand, smelled profit. 'If the Bundesliga is the only league around the world to be broadcast on TV, then I assume that we will have an audience of billions all over the world,' he told *Sport Bild*. The DFL produced a huge document of stringent rules that had to be followed, covering everything from training to matchdays and how the media coverage would work. Only 322 people would be allowed in the stadiums, and of these only a maximum of 98 would be allowed into the 'interior' of the venue, the pitch area. This would include players, coaching and medical staff, and referees. A further 115 would be allowed in the stands, which is where members of the media would find themselves, and a further 109 would be allowed within the stadium perimeter.

Archie Rhind-Tutt was one of the reporters who had the very strange experience of covering these games. 'It was very surreal, because of the way you're used to seeing German stadiums. The way it bounces. The fact that German football is built upon its fans, and then there was no one there. It was eerie.' He remembers the clear ambivalence within the German football scene, and how many fans simply were not having it.

There was more respect for going ahead with the games abroad than there was in Germany. I remember there were protests outside the stadium in Cologne, someone left banners, someone left an empty sofa. People were against the idea of ghost games. The ultras didn't want them to happen, to the point where they didn't come back to the stadiums until 100 per cent of fans were allowed back in. It was definitely missing something, it was missing the core element of German football. There was no atmosphere, and given that German football really feeds off the atmosphere it was really weird. It felt like we were in some sort of dystopian film. It just had an uncomfortable feeling.

Another reporter who saw it all up close was Oliver Müller. 'It's so strange, especially when you're working in Dortmund,' he remembers.

Normally you have the Yellow Wall. Lots of noise. Great atmosphere. In regular matches in Dortmund it's very, very loud, and sometimes you even have difficulty understanding the answers when you're doing interviews because it's so loud in the stadium. But now the whole atmosphere during the match was spooky, in a way the name *Geisterspiele* was very well chosen for it.

Geisterspiele means 'ghost games', and is the German word for games played without supporters in the stadium. 'For me, personally, this zero atmosphere was really hard to swallow,' Müller adds.

German football particularly prides itself on its fan culture, and Bundesliga clubs have some of the most rambunctious atmospheres in European football. This silence was no one's idea of what football should be like. Though for occupationally curious reporters, it did open up a window to a side of elite football they usually don't get to experience. 'Suddenly you could understand more or less every word from the players and the coaches on and beside the pitch. It felt very unreal,' Müller says. Rhind-Tutt echoed this: 'It was fascinating hearing the kind of things coaches wanted to get across to players, and hearing the players talk to each other. It was unique.' According to Müller, there was also a tangible sense that the game was being played differently without the crowd egging the players on. 'I personally think the game changed, compared to normal Bundesliga matches,' he says.

> Because when Dortmund play, the team gets a lot of energy from the crowd. And that has an influence on how they play. I think that when there were no spectators in the stadiums, the game changed more in a direction of a game that was more calculating, more strategic. But I wouldn't say the quality was bad. And you had almost no discussions on the pitch, even after close decisions by the referee. Somehow the players were really really calm, accepted the decision whether it was right or wrong. So it was something totally different. When you talk about these 'corona times' and these 'ghost matches', you can see that clubs with a lot of tradition and who were really strong at home, they suffered a little bit. Clubs that usually have a less atmospheric crowd for their home matches, they were able to show more of their footballing ability. I think it had a really really big influence on the game.

Müller's theory would seem to have merit. The next season, which was played mostly behind closed doors, saw three teams with a strong home support take the bottom three places in the league. Schalke, Dortmund's local rivals who normally sell out their 62,000-seater stadium every week, put in one of the worst seasons in Bundesliga history. They went 30 games without winning, falling one game short of the all-time record set by the profoundly awful Tasmania Berlin team of the 1965/6 season. Werder Bremen, another club with a proud history and a big home crowd, followed Schalke down. Cologne, who have some of the most passionate fans around, ended up in the relegation play-off spot. At the other end of the table, VfL Wolfsburg – who in a normal season have one of the lowest attendances in the league – secured an unexpected Champions League spot.

So many things were different, but one thing stayed the same: Erling Haaland scored goals. In fact he was the first player to score in the Bundesliga after football resumed, netting the first in a 4–0 win for Dortmund against rivals Schalke. He added three more before the end of the season, which put him at 13 goals in 15 games. A reasonable return for a teenager who had only just joined a new club. Given his explosive success on the field, it's easy to forget that at this point he was still very young and he'd just joined a new club in yet another new country. Added to all this was the isolation of living through lockdown. As his youth coach Alf Ingve Berntsen put it: 'Erling Haaland was not designed to sit still.' But here he was, mostly trapped at home, in a town and a country he had only just moved to.

Patrick Owomoyela played for Dortmund between 2008 and 2013, was part of the squad that won two Bundesliga titles under Jürgen Klopp, and got 11 caps for Germany. He now works for the club as an international ambassador, and does co-commentary for the Bundesliga's international broadcasts. 'Being young, coming to a new country and a new city, you want to explore,' he says.

You want to get to know people, you want to go out and celebrate after games, maybe meet people. That was all taken away from him. And these guys are professionals, probably more than players in my time. So they don't go out like we used to do, not even for lunch, they have perfect surroundings. They kinda lived in a bubble even before Covid. But as a young player you sometimes break out of it and you want to experience things, and he couldn't. Of course this makes it hard. The club did a perfect job making the best possible situation, having everything you need at the training ground so the guys could hang out there. And once you're in that bubble you could act freely, but outside of that, going home, everything was different. Everything was shut down for a big amount of time.

In the first couple of games he played for Dortmund at home, Haaland had appeared to revel in the spotlight and the excitement of playing in front of 80,000 people. Suddenly that was no longer possible. 'There is something special about Borussia Dortmund, especially playing at home in this stadium when it's at full capacity, when everybody is there and being loud,' says Owomoyela.

He didn't really get to feel that. So it wasn't the easiest bonding phase between him and the club. He knew about it of course, and he did experience a little bit of that, but then it was gone. And playing in front of empty stands, especially in that stadium, it is something strange. It doesn't make it easy for you as a player to play at your highest level.

Still, Haaland did continue to play at a very high level. And Owomoyela, like everyone else at Dortmund, was convinced early on that the club had something special in the Norwegian.

> I watched his first training match for the club, and he was acting the same way as he does in games. And this is something very unique and very special about Erling, I would say. For most of the players there is a difference between training and a real game, but not for Erling. As long as there are two goals and two teams on opposite sides, Erling wants to win. He wants to score, of course, but even more he wants to win. You know, sometimes in training players will be like 'come on, it's midweek, we have a game at the weekend, let's just hold back a little bit.' This is a normal thing, I did it myself. But not with Erling, he always goes at full throttle. And there are just very few players who do that. Especially when you're that good, everything is going your way, it's easy then to just do as much as you need to do but not more. But he was always investing more than the usual.

That hard work would quickly pay off. He was an extraordinary talent, as anyone could see, but he was still raw. There were aspects of his game that still needed to improve, so Haaland set about working to improve them. 'He improved a lot, and it was necessary,' Owomoyela remembers.

> You're playing in the Bundesliga now. You will be analysed by opponents, they will know what your biggest strength is. If you're a guy with only one weapon, they will then put their fastest player or their strongest player against you and try to

take that weapon away from you. But then you have to find different ways, and he worked on that. He tried using his right foot more. He tried to be involved in the build-up play a little more. Of course he used his speed and his strength. Heading was something he was actually really poor at, but he added some goals there. He was still looking for improvements, he was still working. In every training session he was going to the limit. This allows you to improve. He's a young man still and he will probably improve even more. But a major part of this improvement he made at Borussia Dortmund. He was able to play at the highest level, being surrounded by very good players, better players than at Salzburg, better players than with the Norwegian national team. And he had to face the best players in the world playing in the Champions League for Dortmund.

The Champions League remained a happy hunting ground for Haaland. The next season, in the autumn of 2020, he played four group-stage games and scored six goals. Experienced reporter Oliver Müller also noticed rapid improvements to Haaland's all-round game.

When he came he already had very high quality when he had space in front of him and could run towards the goal of the opponent. But one thing that was weird was that he was not the best header of the ball. And he worked on it, he really worked on it. At that time the manager was Lucien Favre, who is an older manager, and he is someone who was always talking very critically about the advantages and disadvantages of his players. But he said frankly, that it was just amazing, because when the training session was over

Haaland stayed on the pitch, he worked on his weak points. And we all saw him progress, from week to week.

'He has this hunger, this fire that is burning in him,' Müller remembers. 'It's unbelievable. There were times when he had already scored three or four goals, and when the coach took him off ten minutes before the final whistle and the game had already been decided for a long time, he was pissed! This shows how ambitious he is.' One game in which Haaland was displeased to be taken off was against Hertha Berlin in November 2020. The game was won, there were five minutes left, and Haaland had scored four goals already. The giant Olympiastadion in Berlin was almost entirely empty, but Archie Rhind-Tutt was one of the few people there. 'When he scored four goals against Hertha, that for me was when it truly dawned on me how special he was,' he remembers.

When you were watching these things you didn't have an idea of the scale of it, because there were no fans. Fans act as a good sounding board for how special the moment is. It's 1–0 against Hertha at half-time, and Dortmund were playing terribly. So, so bad. And Haaland is coming on. Haaland had just won the Golden Boy award. And I remember he came on, he scored four, and I remember looking at each goal going in thinking, God, Hertha are really bad, why can't they stop him? And then it slowly crept up on you that actually, no, it's him being that good. He makes it look like when you have a school team and you have one guy who is just so much better than everyone else. You lose track of the context. It was insane.

When the Bundesliga was initially paused because of the pandemic in early April 2020, Dortmund were four points behind Bayern with nine games left to play. One of those nine games was at home against Bayern. If Dortmund could win that one it would leave the Bavarian giants with a very slim margin of error. Normally Dortmund's players would have had the noise of 80,000 people pushing them on. But now, of course, they did not. Instead they had a massive, cavernous stadium in which the sound of every shout and kick of the ball rang out and was left hanging in the air over the empty terraces. The biggest game of the domestic season somehow looked and sounded like a training session. In the 46th minute Joshua Kimmich caught the Dortmund-keeper Roman Bürki unawares with a delicate chip from the edge of the box. The Swiss goalkeeper made an acrobatic attempt to recover but couldn't quite get to it, and in truth the effort from Kimmich was a thing of exquisite beauty. 'It was maybe the most beautiful goal of my life and also very important,' Kimmich said after the game. 'I didn't see him off his line but we were told before the game that Bürki stands a bit off his line so I went for it and with a bit of luck it went in.' There was some redemption for Bürki in the second half as he did well to get down and stop a shot from Leon Goretzka but, down the other end of the pitch, Dortmund were struggling. Haaland didn't have a good game. His best chance came in the 58th minute, when Thorgan Hazard set him up for a shot in the box. Haaland's finish hit Bayern defender Jérôme Boateng, who had slipped and fallen over in the box. On replays the shot looked goal-bound before being blocked by Boateng's arm, but VAR took no action. Then, 20 minutes before full-time, Haaland limped off with a knee injury. The game ended 1–0 to Bayern. 'We were too wasteful around the penalty area in the first half,' said Mats Hummels after the game.

We had two or three opportunities to shoot. It was that all-important final ball. It was missing in certain moments, otherwise we would have had chances. When we did have the chances, then our finishing wasn't good enough. It was not a poor performance. We fell just a little short.

The defeat left Bayern seven points clear at the top of the table with six games to go. And after stuttering under Niko Kovač at the start of the season, Bayern were now flying under Hansi Flick. Beating Dortmund meant the team had won 13 out of their last 14 games in the Bundesliga. There was simply no way they were going to give up a seven-point lead over the last six games. Dortmund finished second in the Bundesliga for the fifth time in eight seasons. There is no shame in being the best team in Germany not named Bayern Munich, but these constant near misses were becoming hard for Dortmund to swallow.

18

MEDIA STUDIES

The first *Geisterspiele* Borussia Dortmund and Erling Haaland were involved in was, of all things, a derby against local rivals FC Schalke 04. Ordinarily one of the most heated and passionate derbies in world football, a fixture that should be on the bucket list of any self-respecting football connoisseur was played in near silence in front of tens of thousands of empty seats. Everyone, aside from the 22 players on the pitch, was wearing a mask. Players on the bench had to practise social distancing and so were spread out. Many German fans felt the games shouldn't go ahead at all. It was surreal. The defeat in Paris aside, Dortmund had been in good form domestically when the season was paused, and against Schalke they picked up where they left off. There was very little about this game that felt normal, but Dortmund's opening goal after 29 minutes at least had some very familiar sporting ingredients to it: a clever flick from Julian Brandt linked midfield and attack, this time sending Thorgan Hazard off into space on the right-hand side. His perfect cross found Haaland's well-timed run in the middle: 1–0. A fairly typical Dortmund goal, and a very typical Haaland goal. Dortmund added three more to win the game 4–0, and after the game the players made a point of celebrating in front of the Yellow Wall – just as they would have if there had been 25,000 people in Dortmund's famous south stand. Ghost game or not, a 4–0 win over Schalke is a 4–0 win over Schalke. Having scored the first goal in the game, and the first in the Bundesliga since the restart, Erling Haaland was made available for a post-match interview. On the reporting side, the honour fell to Oliver Müller.

> **Müller:** Congratulations. Maybe the strangest derby in the history in these two clubs, but a very, very strong performance of Borussia Dortmund. Are you surprised how strong?

> **Haaland:** No I'm not, I know that many guys on my team have been working hard in this period. And I'm not surprised, no.

> **Müller:** It seems that Borussia Dortmund was in the match pretty much from the beginning, did you always feel secure? Also it's a really strange surrounding for a Bundesliga match.

> **Haaland:** Yeah of course, normally it's 80,000, but we knew that we had the support at home from the fans. We were never afraid of anything. We knew that we're going to win. And yeah, you saw today that we had full control. So a good start.

> **Müller:** And you started there where you stopped seven weeks ago, another Erling Haaland goal. Are you already in the shape that you have been before all this corona crisis?

Haaland: Of course I'm not in the same, I haven't been playing games for seven weeks. So of course not. But I know that I've been working hard this period and I'm not surprised, no.

Müller: After the final whistle, you and the whole team-mates, you were going to the south stand, the famous Yellow Wall, which was empty today of course, why did you do that?

Haaland: Why not?

Müller: Is it a kind of message you want to send out?

Haaland: Yes.

Müller: Would you tell us the message?

Haaland: To my fans. To our fans.

Müller: They are everything for you and for Borussia Dortmund.

Haaland: It is.

A slightly awkward conversation between two people, neither of whom speak English as a first language. Erling Haaland had already established a reputation for giving somewhat monosyllabic interviews, and in the Norwegian media he had been frank and honest about why. After playing a Champions League game for Salzburg, he had told Norwegian newspaper *VG* that he was hoping to speak less to the media going forward. 'The club is good at protecting me a bit, I hope there will be more of that going forward. It's difficult, but we will try. I want to be protected.' The Norwegian word he used was *skjermet*, which literally translates to being screened, though in this context to be sheltered or protected would be a more useful translation. The reporter asked him why he wanted to be screened. 'It's *dritkjedelig.* I'm bored right now.' The word *drit* means shit or crap, while *kjedelig* is the Norwegian word for 'boring'. Haaland, when he has to speak to reporters, is often very bored. Bored as shit, to be exact. 'On a scale from 1 to 10, how bored are you right now?' the reporter asked. 'Nine point nine,' Haaland replied.

Aside from his general disinterest in speaking to the media, there is also the element of Haaland's background. Author and fellow Bryne native Nils Henrik Smith explains:

> I would say that it's typical for people from Jæren to be quite taciturn. Pretty much every time a journalist from outside of Norway has contacted me to ask about Erling Haaland, one of the things they ask about is how he approaches media interviews. Some people interpret it as him being painfully shy, which I definitely don't think he is. Others perceive it as a kind of arrogance. Which perhaps is something you might become from being a footballer with that level of fame. But I always answer that this is quite typical for where he's from. If someone asks you a question that has a yes or no answer, you will most likely get a yes or no answer – and not some long explanation about why you think yes or no. Especially if you're speaking to someone you don't know very well.

This tendency to provide the simplest and shortest possible answer can be frustrating for journalists – print journalists in particular, who are looking for quotes they can use, ideally complete sentences that will make sense in writing. After playing against Liverpool in the Champions League for Salzburg – the game at Anfield where he came on and scored – the Norwegian press attempted to draw Haaland on one particular question. Haaland's old manager famously used to sit on the bench at United and look for weaknesses in the opposing defence that he could exploit if he was brought on. When asked by *VG* if this was something Solskjær had passed on to him, Haaland replied, 'Yes.' In what way? 'Like you said.' Can you put it into your own words? 'No, you just said it, you've put it into words.' What is it that Solskjær has taught you? 'What you just said.'

So by the time Haaland was playing for Dortmund and had scored the first Bundesliga goal after football had resumed, he already had a bit of a reputation for this sort of thing. And then, with almost no other professional football being played anywhere else in the world, and with millions and millions of people stuck at home with nothing to do but look at their phones and laptops, an edited version of the interview with Oliver Müller – which included only the last 26 seconds – was published. The video clip didn't include the first part of the interview, for which Haaland had provided perfectly reasonable answers to the interviewer. It only showed his clipped answers about celebrating in front of the Yellow Wall. 'ERLING HAALAND SAYS JUST 11 WORDS IN POST-MATCH INTERVIEW AFTER DOWNING RIVALS SCHALKE AS BORUSSIA DORTMUND WONDERKID GIVES INTERVIEWER SHORT SHRIFT BEFORE WALKING AWAY,' said an online newspaper headline. 'ERLING HAALAND GIVES BIZARRE 11-WORD POST-MATCH INTERVIEW AS DORTMUND THUMP SCHALKE ON BUNDESLIGA RETURN' said another. There were many, many more. Adding fuel to the fire, a compilation video showing other examples of Haaland being unenthusiastic in interviews surfaced and was spread far and wide. Social media, already a heightened focal point during the pandemic, went into a bit of a frenzy. Some people, such as Piers Morgan, suggested that Haaland 'isn't programmed for basic manners' and that his 'arrogance with the media is unedifying'. On the other hand, there was also no shortage of fans who applauded Haaland's approach to interviews, and praised him for what appeared to be a hostile attitude towards reporters. Others still, like former Norway forward Jan Åge Fjørtoft, enthusiastically leapt to Haaland's defence.

The man who conducted the infamous Schalke interview remains slightly baffled by it all. 'My recollection of this is still very strong,' Oliver Müller says.

I'm quite an experienced reporter, but things like this don't happen very often. Normally you can more or less predict what a pre-match interview is going to be like. A lot of players have their phrases, their sentences, and also they more or less can expect what kind of questions they are going to get.

The setting for the interview, like a lot of things to do with these ghost games, had a slightly surreal feeling to it. 'At the time it was done with the player standing on the pitch, and I was 5–6 metres away from him,' Müller remembers.

I was standing on the lowest step on the main stand. He had an ear plug so he could hear my questions, and in order to get his answers we had to use a very long microphone. So it was not like a normal, personal interview. The situation was perhaps a little weird for him.

Müller knew a little bit what Haaland was like. He had spoken to a colleague who had interviewed Haaland before, and had been warned that he could be difficult,

> so I kinda knew what to expect. Also it was a live situation, so I tried to prepare myself a little bit. I tried to give him questions that were open questions. For example, when they went to celebrate in front of the empty Yellow Wall, I asked him if he could explain why they did that. So he couldn't give the answer 'yes' or 'no'. Because he had a kind of reputation. My impression was that he sometimes likes to make fun of the reporter, and of the journalist. So I gave him open questions, but then what he did was he answered back to the journalist, 'Why not?' And so I tried again, and I continued, and the situation really was quite funny.

He came away from the interview thinking he hadn't gotten much out of Haaland, but thought no more of it.

> Then some hours later I got a phone call from a colleague, who was saying, 'Oh have you seen this, this is going viral on the Internet.' And I looked at it again, and I was really amused. There was not a second where I thought that he had taken offence … I really never thought in that direction. Then one or two days later I heard that the interview was somehow analysed [as] bad behaviour from Erling. Personally I have another point of view on this subject. At the time he came to Dortmund he was very, very young. There is a lot of pressure on these young players, we expect from them not just good performances, but to be eloquent

in interviews and so on. I thought that he always kept his sense of humour. We talked about it some months later, the conversation was not much longer than the interview, but he started to grin when he saw me again and we got along very well even after this interview.

Müller understands how incidents like this one inspire conflicting opinions.

The funny thing for me was, of course, when things like this happen and they go viral, there are many reactions. One reaction was people saying 'that was funny, that was cool', then there were other kinds of reactions that said 'Haaland is stubborn, it's unfriendly, he's rude,' then there were also reactions saying 'It's right that this has happened to this journalist, they ask a lot of nonsense, that was a nonsense question,' and this is not so nice for me. But I never worried about these kinds of reactions. It surprised me a couple of days later when I heard that there had been a discussion, a controversy. People were saying that he should grow up, this is disrespectful, he can't present himself like this. I always say, 'My God, this is just football.' OK, the players earn millions, but we are still dealing with very young people. They are human beings, and sometimes they like to make a bit of fun.

Müller is also keen to stress that he saw another side of Haaland soon enough when he had the chance to interview him and Giovanni Reyna, Dortmund's young American player. Reyna had played magnificently in that match, and Haaland was talking about [him]. And he said some amazing things: the future belongs to this guy, for me he is the American dream and so on. So you can see, if he wants to then he has the ability to be more eloquent. But I think at that time, when he was new in the Bundesliga, he liked to tease the reporters a little bit. I frankly quite enjoyed it.

Archie Rhind-Tutt also had the experience of interviewing the young Erling Haaland. 'For me it was a challenge,' he remembers.

I realised that I needed to match him with his energy. If you act very upbeat towards him, and that's not the mood that he's in, then you're not going to get much out of him. I think you have to fire questions in the same kind of flat, straightforward nature that he has. There are also just some days when you accept that he doesn't want to say anything. I had an interview with him once when he'd scored, where I said 174 words and I think he was around the 160 mark. But I didn't think ill of him. The joy of football is that many different characters play it. I find it more authentic that he's like 'you know, I just have no time for this.' You get some players who are trying to answer every question diplomatically, you get some who are laid back and happy to show their character a bit more. And I think it needs to be taken into account for him in particular, to be as good as he is, it's not because he spends his time going to improv classes to give himself an extra shade of kooki-ness. He spends his time conditioning his body and mind with unbelievable hours of dedication. With players who are that focused I think you're going to get characters like Erling Haaland.

Patrick Owomoyela, being a former Bundesliga winner with Dortmund and a current Dortmund employee, got to know Erling Haaland in a very different way during this time. 'Whenever I met him, and it was mostly at the training ground, we'd have small talk about Norway, about fishing, about so many things. It was always just normal conversations, he was always polite and funny and open,' he says.

> So all these interviews where he just answers with a yes or no, that's not Erling Haaland when he's in his comfortable zone. You have to accept that. I also work with television and broadcasting, so I know what a pain in the ass it is when you have someone who isn't willing to talk. But on the other hand, he just wants to play football. He just wants to be successful. And he just wants to have fun as well. That's a big part of it, he's a really fun-loving guy. And a funny guy as well. Whenever the cameras and the mics are off, it's always fun.

Owomoyela also believes there was an element of mischief to Haaland's infamous interviews.

> I think, and this is just my opinion, I don't know it for certain, but I think he was kinda playing with the media and making fun of the media by doing this. Because they were maybe pushing it a little bit too far, or putting it in the wrong perspective. So maybe he just took it on and built

on it. 'OK, you think I'm that kind of guy? I'm going to be that kind of guy now, I will answer yes or no. Ask the right questions or you get yes or no.' I think he laughs himself to sleep afterwards. This is also something about him, he doesn't care about his perception in the media. He doesn't care about other people's opinions. This is also Erling.

Haaland himself has addressed his somewhat taciturn media persona. Speaking to the *Top 3* podcast a couple of months after the Schalke interview went viral, Haaland explained that his background plays a part. 'To put it simply: if a *Jærbu* is asked how it's going, if it's going well you will reply, "It's going *grævla* well," and that's the end of that. You don't need to say more than that.' Though he did reject the notion that his curt answers were meant as a kind of criticism of the questions. 'It doesn't have to be a bad question. If you ask a yes or no question, you will have a yes or no answer. You're getting an answer to the question you asked.' So this is a challenge to the journalists to ask you more open questions? 'Yes, you can say that. If you'd asked me a yes or no question now, I would give you a yes or no answer. It's like that for everyone.'

'My God!' Oliver Müller exclaims years later, laughing ruefully. 'I did everything to avoid this situation! I avoided giving him a question where he could only say "yes" or "no". So I gave him an open question, and he just answered, "Why not?"!'

Throughout his time in the global spotlight there have been a handful of interviews where fans have seen the real Erling, the person who Patrick Owomoyela had small talk about fishing with, the person former coaches and teammates describe as warm, funny, even approachable. It's not unreasonable for fans to wish that they could see that side of him more often, but at the same time perhaps he is right to be guarded. There are sections of the modern media that combine an insatiable hunger for clickbait with a total lack of scruples, the net effect of which is that any and all things someone like Haaland says can and will be taken out of context. 'It's also the media's fault that you don't get the full picture,' says Martin Ødegaard in Viaplay's documentary *Haaland: The Big Decision*. 'If you do one thing wrong, suddenly there are ten headlines. And you don't even need to do anything wrong, it could just be a funny thing, and it suddenly becomes a big deal. So you think about that and you have to protect yourself.' And at the end of the day it's not Haaland's job to be a public personality. That part of global stardom is a potential distraction one suspects Haaland wishes he could do without. His job is to score goals and win football matches. In the same documentary he explains his approach to the media in characteristically simple and direct terms: 'In front of a camera I don't feel the need to show who I am. Why should they know who I am? I prefer to put on a front.' Straight to the point. No words wasted. No embellishments. Typical Erling Haaland.

19

THE GOLDEN BOY

Erling Haaland's second season at Dortmund started later in the year than usual for the football calendar, as the pandemic had forced a shift in fixtures. The games were still ghost games, the atmosphere was still eerie, but Erling Haaland was straight back at it. He scored ten goals in his first seven league appearances for Dortmund that autumn. On the same day that he scored four goals against Hertha Berlin, Haaland also received the Golden Boy award – a kind of baby Ballon d'Or awarded annually to the best under-21 player in the European leagues. Past winners include Lionel Messi, Cesc Fàbregas, Sergio Agüero and Kylian Mbappé. 'I'm happy and when I got the message it was free motivation for me,' he told Dortmund's in-house media after the Hertha game. 'I had to show some people that I'm the golden boy. I feel I did it today. We go again in the Champions League now.' His manager, Lucien Favre, was joking with Haaland that in the next game he should go for five goals. Haaland scored 'just' two, as Dortmund beat Club Brugge 3–0. This took Haaland's tally to six goals in four Champions League appearances that autumn. But when Dortmund announced the line-up for their next Champions League fixture, against Lazio on 2 December, Erling Haaland was not in it. The club confirmed that he had suffered a torn hamstring and would be out for the rest of the year. These injury setbacks would continue to frustrate Haaland during his time at Dortmund. 'If he hadn't been held back now and again by minor injuries, who knows what kind of records he could have set,' says Owomoyela. 'And of course there was Covid going on, there was no one in attendance … Just imagine if everything had been perfect, it would have been incredible to watch.'

With the injury keeping him out for the rest of 2020, Haaland travelled to Qatar to work on his rehabilitation. While he was away, Dortmund manager Favre was sacked. In spite of Haaland's goals, it had been an iffy start to the season for the team overall. A disastrous 5–1 defeat to newly promoted Stuttgart on 12 December left Dortmund six points behind Bayern in the table after only 11 games. 'It is very difficult to take this step,' said the sporting director Michael Zorc. 'But we believe because of the negative developments lately that there is a need to act.' CEO Hans-Joachim Watzke added that 'as a professional and as a person, Lucien Favre is beyond any doubt.' Assistant manager Edin Terzić, a lifelong Dortmund fan who had cheered the team on from the Yellow Wall many times himself, was put in charge until the end of the season. The year 2020 became 2021, and Erling Haaland returned to full fitness. In late February Dortmund faced Sevilla in the Champions League's round of 16.

'It's been a long time since I felt like this in a stadium watching a player,' Sid Lowe, an English football journalist and author who reports on Spanish football, said on the *Spanish Football Podcast*. 'He kinda imposes on everybody and conditions everyone. It's almost like he warps the reality that's going on around him. When he set off running, you could feel the fear. It was an extraordinary thing to see.' The first leg was played in Seville. The hosts took the lead, but just over ten minutes later Haaland set up an equaliser for Mahmoud Dahoud.

> He started running, and you could see. I don't know if it's in his style, the way he pumps his arms, or what it is, but as soon as he started running you could feel that this was different ... It felt like a machine, you could imagine in your mind the speedometer going up.

Haaland didn't do anything fancy ahead of the goal, he simply accelerated away from his opponent and left the ball for Dahoud. 'But it's just that little surge, you can tell everyone went, *shit*,' Lowe observed. In addition to his obvious physical gifts and his steadily improving technique, Haaland was starting to develop an aura. Defenders knew about him, and they worried about what he could do to them. He was starting to spread fear just by making runs. For Dortmund's second goal, Haaland picked up the ball, advanced through the middle, played a one-two with Jadon Sancho and scored. Sevilla's defence had backtracked all the way to their penalty area, yet no one came to challenge Haaland. Sevilla had the second-best defensive record in La Liga at the time, but here their backline panicked at the mere sight of Haaland. Central defender Diego Carlos, who was having an otherwise excellent season, looked particularly flummoxed. 'Haaland turns and runs at them, and Diego Carlos ran away!,' Lowe marvelled. 'He didn't want to go in and get beaten and have loads of space behind him, or he just didn't want to get in the way. It felt like they were frightened of him!' Haaland then made it 3–1 after a turnover by the home team gave Dortmund a brilliant chance on the counter, and the unfortunate Carlos was left trying to deal with Haaland and Marco Reus on his own. Sevilla managed to get a goal back in the 84th minute to make it 3–2, but the result set Dortmund up nicely for the return leg. 'I was motivated by watching Mbappé score nice goals on Tuesday,' Haaland said after the game. The French superstar had put three past Barcelona the night before. In the return leg against Sevilla, played at Signal Iduna Park, Haaland promptly scored another two goals, taking his Champions League tally for the season to ten in six games. Dortmund being Dortmund, the team squandered this lead by conceding two goals in the second half. The 2–2 draw was enough for the German side to progress to the next round, where they would face none other than Manchester City.

The first leg of the tie was to be played in Manchester, and City came into it in ferocious form. The English club had won 26 of their last 27 games and were running away with the Premier League. Dortmund, by contrast, continued to be maddeningly inconsistent. Three days before facing City, Dortmund had lost 2–1 to Frankfurt, and *The Athletic*'s Raphael Honigstein was scathing in his assessment:

> It was the usual, deeply unnerving combination of disembodied, half-baked attacks and lack of focus at the back. Dortmund had enough opportunities to win the game twice over, but their 'technical deficiencies' (Hummels' words) and propensity to make the wrong decision rendered their attempts hapless. Every one of their 10 Bundesliga defeats this season has followed the same pattern.

Erling Haaland may have startled Sevilla, but he had recently drawn a blank across a three-game international break with Norway and cut a frustrated, goalless figure in the defeat to Frankfurt. For the second season in a row, Dortmund's Champions League hopes came down to a tie against a team representing the new money of football. Like PSG, Manchester City have been turbo-charged by vast sums invested by owners from the Persian Gulf. But whereas PSG has used its deep pockets to create a fashion brand and buy a guest list, Manchester City has used its funds to build a football club. City had already won the Premier League several times, and under the leadership of Pep Guardiola the Manchester side developed into one of the most impressive teams on the planet. There was a sense that against a rampant Manchester City, this could easily get very ugly for Dortmund.

With that ominous backdrop, Dortmund showed a lot of defiance in the first leg, away from home. The hosts took the lead after Emre Can had given the ball away cheaply in midfield, and City's counter eventually ended in a goal from Kevin De Bruyne. But Dortmund didn't crumble. The players showed plenty of spirit and endeavour, and were soon denied an equaliser by a refereeing error: Jude Bellingham nicked the ball from a complacent Ederson, but before he could put the ball in the net the referee whistled for a foul. There was no foul, as replays clearly showed. VAR technology was available but, because the whistle had blown and the game had been stopped before Bellingham put the ball in the net, there was nothing the referees with the video monitors could do. The on-pitch referee, Ovidiu Hategan, had mistakenly given Manchester City a penalty earlier in the game as well, though that time VAR had been on hand to correct him. 'This Ref needs checking!' tweeted a grumpy Jadon Sancho, who was unable to play in the game because of injury. Dortmund would eventually get the hard-fought equaliser. In an interesting little role reversal it was Erling Haaland who slipped a clever ball through for Marco Reus, and the Dortmund skipper finished expertly. For a while it looked like Dortmund might hold on, but in the 89th minute Phil Foden popped up with a late winner. It was not undeserved – City had the better chances in the game – but Dortmund had shown spirit and the Bellingham non-goal left a sour taste. Haaland didn't score and only had one shot all match, but he was still singled out for some slightly unconventional praise by Pep Guardiola after the game. 'When you want to press, they play long balls,' Guardiola told *DAZN*. 'They play long balls to Haaland, Haaland is a bastard. Link-up is always perfect and they have the pace, so we knew it was not easy to control them.'

Dortmund came away feeling that there was still something for them in the tie, even though they had lost this leg. They got the away goal – this was the last season before UEFA scrapped the away-goals rule in the Champions League knockouts – and there had been enough times where they had carved City open for the team to believe that it was possible to get a win in the return leg. 'The belief here is great, but that alone will not be enough,' Terzić warned before the game. 'We have shown that we can hold out against top teams. It will be a brutally difficult task. We have to work hard and be coura-geous tomorrow.'

The second leg started well. In the 14th minute Erling Haaland ran onto a long ball from Emre Can. He was too far wide to score himself, but he easily held off City defender John Stones and left the ball for Mahmoud Dahoud. The shot was blocked, but the ball dropped kindly for Bellingham, who swiftly launched it into the top corner. The emergence of the then 17-year-old Bellingham had been one of the stories of the season for Dortmund in Germany, and the two games against City showed the English audience that their national team could have a new superstar on its hands. Ten minutes later, Kevin De Bruyne rattled one off the crossbar, almost as if to remind the jubilant Dortmund players that this was still Manchester City they were playing against. And there was a lot of time left on the clock. Keeping Manchester City at bay for over an hour is something very few teams are capable of doing, and this Dortmund team was not exactly known for its defensive resilience. With half an hour played, the goal-scoring hero Bellingham had to block a goal-bound shot from Riyad Mahrez that had beaten the Dortmund goalkeeper Marwin Hitz. The resulting corner ended in Hitz saving a close-range header from Oleksandr Zinchenko. City players were knocking on the door. In the second half City finally got a breakthrough, and it was an immensely frustrating one from Dortmund's perspective. Emre Can, contorting his body to clear a cross, ended up heading the ball onto his own shoulder. The modern handball law and its application could befuddle the most learned of scholars, but punishing Can with a certain goal against seemed wildly disproportionate to the offence that had taken place. But that's what happened, and Mahrez hit a superb, unstoppable penalty kick. With the game back in City's favour, the visitors looked comfortable. In the 73rd minute Kevin De Bruyne nearly scored a brilliant individual goal, and from the resulting corner kick City made it 2–1. The ball had been worked to Phil Foden just outside the corner of the box, and he beat Hitz at his near post with a surgical left-footed strike. No one could argue that City weren't the better team. In both games, they had created more chances. But it was still a tie that left an awful lot of 'what ifs' for Dortmund. 'Well done City. Congrats But, some strange ref decisions over the two legs. All the best in the next round,' Alfie Haaland tweeted. 'We haven't been very lucky with the refereeing decisions over the last seven days,' Edin Terzić observed. Above all, Dortmund were left to wonder what that second leg could have been like with 80,000 home fans driving the team on.

For Erling Haaland it had been another frustrating evening against Manchester City. Though he had provided a fine assist in the first leg, he had only managed two shots over 180 minutes against his father's old team. In the first leg he had been through on goal but never seemed to fully get the ball or even his body under control and he was unable to beat Ederson with the finish. For a young man who lives for the big occasions, it was galling. But something else had been going on with Erling Haaland during the course of this tie. 'I'll be totally honest. When we played City, after those two games I think it was 15 guys who had told me I should come to City,' Haaland told Viaplay about a year later. 'Stones and Ruben Dias said it, Gündoğan said it, Foden said it. De Bruyne said it. There were many of them who said it.' Haaland also revealed that after the end of the season, when he was on holiday in Mykonos with his friends from home, they bumped into Riyad Mahrez who had continued the informal recruitment efforts on behalf of City.

Dortmund may be an ideal place for a world-class talent to develop, but the club has certain limitations. Haaland may have drawn a blank against City, but he was still on 21 goals in 23 games in the Bundesliga that season, and ten goals in eight in the Champions League. Dortmund's team was flawed, but Haaland's credentials as one of the most exciting players on the planet were clear.

Erling Haaland broke his mini goal drought in the next game with a brace against Werder Bremen, and added four more goals before the end of the season, taking his Bundesliga total to 27 goals in 28 games. Robert Lewandowski had scored a scarcely believable 41 goals in 28 starts for Bayern, but Haaland was voted the Bundesliga player of the season by fans. After that poor defeat to Frankfurt ahead of the first City match, Dortmund actually went on to win the rest of their games in the Bundesliga. It was only enough for them to finish third, but at least they secured a Champions League spot for the following season. And at the same time as all of this was going on, Dortmund were still alive in the German Cup. The team had sailed past Duisburg and Eintracht Braunschweig – second- and third-division sides, respectively – in the first two rounds. Extra time was needed to dispatch Paderborn in the third round, with Haaland scoring the winning goal, and in February Dortmund beat Borussia Mönchengladbach 1–0, which meant that the club had made it to the semi-finals. For this knockout game, Dortmund met Holstein Kiel, a second-division Bundesliga side that had shocked the nation by eliminating Bayern Munich in the second round. No such slip-up from Dortmund, who beat Kiel comfortably 5–0. And so, after a season of ups and downs, Dortmund had a chance to win a cup final in Berlin against RB Leipzig.

It was a strong Leipzig team. The club had finished second in the Bundesliga, ahead of Dortmund, and the players were led by the young coaching star Julian Nagelsmann. The team had no obvious superstars, perhaps, but the squad included an array of athletic, skilful, hard-working players – most of whom were well drilled in the high-intensity football of the Red Bull football empire. But Dortmund were on the up. In a strange twist of fixture scheduling, they had beaten Leipzig 3–2 in the league just five days earlier. They were on a winning streak. The team was confident. After only five minutes, Jadon Sancho gave Dortmund the lead with a lovely finish from just inside the box. Later in the first half Marco Reus released Erling Haaland, who made Dayot Upamecano look silly and made it 2–0. Just before half-time Reus beat the high Leipzig line and raced towards goal. He eventually squared it for Sancho, who made it 3–0. The linesman mistakenly flagged for offside, but VAR corrected the error and confirmed the goal. Nagelsmann made changes at half-time and Leipzig improved after the break, but Dortmund were already too far ahead. Dani Olmo grabbed a consolation goal with a superb hit from the edge of the area in the 71st minute, but for once there was no suggestion of Dortmund throwing anything away. A couple of minutes before full-time Erling Haaland added a fourth.

With COVID-19 rules still in place and the stands still empty, Haaland and Dortmund were denied a proper celebration with their fans. But it was still a huge moment for both the club and Haaland. It was Haaland's first major trophy, and it was only the fifth time in Dortmund's history that the club had won the Cup. In recent years the team had finished second in the Bundesliga twice and now third. In the Champions League they'd been knocked out by the vast wealth of PSG and Manchester City. It was hard to shake the feeling that the team had hit a glass ceiling, but lifting a trophy was a just reward for a period of time in which Dortmund actually had gotten quite a few things right. Certainly, a team that can field Erling Haaland, Jude Bellingham and Jadon Sancho has a lot going for it. 'Just imagine, if we could have had another year with a healthy Erling Haaland and Jadon Sancho,' Patrick Owomoyela says wistfully.

> Just imagine if we had kept Ousmane Dembele, instead of him going to Barcelona. Or even Lewandowski, and not let him go to Bayern Munich. Who knows what kind of team we would have had, and what that would have done for Borussia Dortmund. But we work with what we have.

Sancho was widely expected to be sold to Manchester United that summer. Haaland had suitors as well, but by now it was the worst-kept secret in football that he had a release clause in his contract that would become active the next summer. It would take an astronomical offer for Dortmund to consider a sale before then. This is the model of Borussia Dortmund: attract the most promising youngsters, develop them and let them go for the right price when the time is right. Dortmund does this successfully, time and time again. 'I don't think there is a secret,' Owomoyela says, laughing. 'There is nothing in the water. It's part of the DNA of Borussia Dortmund, to take young players, give them a chance and develop them. And then of course sell them, so we are able to do it all over again.' Borussia Dortmund has repeatedly sold its best players and still been able to compete in the Champions League, as well as win a couple of titles. 'This is such a good place to come for good young players. They want to come to Borussia Dortmund, and that of course makes it easier for Dortmund to pick the best ones.' Once players have joined Dortmund, Owomoyela says,

with a little bit of help and a little bit of correction, you know that they will do the rest. It's all about the players. We have proper youth development coaches of course, but nowadays all of the good clubs have that. We are maybe one or two steps ahead because we started early, using our own talent, and were able to then be successful with it. So now we're the first club that young, promising players talk to when they want to go to the next stage. Here they get to compete at the highest level, and get the right footballing education, and get the right playing time.

Borussia Dortmund has become so renowned for bringing through youth talent and allowing young footballers to play regularly in elite competition that it means the club can choose between the very best talent in the world, according to Owomoyela.

[Players] know they'll get to play in the Champions League and to compete for titles every year. And they know that the even bigger clubs have their eye on Borussia Dortmund because they know that we do this. Every season there will be a couple of players here that are very, very interesting for clubs like Real Madrid, like Barcelona, you name it. For some players the goal is to play in a top club in the Premier League, and they know that these clubs pay attention to Borussia Dortmund. It is, on the other hand, a little bit difficult for Borussia Dortmund because we would love to keep some of those players for longer.

Erling Haaland certainly had developed. Quite aside from all the goals and him gradually becoming a slightly more rounded player, he looked different. He looked bigger. In an interview with Viaplay at the end of that season, Haaland revealed that since joining Dortmund he had put on some serious muscle.

I've become more of a man now. I've added eight kilos, and I've become faster. I was 86 kilos when I came to Dortmund, now I'm almost up to 94. I'm not the best at maths but that's eight kilos in a year and a half. If you look at my body, you see an extreme change. I'm totally different.

He had become bigger, he had scored a lot of goals and he had lifted his first major trophy. And after a short holiday, he was heading into what was always likely to be his last season with Dortmund.

20

GOALS AND INTERRUPTIONS

Amid falling infection rates and the roll-out of vaccines, the German authorities decided that fans could return to Bundesliga matches from the start of the 2021/22 season. Restrictions would still have to be in place, but initially Bundesliga clubs were allowed to fill their grounds to 50 per cent capacity, although with a maximum of 25,000 people in attendance. Author and Dortmund season-ticket holder Uli Hesse was one of the 25,000 fans who were able to witness Dortmund's season-opener against Frankfurt.

I was lucky, you couldn't just go out and buy tickets, there was a lottery and you had to apply for a ticket … And I remember that when the teams came out to warm up, Haaland was the first man out of the tunnel, and he ran straight across the pitch towards the stand and waved at people. He was so happy to see people at the ground and play in front of people. That was one of the sad aspects, because he's such a crowd-pleaser and he feeds off the crowd. It's a shame that he missed out on that for so long.

The ghost games had allowed football to continue throughout most of the pandemic, and some players might have become used to the strange unreality of these games. It's even possible that some players found an upside in the absence of a crowd, as they could try difficult things on the pitch without the risk of having tens of thousands of people immediately complain and moan if those actions didn't work. But Erling Haaland was emphatically not one of those players. This is, after all, the guy who at the age of 17 ran straight over to goad the Viking fans after scoring one of his first senior goals in Norway. He doesn't just play to the crowd, he feeds off it. Throughout his career so far one trend has been clear: the bigger the occasion, the bigger the crowd, the bigger the noise, the more excited Haaland has been. During lockdown he had made the best of a bad situation, engaging a private fitness coach to help him at home via video conference. When the ghost games came back he had performed, and he had kept performing. He had worked meticulously on his body, becoming both stronger and faster. But now, with fans back in the stands, this was real football again. So in Dortmund's opening game against Frankfurt, Haaland ran riot. He scored twice and made three assists, as Dortmund won 5–3. 'Today, it was easy to be motivated,' he said after the game. 'I had goosebumps when I went out on the pitch. It was amazing to play in front of fans today. It's free motivation, I've missed them a lot. It's a good feeling, I can't explain it. When I scored, it was amazing.'

Jadon Sancho had departed for Manchester United that summer, but Dortmund had held on to Haaland. There had been no shortage of interest, but the club hadn't budged. 'There were a lot of rumours, a lot of discussions, but internally we were always clear with Erling, with his father, with Mino Raiola,' said Sebastian Kehl, the former Dortmund player who was now set to take over as sporting director when Michael Zorc stepped down at the end of that season. 'So for that reason we were very calm. And the guy is here, you can see him, he's very motivated and very engaged, and he wants to play a great season for Borussia Dortmund.' Haaland himself had said all the right things. When he was asked about his future at the end of the previous season he had simply said that he was under contract with Dortmund for 'a few more nice years' and that he wasn't thinking beyond that. One of the more persistent rumours during the summer was that Chelsea wanted to make a move. Knowing that there would be competition from even more attractive clubs when Haaland's release clause became active the following year, Chelsea reportedly considered stealing a march on their rivals by offering Dortmund €175 million for the Norwegian that summer. When asked about it by Sky Germany during Dormtund's summer camp, Haaland simply said, 'before yesterday I hadn't spoken to my agent for a month, so there you have the answer.' While Erling Haaland was doing nothing to stoke the fires of the transfer rumour mill, the same couldn't quite be said for his entourage.

Back in April, as Dortmund's staff and players were getting ready for important fixtures against Frankfurt and Manchester City, Mino Raiola and Alfie Haaland had gone on the road. Or, more specifically, they'd taken to the skies. On the morning of 1 April, a Cessna 680 private jet had taken off from Nice airport at 9.40am. It landed in Barcelona less than an hour later, where according to Spanish sports daily *Mundo Deportivo* Raiola and Haaland senior were met by Barcelona president Joan Laporta's private chauffeur. After meeting with Laporta, it was back to the airport, where the jet left again just after 2pm. But it wasn't heading back to Nice; this time the destination was Madrid. Here, they met with representatives from Real Madrid, before the plane left again at 6.11pm and landed back in Nice at around 7.30pm. The suggestion in the Spanish press had been that the travelling twosome were planning a similar trip to England the next day, though this would have been impractical owing to the UK still having strict quarantine rules in place. At the time, any new arrivals in the UK had to travel directly to the place they were staying and not leave that location for ten days. Probably not quite what Messrs Haaland and Raiola had in mind.

It's entirely common for players' representatives to have a dialogue with potential future employers, but this trip was something slightly different. Mino Raiola and Alfie Haaland were not exactly innocuous, indistinctive characters who could easily blend into a crowd outside an airport. It would have been difficult to keep the trip a secret even if they had wanted to, something an experienced operator like Raiola will have been well aware of. And the Spanish press did seem curiously well informed about it all. Having an ongoing dialogue is one thing, but being seen to publicly court potential suitors in the middle of a season, that was something rather different. The timing wasn't great either. Dortmund's form was patchy, and the upcoming game against Frankfurt was seen as crucial to the club's season. The team lost, leaving Dortmund a full seven points outside the Champions League spots. 'The behaviour of Haaland's father and Raiola is unspeakable, disrespectful, a cheek. If he wants to go, let him go,' Dietmar Hamann told Sky Germany. 'It's the most important game of the season and you are not able to address this behaviour because you are afraid to upset the player. Dortmund should think about why the players are always walking all over them. They lack leadership there.' According to the German tabloid *Bild*, the club had been informed beforehand of Alfie and Raiola's Spanish sojourn.

'I can't stop Mino Raiola and Alfie Haaland from travelling. They're grown-ups and they can choose whatever they want to do,' said caretaker manager Edin Terzić.

Speculation about Haaland's future intensified after what ESPN referred to as the 'Haaland roadshow', but Dortmund were determined not to let more than one of their crown jewels go at a time. Jadon Sancho was permitted to leave, but Haaland was going nowhere. There was also a change in the team's coaching staff. Terzić's time as caretaker boss came to an end and former Red Bull Salzburg boss Marco Rose was brought in from Borussia Mönchengladbach. Rose's remit was clear: reintroduce the energetic, front-foot football Dortmund has been known for in the past. For the opening-day win against Frankfurt the team looked much more like a classic Dortmund team, and with two goals and three assists Erling Haaland was enjoying himself immensely. Even though it was just the first game of the Bundesliga season, Haaland looked as physically sharp as he ever had. His movements were snappy and he was terrorising the Frankfurt defence. Before the Bundesliga kicked off he had scored a hat-trick against Wehen Wiesbaden in the first round of the German Cup, and he went on to score seven goals in Dortmund's first five league games. He also scored yet another goal in the Champions League when Dortmund beat Beşiktaş 2–1 in the first game of the group stage. The only false notes from the start of Dortmund's season were another defeat to Bayern Munich, this time in the German Supercup, and a surprise 2–1 defeat to Freiburg. Still, after eight games in all competitions, Haaland had scored 11 goals and he was looking better than ever. Then the injuries started.

First, he missed three games for Dortmund with a muscle injury, which also kept him out of Norway's crucial World Cup qualifiers against Turkey and Montenegro. He came back and scored a brace against Mainz, before being part of Dortmund's surprise 4–0 defeat to Erik ten Hag's Ajax in the Champions League. Then he had a problem with his hip flexor, which caused him to miss out on four games in the Bundesliga, two in the Champions League and the second round of the German Cup. He also had to watch from the sofa as Norway's World Cup dreams were ended by a 0–0 draw against Latvia and a 2–0 defeat to the Netherlands. The two games he missed for Dortmund in the Champions League ended in defeat, which meant that they were knocked out in the group stage for only the second time in the last nine years. Haaland returned in late November, playing 17 minutes off the bench in a 3–1 win against Wolfsburg. He scored, of course, and he proceeded to score six goals in his next seven appearances in the Bundesliga. He also added another two in the Champions League during a 5–0 win against Beşiktaş, not that it counted for much. In February he was hit by another muscle injury. It meant he missed another four games in the Bundesliga, including a 5–2 defeat to Leverkusen and dropped points in a draw with Augsburg. He also missed both games of a Europa League tie against Rangers, in which Dortmund were knocked out. By the time he could return to first-team football for Dortmund in March, the team was not only out of Europe and nine points behind Bayern in the league, but they had been dumped out of the Cup by second-division Bundesliga club St Pauli in January. It already looked near impossible for Haaland to achieve any of his big objectives with Dortmund before his inevitable departure that summer. When he'd been fit he had done the business. Before his return from the third injury he had scored 16 goals in just 13 starts in the Bundesliga. And with three goals in three games in the Champions League, Dortmund's group-stage exit was hardly his fault. But he'd missed too many games, and Dortmund had dropped too many points.

'I've had various problems this season,' Erling Haaland told Viaplay. 'It's been a frustrating season, but that's life. It could be a factor that I've overloaded myself. That I didn't do enough to look after my body. A lot of things play a part, a lot of small things.' Marco Rose's high-pressing style suited Dortmund as a club, but Haaland is 6 foot 4 and carrying almost 94 kilograms of mostly muscle around the pitch. No one has ever doubted Haaland's work ethic, but for him to be explosive in the right moments he does need to manage his energy on the pitch. He also thinks that his doggedness and determination may have counted against him that season, suggesting that there were situations where he should have asked to be rested or substituted. 'Maybe I've felt something, but figured it would be fine,' he said. 'You're a footballer. If you feel something, so fucking what. Go out and play. That's the only thing on your mind.' ESPN reporter Archie Rhind-Tutt suggests that manager Marco Rose may have been a factor here, as Rose may not have seen the signs or listened to Haaland's concerns. 'I'd say that's a weakness of Marco Rose, in terms of not listening. Older players he would listen to, younger players he wouldn't.' It was the same story with Christopher Nkunku at RB Leipzig, according to Rhind-Tutt. The French attacker, bought by Chelsea in 2023, had no serious history of injuries but, like Haaland, started picking up muscle injuries when playing under Marco Rose. But beyond Rose, there was one very clear indication that the Dortmund board was unhappy with how their players had been handled that season: 'The fact is Dortmund did a big overhaul of their medical department the next summer,' Rhind-Tutt explains. 'I think that tells you they recognised those problems just a little bit too late.'

Haaland returned from injury on 13 March, coming off the bench for the last 27 minutes in a 1–0 win against Arminia Bielefeld. But almost more importantly, that same weekend Bayern Munich fumbled and could only draw 1–1 against Hoffenheim. The gap was down to seven points. Dortmund had a game in hand, against Mainz, to be played a few days later. They managed to win it, cutting Bayern's lead down to four points. Could it be? There were eight games left of the season, and one of those was against Bayern. A Bayern team that had just drawn consecutive games, and was not looking fully invincible. Could the title race be on? Dortmund's next game was away to Cologne on a Sunday night. Bayern had already done their job that weekend, beating Union Berlin 4–0. It was a full house and a loud, hostile atmosphere in Cologne, and the pressure was on. Dortmund took the lead but were not at their best. They conceded an equaliser, and the game ended 1–1. The gap was back to six points, and any lingering hopes of catching Bayern were snuffed out the next weekend as Dortmund were trounced 4–1 at home by RB Leipzig. The game was the first time since the pandemic that Signal Iduna Park had been full of fans again, with a crowd of 81,365 in the stands. 'It was a really tough result to take and we're really, really disappointed because we really had other ideas,' Marco Rose said after the game. 'We were so excited about playing in front of a packed crowd again.' The end of Dortmund's title challenge meant there wasn't all that much to play for in Erling Haaland's final weeks with the club. However, after the Leipzig debacle, he did score six goals in six games. There was no suggestion that Haaland ever gave less than 100 per cent for Dortmund in this period, but Archie Rhind-Tutt believes Dortmund's travails affected him all the same.

> The situation Dortmund were in probably sucked something out of him. They weren't really challenging Bayern for the title, and that's not what Haaland is about. That probably took something out of him. Seeing that his teammates

were not quite up to his level. There were times Bellingham and Haaland looked at each other as if to say 'what are we doing here?' They never said it, but you just felt it sometimes in the looks they exchanged.

Haaland's last big game for Dortmund came on 23 April, as the team took on Bayern away from home. The gap was now up to nine points, but with a win Dortmund could at least give Bayern the opportunity to trip over their own feet and lose the title in the final three league games after that. But Bayern won 3–1, making it the seventh time Erling Haaland had lost against Bayern as a Dortmund player, in seven attempts. Though, in fairness to Haaland, during the course of these seven encounters he did score five goals. Five in seven against Bayern Munich is a better record than most strikers can point to. But a big part of the reason why Dortmund could never win these games was named Robert Lewandowski. Over the seven games in which Erling Haaland faced Bayern with Dortmund, Robert Lewandowski scored nine goals. 'That man is crazy. He is just crazy,' Haaland said back in 2021. 'When I score a goal it's like "One goal closer to catching up to him." And then he just scores another hat-trick like it's an everyday thing. What he does is so crazy.' For Dortmund fans, seeing their former hero come back to haunt them again and again must have been particularly vexing. Uli Hesse is one of the fans who was at his wit's end with Lewandowski. 'Sometimes I think that, these ten years, this dreadful Bayern dominance, I sometimes think that it basically came down to one single transfer,' says Hesse. 'Robert Lewandowski leaving Dortmund for Bayern. Because from that point on Bayern had a guy who scored 30-plus goals every year. How can you compete with that?' Well, the hope was that with Haaland in the team they would be able to compete with that. And as Patrick

Owomoyela said, you have to wonder what Haaland and Dortmund could have done together if circumstances had been less complicated. The first season, interrupted by COVID-19. The first full season, played behind closed doors, and with Dortmund having to go through a managerial change. The second full season interrupted by injury. In the end, Erling Haaland's individual numbers with Dortmund were remarkable: 86 goals in 89 appearances in all competitions. In his last full season he scored 22 goals in the Bundesliga in just 21 starts, and that was with three significant injuries interrupting his flow. It was obvious that he was ready for the next step.

· · ·

Having a star striker who is constantly linked with other clubs the way Haaland was during his time at Dortmund might frustrate some football fans, but, according to Uli Hesse, the Dortmund faithful accepted this as part of the deal. 'Normally losing a player like that would be very hard, would be a major talking point among the supporters. But with these players, you just know from the get-go that you're going to lose them,' Hesse says.

> This is the downside to this business model. You try to become attached to these players and sometimes you do, but at the same time you know that they're only here for two to three seasons so it's best not to get that emotionally attached to them. Haaland has never been one of those badge-kissing guys. He never went around saying that he was going to be there until the end of time. Everyone always knew what was going to happen. We knew he would score lots of goals, and we knew he would then leave. And he did.

With Dortmund's season effectively over and Haaland's summer departure a foregone conclusion, the rumour mill went into overdrive. Scarcely a day went by without a cluster of Erling Haaland transfer news of dubious origin making its way to the Internet. The irrepressible Jan Åge Fjørtoft provided constant updates on Twitter, in multiple languages. On 10 May, a couple of days before Haaland's last game for Dortmund, the identity of his next club was officially announced.

21

THE DECISION, PART TWO

The Norwegian obsession with English football started well before the Premier League became a global broadcasting phenomenon, and it started in a most peculiar way. Lars-Gunnar Björklund, a Swedish sports reporter working for the Swedish public broadcaster SVT, visited England in 1967 with the idea of producing a report about fox-hunting. But an outbreak of foot and mouth disease meant the hunt was cancelled. Björklund, finding himself in England with some time to kill, decided to go to a football match. On 18 November 1967 he was at White Hart Lane to watch Tottenham beat Chelsea 2–0, with goals from Cliff Jones and Alan Gilzean. Björklund thought the spectacle was pretty good, and had a bright idea: why not put this on TV? Sweden, like Norway, has to play its club football in the warmer months of the year, and so in the winter months people have no access to football of any kind. Maybe this is where television could come in?

It took a while to get things together. The public broadcasters in Sweden, Norway and Denmark decided to pool their resources, and in 1969 they struck a deal to broadcast live games from the English top division in the three countries. On Saturday, 29 November 1969, the undeniably glamorous fixture between Wolverhampton Wanderers and Sunderland became the first English league match to be broadcast live in Scandinavia. At a snowy Molineux, Sunderland won 1–0, with Hugh Curran scoring the winner with a header. It was a strange place for English football's eventual domination of the global sporting landscape to begin, but everything has to start somewhere. Norway had only one TV station at the time, so anyone wanting to watch TV on Saturday afternoon would have to make do with whatever was on – in this case, an English football match. Advertising on television was strictly forbidden, which prompted fears that enterprising Norwegian companies would buy up pitch-side advertising hoardings in England and thus have their brands broadcast to the nation through the back door. To avoid this most perilous of outcomes, the exact fixture being shown was initially kept a secret until Saturday. Sometimes games would even be switched at the last minute due to the nefarious presence of Scandinavian advertising. So every Saturday Norwegians would sit down in front of their televisions to watch some kind of game from England, though which teams would be involved was for a period entirely unknown. This meant that a wide array of teams were shown, not just the most successful or popular ones. Perhaps this helps explain why so many different English teams still have some kind of fan base in Norway. Perhaps it at least partially explains why Erling Haaland's great-uncle Gabriel Høyland is, to this day, a passionate Burnley fan.

Either way, English football came to have a huge cultural imprint in Scandinavia decades before it attained global popularity, and several generations of Norwegian kids grew up dreaming of playing in England. The influence of English football on how the sport was played in Norway is obvious. There is a 'chicken or the egg' element to this: did Norwegians become obsessed with English football because the robust and physical nature of the English game resonated with our sporting culture, or did our own football develop the way it did because everyone grew up watching football from England? Either way, when Alfie Haaland and the other Norwegian players started arriving in England in the 1990s it was a perfect storm. Players who had grown up watching English football had a chance to make their mark in the league, and a country that was already obsessed with English football suddenly had their own representatives in the league. This is the culture that Erling Haaland grew up in. For him the dream had always been to play in the Premier League. Not just because his father did, not just because it's the biggest league in the world, but because it's been the dream of near enough every Norwegian kid who has kicked a ball since the late 1960s to play in England's top flight.

Fast forward to the spring of 2022, and Erling Haaland again has a big decision to make. His performances and goals had demonstrated one thing clearly: he belonged in the absolute elite of European club football, the top tier that Dortmund can never quite reach. Mino Raiola, showing the benefits of players working with experienced agents, had insisted that Haaland have a release clause in his contract with Dortmund. He saw what Haaland's potential was, and knew the Norwegian would soon outgrow even Dortmund. But by the time that moment came, Raiola was sadly not around to experience it. He died in April 2022 after a period of battling illness. Erling Haaland posted on Instagram a photograph of the two of them in better times, with the simple caption 'the best'. Like other Raiola clients, Haaland continued to work with long-time Raiola associate Rafaela Pimenta, whom he has described as 'in many ways a female Mino'.

Haaland credits Raiola with putting him in a position where he was in control of his own destiny, because he managed to secure that release clause in his contract with Dortmund. The clause was set at €60 million, which by now was far less than Haaland's market value. The Dortmund CEO Hans-Joachim Watzke has said that the club allowed the release clause in Haaland's contract because if they hadn't he would have gone to Manchester United rather than them when he initially left Salzburg, though the Haalands have always maintained that they favoured a move to Dortmund for sporting reasons. As much respect as Erling Haaland has for his old boss Ole Gunnar Solskjær, who was the manager of Manchester United at the time, it will not have been lost on the Haalands that a lot of good players have struggled at Manchester United during the last decade.

This time around, Manchester United was certainly not an option. Haaland's performances for Dortmund and the presence of a release clause in his contract meant he could more or less pick and choose from any club in Europe, and in early 2022 there were more attractive options out there than United. In the Viaplay documentary *Haaland: The Big Decision*, Alfie Haaland explains how they devised a points system to rank Erling's potential new employers. In early 2022, they scored various criteria from 0 to 10, and the club that received the highest score was considered the most desirable. 'Which is the best team, as of today? And another criteria is who needs a number nine,' Alfie Haaland explained.

So Liverpool, for example, are way up there on some things but they play with a half-way number nine, do they need a number nine or not? City is [a] clear ten in this, they need one. While Real Madrid might be a five or a six, because they have Benzema. Do they get Mbappé? Bayern Munich get one point. They don't need a number nine. Their best player is their number nine. But if he leaves? Then they have no one else. It would be controversial to go to Bayern Munich, but you would also be going to one of the best teams, there's no doubt about that.

The Haalands also ranked the quality of the leagues: the Premier League was seen as the best and La Liga as the second best. In an interview dated 21 February 2022, Erling Haaland said he didn't know what his next club would be and admitted that he had even lost sleep over the question. 'Before I go to bed I think about this,' he said. 'You can say what you want, but sometimes I struggle to sleep because I'm pondering it.' He added that, at that point, realistically it was down to three clubs. 'I would say five to six, but to be honest I think we can cut it down to three.' Eventually, for all intents and purposes, it came down to two: Real Madrid or Manchester City.

The attraction of Real Madrid was obvious. It's Real Madrid. With Erling Haaland's terrifying physique and his single-minded efforts to constantly improve himself, it wouldn't be too much of a stretch to paint him as a spiritual successor to Cristiano Ronaldo at the Santiago Bernabéu. The slightly less physical nature of La Liga could also be seen as an advantage for Haaland, especially as he was enduring an injury-hit season with Dortmund. 'The Premier League is tougher. I think the tempo is higher, there are more games,' Haaland said.

There are more games in England because you have the league [EFL] Cup, the FA Cup, the Champions League and 38 games in the Premier League. So for a top team you're looking at 60 games. Then with the national team that's 70, if you play everything, which I hope that I will. So that's a plus, but it can be a minus as well. If you play every game you risk getting injured in the end if you can't handle it.

But there were a number of reasons why Manchester City could be a better fit. As Alfie Haaland pointed out, they had no striker. Going to a club that had a vacancy up front had worked well for Haaland when he moved to Dortmund. Real Madrid still had Karim Benzema, and Florentino Pérez was known to be a long-time admirer of Kylian Mbappé. Would Haaland truly be the team's focal point at Real Madrid? Not to mention that Manchester City was now a far cry from the club Erling's father had played for back in the year 2000.

The football club that eventually became Manchester City was founded in 1880, but the modern iteration of the club was, to all intents and purposes, born in 2008. After a short and chaotic period under the ownership of Thaksin Shinawatra, the former prime minister of Thailand who was exiled from his home country and at one point had his assets frozen, the club was bought by Abu Dhabi United Group. ADUG is owned by Sheikh Mansour bin Zayed bin Sultan Al Nahyan, a member of the royal family of Abu Dhabi and a powerful figure in the United Arab Emirates. Before this, Manchester City had achieved some success in English football, winning the old First Division in 1937 and 1968 – as well as winning the FA Cup four times. But there had also been a handful of relegations, and as recently as 1999 City had been all the way down in the third tier of English football. For a very long time the club existed in the shadow of its more successful cross-town rival Manchester United, but it still retained a loyal and passionate fan base.

Fans even came to revel in City's role as Manchester's underdog; when United became a commercial juggernaut in the 1990s, City came to define themselves as being the opposite of the sell-outs across town. While Manchester United was for the tourists, Manchester City was for 'real' Mancunians. While Manchester United had success, money and glamour, Manchester City had, well, other things. City fans learned to embrace adversity, as evidenced by the fact that the club still had home attendances of around 30,000 people during the season spent in the third tier. Owing to decades of inconsistent results, City's support became tinged with a sense of fatalism. This is not uncommon for football fans, but as *The Athletic*'s Manchester City correspondent Sam Lee writes:

> 'Typical City', they call it. Urban Dictionary have summed it up well: 'When Manchester City somehow mess up an easily winnable situation and everyone is disappointed but not surprised.' Fans of other clubs might recognise it in that routine feeling of 'if something can go wrong, it will go wrong'. 'We don't do it the easy way, do we?!' say fans of every club on the planet. And yet it is part of the fabric of Manchester City, because it is living and breathing in every single one of the fans who can remember anything before around 2010.

City has been seen by its fans as the more authentic alternative to the slick marketing machine across town. Historically it was a team that failed far more than it succeeded, but its fans embraced the journey with fatalistic loyalty. It will have been some gear change for the fans, then, when in 2008 Manchester City suddenly became the richest club in the world.

With the wealth of Abu Dhabi behind the club, Manchester City started spending a lot of money. Though, with due reverence to the club's previous culture and identity, there were some early bumps in the road. Even with a near-unlimited budget it's hard to make a team successful overnight. The new ownership had inherited Mark Hughes as the team's manager, and he was perhaps not the right man to lead a glitzy outfit with global ambitions. In December 2009 he was sacked after a run of just two wins in 11 games, and replaced with Roberto Mancini. The Italian came within three points of qualifying City for the Champions League that season, led them to third place the next season, and then to a first league title under Abu Dhabi ownership in 2012, only four years on from the takeover. A few months later, City recruited Ferran Soriano and Txiki Begiristain to be the club's CEO and director of football, respectively. The two had held key roles at Barcelona during Pep Guardiola's hugely successful spell in charge of the Catalan club, and from the day they arrived at City it seemed inevitable that some day Guardiola would follow. He did, in 2016, and after a season of bedding in and shaping the team to his liking, Guardiola set about doing what he and his teams usually do: breaking records and winning things.

Before Guardiola arrived, Manchester City had been a club that was trying to find its feet among football's wealthy elite. Accusations from rival fans saying that City didn't have a history were not entirely fair. Manchester City did have a history, it just looked very different from what the club was now. Additionally, in terms of an identity, it was no longer entirely clear who Manchester City were. When City had sacked Roberto Mancini in 2013, club officials had stated that the Italian had been removed in part because of 'an identified need to develop a holistic approach to all aspects of football at the Club', a statement that was widely ridiculed at the time. But this was exactly what Soriano, Begiristain and later Guardiola were able to develop. They made the club a fully joined-up entity, with core footballing principles running all the way from the youth teams to the first team. Since the club was bought by ADUG it has had no shortage of critics, but few would dispute that on the footballing side of things Manchester City has developed into one of the most well-run clubs on the planet. According to his biographer Martí Perarnau, Guardiola saw the fact that City didn't have a history of being an elite club as a strength rather than a weakness. At Bayern Munich, Guardiola's previous club, he had wrestled with the fact that there were a lot of big, authoritative personalities both inside and outside of the club who had very strong views on how he should do his job. 'Pep took on the job at City because he knew that he would be able to work without feeling that he was shattering long established customs and practices,' Perarnau wrote in *Pep Guardiola: The Evolution* (2016).

> City was a blank canvas and he would be free to create as he saw fit. In practical terms he'd be able to sign players of his choosing and hire the best technical and coaching talent available. City's generous budget also means that he can make crucial changes to the club's youth training programme.

And it turns out that if you give Pep Guardiola a blank canvas and a huge budget, success will follow.

By the time Erling Haaland had to decide what the future held, it just so happened that one of his father's old clubs was now one of the wealthiest in the world, one of the most successful in the world and was coached by an era-defining manager. And oh, they didn't really have a striker. In hindsight, it all seems so obvious. Of course Erling Haaland was going to Manchester City.

22

CITIZEN HAALAND

On 10 July 2022, under a blazing Manchester sun, Erling Haaland was officially presented to the Manchester City fans. The club had put on an event at City Square just outside the Etihad Stadium, where the club's four summer signings were introduced to an excited crowd of fans. And with apologies to Stefan Ortega, Kalvin Phillips and Julián Álvarez, it was clear which one of the four was the headline act. 'It's going to be nice, I'm really looking forward to everything, I'm sure we're going to have a good time together,' he told the crowd. When asked which team he was looking forward to playing against the most, Erling Haaland delighted them further. 'I don't like to say the word, but Manchester United.' At a press conference the same day, he said that in the end his decision to move to City had come down to his gut feeling. 'In the end I just had a feeling in my stomach. The feeling, the way they play, everything. I just had a feeling for City.' Haaland's feeling for City was good, City and their fans had good feelings about Haaland, but back in his native Norway there were some dissenting opinions.

Brann, the team Haaland had had his big breakthrough playing against back in 2018, had been relegated and had to spend a year in the second tier. This meant an away trip to Bryne, who were by now back in that division after spending four unpleasant seasons in the godless wastelands of the Norwegian third tier. When Brann visited Bryne that summer, the away fans from Bergen unfurled a banner that read 'Hello farmers, Braut plays for filthy blood money! There is only one Haaland'. The Haaland in question was Markus Haaland, a youngster in Brann's youth team and of no relation to Erling. Braut, of course, is Erling Haaland's surname from his mother's side. The issue of sportswashing has been hotly debated in Norway in recent years, culminating in a considerable grassroots campaign calling for the national team to boycott the 2022 World Cup in Qatar. The boycott proposal was eventually defeated in a vote at the Norwegian FA's general assembly, but a considerable segment of Norwegian football supporters continue to have strong feelings on the subject. Human rights organisations have repeatedly accused Manchester City's owners of using football to launder the public image of their nation. 'The UAE's enormous investment in Manchester City is one of football's most brazen attempts to "sportswash" a country's deeply tarnished image through the glamour of the game,' Amnesty International's Gulf researcher Devin Kenney said in 2018. 'As a growing number of Manchester City fans will be aware, the success of the club has involved a close relationship with a country that relies on exploited migrant labour and locks up peaceful critics and human rights defenders.' The banner unveiled by the Brann fans caused headlines, both in Norway and abroad. The leader of Brann's supporters club 'Bataljonen', Erlend Ytre-Arne Vågane, was emphatic when asked about the banner. 'Haaland can't escape the criticism. He could have chosen any club in the world. He didn't need to go to the club that's one of the worst in terms of sportswashing,' he told NRK. But Haaland also received vociferous support following the incident. Former Brann player-turned-pundit Yaw Ihle Amankwah called the banner 'embarrassing'. 'We should all, as fans, players and coaches, be aware of the mechanisms in football to do with sportswashing. But I think Haaland, because of his level and his way of being, has become an easy target,' Amankwah said.

> Players have to live in the world they live in. He becomes an easy target when he's made the best decision for his career … And I would ask the question back to you, where do you draw the line? Martin Ødegaard is the captain of Arsenal. He plays with Emirates on his chest, at the Emirates Stadium. Where do you draw the line?

It's been a thorny issue for the Norwegians, and a tricky one for Haaland to navigate. In September 2021 the Norwegian national team played games against Gibraltar, Latvia and the Netherlands, and ahead of each game the team held up a banner with the slogans 'Fair play for migrant workers', 'human rights on and off the pitch' and 'make the changes count! Human rights on and off the field'. Haaland, noticeably, was the only player not holding on to the banner. All three times. Once can be a coincidence, three times not as much. Neither Haaland nor his advisors commented publicly on the matter. But given that both he and his advisors knew that was always likely to be his last season at Dortmund, and that Manchester City would be a possible next destination, it's hard not to conclude that they felt it was an awkward time for Erling Haaland to be standing up for human rights. During his first international week after joining City, Haaland was asked about the subject at a press conference. 'The owners of

Manchester City have been accused of massive human rights abuses, they've been accused of imprisoning their own citizens. You now play for Manchester City, what do you think about the owners of the club you represent?' a reporter asked. Haaland, flanked by national team manager Ståle Solbakken, gave a quick reply.

> First of all I've never met them, so I don't know them like that. You've made some very serious allegations. When you put things like that there isn't much I can do except not say much about it. I think your words are too strong.

He added that he had joined City for sporting reasons. 'I've joined City for my development, I've done that with every club I've gone to.' His aim, he said, was to 'develop as much as possible, in a positive way, so that I can become a better footballer and one that Norway can get use out of, just as the club I'm at can get use out of me'. Solbakken, a vocal critic of FIFA's decision to award the World Cup to Qatar, backed his player: 'Manchester City have been approved by the Premier League. I think this is a much bigger question than just the individual, whether that's Pep Guardiola, Kevin De Bruyne or Erling Haaland.' Solbakken stated firmly, 'It's too big a political question for one individual to be held to account.'

The next day, having slept on the question, Solbakken expanded on this view.

> It's not that I think he should be protected from questions like that, or that he shouldn't have to answer them, but it's my opinion that some of the things in that direction are out of proportion. What is not justified is that there is a 'feeling' that Erling Haaland now has to be held responsible, or

participate in a debate, or be the one who gets criticism for what is a massive political question … For me it's overkill, and I say that with the greatest of respect for your right to ask the question. But it's to do with the corporate world, it's governments, it's the international community. If you're going to shine a light on the issue, Erling isn't the right place to start.

At any rate, Erling Haaland is unlikely to have lost much sleep over his compatriots' concerns regarding human rights in the Persian Gulf. Back in Manchester, he was raring to go. At his unveiling, Haaland also spoke about how he'd been impressed with the Manchester City team before he joined.

I played against them last season in the Champions League. You know, when you see something on TV and then you actually meet them it is completely different. Suddenly I didn't touch the ball for 20 minutes in the game. And I was like 'uh, please Gündoğan, stop playing tiki-taka all the time.' It's a different level, I have to say. How they approach the game, how they play, how they create chances, and that's what I want to be a part of.

But not everyone was fully convinced he would fit in. Alfie Haaland's thinking was simple enough: Manchester City didn't really have a striker, so his son should fit right in. But there was another side to this. Manchester City had won four out of the last five seasons in the Premier League, setting records both for points and goals scored, all without using a typical number nine. The closest player was Sergio Agüero, but the masterful Argentine goal poacher had to adapt his game in a big way to fit into Guardiola's system. City didn't have a big number nine, but what if that was because Guardiola wanted it that way? Throughout his wildly successful coaching career, the only typical number nine Guardiola had ever really worked successfully with was Robert Lewandowski. But the Polish forward was always a more rounded player than Haaland. In fact, Lewandowski's quality in the build-up phase is something Haaland himself had praised and said he hoped to learn a lot from. One of Erling Haaland's idols, Zlatan Ibrahimović, famously did not get along with Pep Guardiola at all when the two worked together at Barcelona. Both in a footballing sense and in a personal sense. On the pitch, Zlatan's size made him ill-suited to Barcelona's rapid, aggressive pressing style. Off the pitch, there was a total personality clash between him and Guardiola, with Zlatan calling Guardiola 'a spineless coward' in his autobiography. Zlatan also felt ill at ease among his Barcelona teammates, who he felt were 'like schoolboys'. Erling Haaland is a rather different character to Zlatan and has been consistently praised by his coaches for his willingness to learn and how well he takes instructions. Still, some comparisons were there, especially concerning his physique.

Guardiola's incredibly successful teams have always been about control. They've conquered all before them by controlling games, by having a lot of possession. They've often been patient with the ball in possession, preferring to keep it rather than playing too many risky forward passes. And when they lose possession, they win it back quickly by immediately closing down the opponent. Guardiola has evolved over the years and there have been variations within the systems, but these are the core principles that his Barcelona, Bayern Munich and Manchester City teams all followed. In Perarnau's 2014 book *Pep Confidential*, written after the author was given total access at Bayern Munich during Guardiola's first season there, Guardiola is quoted saying, 'If there isn't a sequence of 15 passes first, it's impossible to carry out the transition between attack and defence. Impossible.' But this isn't about making passes for the sake of it. Guardiola uses these passes to move players into the right areas of the pitch, to give the team the right structure so that when possession is lost the players are well positioned to immediately win it back. The other reason for all these passes is that you want to create overloads in the right areas of the pitch. 'In all team sports, the secret is to overload one side of the pitch so that the opponent must tilt its own defence to cope,' Guardiola says in Perarnau's book.

> You overload on one side and draw them in so that they leave the other side weak. And when we've done all that, we attack and score from the other side. That's why you have to pass the ball, but only if you're doing it with a clear intention.

This is the secret to why, as Erling Haaland himself put it, Guardiola's opponents can feel like they don't touch the ball for 20 minutes at a time. In order to create these overloads, Guardiola has found over the years that it can be more useful to have an extra midfielder in the team, or at least a forward who is comfortable dropping into midfield, than a classic striker. The season before Erling Haaland arrived at Manchester City the team didn't have a typical number nine, but the club still won the league and scored 99 goals.

At Dortmund Erling had worked on his game and was becoming a slightly more rounded player, but he was still a striker who thrived on the early ball in behind the opponent's backline. He relished situations where he could use his remarkable combination of strength and speed to dominate opponents. And as Sid Lowe observed that night against Sevilla, in those transitional moments, when Haaland has space to move, he strikes fear into opponents with his running and raw power. Pressing was nothing new for Haaland. He had done it since the youth team in Bryne, when Berntsen would substitute him if he didn't work hard on the pitch to win the ball back. Aggressive pressing is a key pillar of the entire Red Bull football philosophy, too. But Erling Haaland, now 195 centimetres tall and weighing over 90 kilograms, simply cannot do sprints for 90 minutes each game for 50–60 games a season the way that some other players can. He has to manage himself on the pitch. How he would fit in with the relentless pressing off the ball favoured by Guardiola was not totally clear. For Erling to find his place in a Pep Guardiola team, there would have to be some kind of adjustment. But who would be doing the adjusting, Guardiola or Haaland? Adding intrigue to the mix, *The Athletic*'s Sam Lee reported after the transfer was confirmed that Pep Guardiola would have preferred to sign Harry Kane, and had to be convinced by the City hierarchy that Haaland was the right player for the club. According to Lee, 'Guardiola felt Kane would be the better fit for his team.'

So these questions were, not unreasonably, being asked before the start of the season. However, it was clear that in at least one phase of play Haaland would fit City like a glove. Manchester City excel at creating little overloads in wide areas and, after a rapid exchange of passes playing a ball into the box, right in front of goal. The upside of having no conventional striker, of playing with a so-called 'false nine', is that it can become easier to create those overloads. You have an extra man in midfield, after all. The downside is that when you eventually feed the ball into the box, well, there isn't always someone there to knock it in. On Manchester City's preseason tour of the United States Erling Haaland scored his first goal in a City shirt, and it was in exactly one of these passages of play. It was City versus

Bayern Munich at Lambeau Field, home of the NFL franchise Green Bay Packers, in Wisconsin. The game had initially been delayed due to lightning storms. Just 12 minutes after the game finally kicked off, Kevin De Bruyne put Jack Grealish through, inches wide of the six-yard box. Grealish squared it, and a sliding Haaland almost tackled it in. Immediately after the goal a thunderstorm passed overhead, and the referee took the players off the field. In the tunnel, a grinning, soaked Erling Haaland told Grealish, 'That's why I'm here, exactly these balls!'

Still, it was only preseason. The real stuff hadn't started yet. There was much intrigue ahead of the curtain-raiser of the English football season, the FA Community Shield. There is some disagreement on whether or not the Community Shield truly counts as an official game, but it is certainly a closely watched event. After all, it pits last season's Premier League champion against last season's FA Cup champion, which means that fans get a first look at two of the best teams in England just before the start of the new Premier League season. With much debate and discussion over how Erling Haaland would fit in at City, this was the first real chance for people to find out. It was also the first proper game for Liverpool's Darwin Núñez, who, like Haaland, had been signed at great expense over the summer. Erling Haaland had scored in his first start for Salzburg, had scored a first-half hat-trick on his debut in the Champions League and had scored a 33-minute hat-trick on his debut for Dortmund. What would he do in his first proper game for City?

Not a lot, as it turns out. Erling Haaland had a very rare off-day that afternoon. He did show his strength, when he collected a lofted pass from Bernardo Silva and a retreating Andy Robertson simply bounced off him. But he couldn't get the finish quite right. In the next attack a perfect cross found Haaland in the box, but he got his attempted finish badly wrong. And right before full-time a rebound from the Liverpool goalkeeper dropped to Haaland, but with the goal at his mercy he somehow hit the top of the bar from just six yards out. Liverpool won 3–1, and Núñez got his debut goal. Haaland's misses did the rounds on social media, to the gleeful cackles of rival fans. Newspaper headlines were predictably unkind. And aside from the misses, there was something slightly off about the whole performance, both from Haaland and from City. That Erling Haaland wasn't 100 per cent match-fit had been known in advance, so some rustiness was to be expected. The misses were good fodder for online banter, but with Haaland's record no sane person would seriously question his general ability to put chances away. What was more worrying was the forward runs he made that were either not spotted or just downright ignored by his teammates. Haaland's quality was not in doubt, but the question had been how he would fit into the team. 'For a while he looked a little lost in this team of interlocking pegs,' wrote Barney Ronay in the *Guardian*.

> It is easy to become blasé, to forget that City play a type of football that is unlike anything else, a pressure wave where the movements repeat and multiply, the parts revolve and elide. Let's chuck a baseball bat into the middle of that and see how it goes.

Well, one thing that can happen is that his teammates could pick up that baseball bat and start battering opponents over the head with it. If the Community Shield had triggered further angst about how Haaland would fit in at City, relief was on its way. Haaland has said many times that overthinking is bad, and perhaps that's what people were doing. Perhaps it was all so much simpler: if you stick the strongest, fastest and smartest striker around up front in a team that has some of the best midfield creators on the planet, goals will follow. It seemed a plausible theory, and it was about to be put to the test.

A week on from the loss to Liverpool, the Premier League kicked off, with City away at West Ham. After just over half an hour, Ilkay Gündoğan slipped a ball through towards Haaland. It looked ever so slightly overhit, but Haaland showed one of the qualities that makes him so unique: a burst of acceleration that's entirely out of keeping with the massive size of his frame. A player his size just shouldn't be able move that quickly, but he does. And because he did, he got to the ball a fraction of a second before the West Ham goalkeeper, Alphonse Areola, who clipped him and conceded a penalty. Erling Haaland's first Premier League goal for Manchester City was 'just' a penalty kick, but it was a penalty kick he created with his very particular qualities. In the second half he scored again, and the second goal was pure Haaland. West Ham had moved their defensive line higher up the pitch and left space to attack in behind. Kevin De Bruyne had the ball at the half-way line, and Haaland was on the move up ahead. De Bruyne played a perfectly weighted pass in behind the home team's defence, Haaland burst onto it and calmly put the ball past the goalkeeper. Two goals on his Premier League debut. 'A good start', a stony-faced Haaland told Sky Sports after the game. And it was pointed out to him that he could have had a hat-trick. 'Yes I could, if you saw Gündo right before I went off, I should have been there. So a bit shit but that's how it is.' When the interviewer encouraged him to be 'steady with the language', Haaland broke into a grin, said 'shit' again and apologised. (In fairness to Haaland, the English word 'shit' is widely used in Norwegian, but is not considered a particularly bad swear word and does not have to be avoided on air in broadcasting. The same goes for 'piss'.) On the subject of getting more used to his teammates, Haaland was confident. 'It's about the connections we do every day in training, and about practising this so we get better. This will come even more, so I'm not worried.'

With his Premier League debut out of the way, Haaland embarked on what can best be described as a goal-scoring rampage. He scored 15 goals in his first 10 league games for City. In the Champions League, his favourite competition, he scored five in his first three group-stage games. In his first derby against Manchester United, the game he was most looking forward to, he grabbed himself a hat-trick. Still, his runs were not always spotted by his teammates – importantly, though, enough of them were. Kevin De Bruyne in particular was not afraid to look for Haaland with an early ball or a long diagonal pass, and there are few players in the world who can see and execute these passes like the Belgian. But City weren't the only Premier League team to start the season in blistering form. A youthful Arsenal, led by Guardiola's former assistant manager Mikel Arteta, were also on the march. On the date that the Premier League was paused, from late November to mid-December, for the 2022 World Cup, Arsenal were top of the league. City's last game before the World Cup was a maddening 2–1 defeat at home to Brentford, in which City had 29 shots but eventually got torn apart by direct balls to Ivan Toney on the counter. 'We struggled from the beginning and we couldn't deal with their long balls,' Guardiola told the BBC. 'Usually you press the balls to win it but this was different. They defended so deep and so well. The game was so difficult, it was so tight. They did really well in the plan they had and were better.'

Club football paused for the World Cup, and the players embarked on adventures with their various national teams. Some had a better time than others, with Haaland's understudy Julián Álvarez going all the way with Argentina. Haaland was stuck watching it from home.

'I will relax my body and my mind a lot and then I will train,' he said. Arsenal had done brilliantly in the first 16 games of the season ... but Manchester City are Manchester City. The club had won four out of the last five league titles for a reason, and there was a certain expectation that the team, and Guardiola, would eventually get it right and reclaim the summit after the World Cup.

It wasn't that simple, however. City did beat Leeds 3–1 in the first game back, with Haaland scoring twice against his father's old club, but this was followed up with a draw on New Year's Eve, 1–1 against a struggling, relegation-threatened Everton. A 1–0 win against a poor Chelsea team followed a few days later, but then City surprisingly lost 2–1 against Manchester United at Old Trafford. Three days before the derby, City had suffered a shock defeat to Southampton in the Carabao Cup. Something just wasn't right. In the next game after the derby defeat to United, City went 2–0 down against Tottenham in the first 45 minutes. But the players rallied and in the second half came back to win the game 4–2. Despite this inspiring turnaround, Pep Guardiola wasn't happy after the match. With a key game away to Arsenal coming up in a few weeks, Guardiola demanded more from his team. In the press conference after the game he suggested that the players might be lacking hunger because they'd had too much success.

There are details. It's not about the way we play, or the quality of the players. Are you going to judge the quality of the players? I love them. They are fantastic players, all of them. They do it, but there are the details. It comes from the success we've had in the past. We have to admit it, we've had a lot of success. People say 'no, it's not a success because you didn't win the Champions League,' bullshit. We won a lot. In this country, two back-to-back titles. And the way we played, the consistency, against this Liverpool? What a success. But we have to look at ourselves, it's not enough. Come on!

He also demanded more, from the fans, from the players, from everyone.

> Our fans have to push us, have to demand more, have to shout. We can't react when we're 2–0 down, today we were lucky. Ten times or nine times, you don't come back … I want a reaction from the entire club, the whole organisation. Not just the players, the staff, everyone. We're a happy flowers team, a happy flowers organisation. No, I don't want to be a happy flower, I want to beat Arsenal. But if we play that way Arsenal will destroy us. They will beat us.

In the next game Haaland scored a hat-trick as City beat Wolves 3–0, but the team was still five points behind Arsenal in the league. The Gunners had a game in hand, and had won 16 out of 19 games so far, so City might as well have been eight points behind. *The Athletic* published an in-depth breakdown showing how Manchester City as a team had done less well so far that season with Haaland than they had the previous season without him. More counter-attacks were being conceded and the team's averages had worsened: 1 goal against per game, up from 0.68 goals per game the season before; 2.25 points per game, down from 2.45 the season before. 'The world's best team signed the world's best striker and got worse,' was the conclusion. One particular concern was tactical. With Haaland's pace and power, and his love of making early runs in behind the opponent, the temptation for City's midfielders would always be to look for him with an early ball. But the purpose of Guardiola's passing game is not just to create chances, it's to create the right structures so that the team can stop counter-attacks when possession is lost. If the players attack more directly, they leave themselves more vulnerable. Guardiola hinted at this after a wild 3–3 draw with Newcastle in the third game of the season. 'The only problem is that when we break the lines and we can run, if you finish the action it's not a problem, but if you don't finish, you don't control [Allan] Saint-Maximin and [Miguel] Almirón,' Guardiola said.

> We should spend more time in the final third, give more passes in that moment, but it's difficult because Erling is going, Phil [Foden] has this aggression to go. If Jack [Grealish] plays there or Riyad [Mahrez] or Bernardo [Silva] play on the right, they are more calm and they help us to be all together, and when we lose the ball, we are there and they [the opponents] cannot run.

Underlining the point, at the start of February, after the 3–0 thumping of Wolves, Manchester City lost 1–0 to Tottenham.

'I think we've only seen 60 per cent of Erling Haaland,' Jamie Carragher told Sky Sports after the game.

> You think of the goal he got versus West Ham when there was space in behind and he gets in … I know that's not there every time due to the way City play. He's come from a counter-attacking league [the Bundesliga], where it's end to end. You saw his blistering pace there – we don't see it here. He might have picked the wrong club to actually get the best out of him. We're not seeing everything of Haaland. City have scored the exact number of goals as last season. He's got

25 of them but City have scored the same number overall. However, they've conceded more and are easier to counter-attack against now. They are a different – and lesser – team with Haaland … That's not his fault. City won't play end-to-end football. That's not Pep Guardiola's way. His players don't have the energy or power to play that way – they build up slowly and push the opposition back to their box and play from there. When they lose it they win it back quickly and keep the team pinned back. Haaland has scored 25 league goals and lots of them are ones that come into the box and he puts them in, but we're not seeing the full package of what the player can do because of the team he's joined.

For Erling Haaland, the situation was bizarre. It was early February, and he had scored 25 goals in the Premier League already. It would have been enough to make him the top scorer in each of the last four seasons. On the primary criteria by which strikers around the world are judged, it had been an outrageous success. But serial champions City were second in the league, their legendary manager was annoyed and pundits were suggesting that Haaland had actually made the team worse. Life at the very top of elite football can be brutal.

23

STARDOM

Erling Haaland has fulfilled his dream, and the dream of young boys and girls the world over. He has become one of the best in the world at the thing he loves to do most. At this point in human history, being exceedingly good at this very specific thing, playing football, comes with almost incomprehensible financial rewards. It also comes with unprecedented levels of fame and attention. A successful elite footballer can in the present time amass generational wealth, but it comes at a cost. Not just the obvious cost in hours spent on the training ground, and in experiences and vices sacrificed and resisted. This kind of stardom also results in a total loss of normality. It is something Erling Haaland's old coach Alf Ingve Berntsen thinks about. 'In the middle of all of this insanity, he has been robbed of a chance for a normal life. Everyone has a need for a certain degree of privacy,' he says.

To help him create some semblance of normality and maintain some degree of privacy, Erling has a tight-knit team around him.

Chief among them is, of course, his father. 'I've told Erling all along that I will try to be a link between him and all the interests around him, including agents, and that I want to have the best team around him,' Alfie told Viaply back in early 2022.

> We want Erling to be able to concentrate on what he has to do, which is to play football and to do things as well as he can on the pitch. So to do that we've put together a small team, so that the decision paths are kept short. Mino and his team are in touch with the club, and then we have others who do more practical things in relation to sponsors, such as Ivar Eggja ... So it's a small team, but we work in a way that we think is right. We don't want too many people involved either.

Eggja, a long-time family friend whom Erling Haaland simply refers to as 'Uncle Ivar', has been a very important presence in his life amid all the noise accompanying his rise to stardom. When asked by *VG* back in 2021 if he had someone in his life he listened particularly closely to, Haaland smiled.

> That's where Uncle Ivar comes in. He's supported me well with various things. We relax well together. It's important to relax as much as possible when you're in the situation I am in, and to be ready when you have to be ready. When I'm not playing, it's all about switching off completely so that my brain can rest. It's full-on at times, so you have to be extreme when it comes to switching off and be extremely switched on when you have to be.

A modern footballer's entourage can get a bad reputation. The public perception is often that these people are hangers-on who are simply looking to leech off the player's money and fame. In the case of Haaland and his team, this is distinctly not the case. In Viaplay's documentary detailing his move from Dortmund to Manchester City, Haaland explains how the team around him helps him perform. 'When I arrived at Dortmund I stayed in a hotel for two days, then we went on a training camp for ten days. When I came back the apartment was ready, full of IKEA things. I think that matters a lot.' And it did matter. A week later, Haaland scored a hat-trick against Augsburg on his debut. 'I think if I had been on my own, and I had to choose my apartment, go to IKEA, buy stuff, I don't think I would have scored three goals against Augsburg.' Not to mention the two goals in the next game against Cologne, and the next two against Union. Haaland wants to make sure that the minutiae of everyday life, which suck time and energy out of people's days, do not affect his ability to perform to his full potential. This includes everything from 'setting up a bank account when you come here to Germany and don't speak the language [to] getting insurance on the car'. A wealthy young footballer can hire people to take care of these matters, but keeping the tasks among family and close friends adds an extra layer of trust and privacy. In 2022, the Norwegian business newspaper *Dagens Næringsliv* reported that Alfie Haaland's old friend and former teammate Egil Østenstad had been brought in to look after the financial side of things. Østenstad pursued a career in private banking after retiring from the game, but he left his job with Norway's largest financial services group, DNB, to become a kind of chief financial officer for the Haalands. Even in Erling's dealings with the media there is an element of keeping things tight, as a considerable proportion of his interviews over the years have been done with Alfie's old teammate and friend Jan Åge Fjørtoft.

Over time Erling has grown more confident and comfortable with such interviews, and he has gradually started to show more of his personality in these public settings. He can still appear guarded, but he has come a long way from the near-monosyllabic answers he initially became famous for. But Erling's most open and forthright interview to date came in a totally unexpected place: it's January 2023 and Erling Haaland is the free-scoring centre forward for one of the best football teams in the world. Every broadcaster and publication on the planet would move heaven and earth for ten minutes with him. Sponsors will pay dizzying sums for just a morsel of his time. Haaland himself mostly seems to avoid these things, granting few interviews and doing very little press in general. But in the middle of all of this, he suddenly decides to sit down and spend the best part of 40 minutes speaking to a niche Norwegian podcast aimed at watch aficionados, *Klokkepodden* (*The Watch Pod*). As far as world exclusives go, it was a good get for *Klokkepodden*.

A genuine and enthusiastic watch collector, Haaland seems more relaxed and at ease when speaking to a pair of fellow watch nerds than to sports reporters. On the podcast, hosted by Jim Fossheim and Joakim Bjerke, Haaland opens up not just about watches, but about his life in Manchester. Recorded the day after he scored a hat-trick against Wolves, Haaland admits to being a little bit tired.

I'm pretty tired right now. I think I just slept five hours. There's always chaos in my head after games, so I don't sleep very well. But I have a good feeling, I took home the match ball. I got everyone to sign it, so I'm happy. It was nice that you guys could come to the match, it's always nice with

Norwegians in the stands. So I'm left with a good feeling and that's the most important part.

When asked about how he felt going into the match, Haaland gives an unexpected insight into his mindset on the pitch.

The first half was a bit ... we had some chances, I had a couple of shots. But really I don't think about scoring goals, I'm just thinking about trying to get chances. Because then there's a big possibility of scoring goals. That's mostly what I'm thinking about, trying to get chances, trying to be a bit faster than the defender, see if I can get there in front of him so I can finish. For example, the first goal, you can see I managed to get in front of him and jump up ahead of him in the duel, which meant I won it and scored. But when we got a penalty I thought, This could be a hat-trick. That was the first thing I thought about. But in the beginning of games I don't think about goals, I think about getting the chances.

On the subject of watches, Haaland cites the influence of 'Uncle Ivar'.

My father and Ivar have always been interested in watches. I always saw my dad's watches but I didn't think too much of it. But I think it was during the pandemic, we spent more time sitting inside, and we were scrolling on our phones or watching stuff on TV. And I read a story about someone who had received a watch from their father, with something engraved, and the idea was that this is something you take with you for the rest of your life. That really hit me. That people collect watches across generations. That hit me,

I thought it was cool, I wanted to do that. So I think it was because of Ivar and that thing I saw.

It's not uncommon for footballers to buy expensive watches, but Haaland has found that not all of his teammates actually know much about them.

You can tell very quickly if people are interested in watches, or if they just buy watches because they think it's cool. You can tell straight away. In the dressing room, I don't have to mention names, but let's say I have a teammate and I ask him about his watch, and he hardly even knows what brand it is. But then you ask someone else and he might know the whole reference number and all of that, when he bought it, the story behind it, all of that.

He mentions his former teammates at Dortmund, Marco Reus and Mahmoud Dahoud, as watch collectors with a genuine interest. And when asked if he has a watch that's particularly meaningful to him, Haaland has a clear answer.

I was given a watch by my agent, who later died. When I won the Golden Boy award – it's a kind of best young player under 20 – he gave me a present. It was a Patek 5712R, rose gold, with a leather strap. He gave that to me, so it's a special watch for me. Of course I'm going to have it for the rest of my life, and I'm going to remember him for the rest of my life.

In addition to collecting watches, Haaland is also a big sneakerhead.

I think it's to do with my lifestyle as well, that I sit at home every day waiting for the next training session, the next game. I'm sat at home, and you have to find things to do on your own, and so shoes. I love shoes. I treat my shoes as if they were my children. I wash them and look after them.

At the time of recording the podcast, Arsenal sat top of the table, above Manchester City. It was a few days after Pep Guardiola's 'happy flowers' rant, and City were about to face Arsenal in the FA Cup. When asked about Martin Ødegaard, captain of both Arsenal and the Norway national team, Erling had nothing but praise for his rival and was excited about his progress.

It's fantastic to watch Martin do as well as he has done at Arsenal. That he's come to the perfect club for him. He's 24 years old, he has 10 years left of his career, we mustn't forget that he's still developing, as am I. He gets to use his best qualities, and he has a manager and a club that gets the best out of him. That's fantastic for us as Norwegians. It's cool to see. And it's extra cool that we're kinda rivals this season, since we're competing with each other. On Friday we'll be playing against each other for the first time this season, and it's my first time playing against Martin. So that'll be exciting … I'm good friends with Martin, he's a fantastic guy. I wish him every success. He had another assist yesterday so that's fantastic. It's fantastic when Norwegians do well … He's a good friend of mine and we speak more or less every day. It's cool, and as a Norwegian it makes me proud.

Back on watches, Haaland confirmed reports that he gave every squad member at Dortmund, as well as members of the backroom staff, a personalised watch when he left the club. According to *Bild*, 33 players in the squad had received a Rolex each, while 20 members of staff were given an Omega. He called his two and a half years at Dortmund a 'fantastic time ... with some fantastic people', so he felt that 'when my time at Dortmund came to an end, I wanted to give something back.'

> To the physios who have massaged my feet every damned day for two and a half years. To the people who washed my clothes every day, made my food every day. I wanted to give them something, personally, from me. So I figured this is what I wanted to do. I thought it was cool, and they deserved it. So I gave them each a watch with their names engraved at the back.

The words he had engraved were *Danke*, the German word for 'Thank you', as well as the person's name, 'BVB', '2020–2022' and the initials EBH.

> It was very emotional for me, the last days at Dortmund. It's hard to think. You're with them every day, you live in a way like a family. You see your teammates more than you see your family. So you become close with many of them. Coaches, staff, physios, the people who print your name on the shirts, everyone who was there ... It was a very special time for me, so I wanted to show something in return. Without them it wouldn't have been possible for me to go to Manchester City.

Towards the end of the interview, Haaland is asked how he spends his days in Manchester.

> I relax. Right now I'm getting a bit tired, I'm consider-
> ing a very short nap now to get through the day. But it's
> about relaxing, having a good meal tonight, and then go
> to bed early since I didn't sleep well last night. Then it's
> about training and treatment, stuff like that. To relax.
> It's much of the same. It's an interesting life, but it's also
> a life of routine. In the daily life you're told what to do,
> what time to turn up, what time you're having treatment,
> when to eat, there's a lot of stuff like that. It's a lot of
> training and rest, which is what I have to do to be ready
> mentally and in my legs for the next training session,
> the next game.

The fame and money that comes with being an elite footballer makes these young men very easy targets for criticism. In comparison with the lives of ordinary people, the financial rewards bestowed upon footballers can seem obscene. But there is a human element to it that should not be forgotten. The advent of camera phones and social media, as well as the increased physical demands of modern football, mean that for much of the year these young men are forced to live an almost monk-like existence. They may have money and fame, but they are effectively barred from the things most young people would do with that money and fame. Pundits and former players who are quick to criticise today's young footballers for how they dress, look and spend their money would do well to remember that, unlike past generations of players, they can't just go out and blow off steam the way regular people do. In the case of Erling Haaland he has so far appeared to be a very reluctant public figure, who mostly wants to be left alone to work on his football.

From an early stage Haaland took an interest in trying to find ways off the pitch to optimise himself, physically and mentally, for the life of an elite footballer. The importance of sleep had been instilled long ago by the youth teams in Bryne. At the age of 18 he was already talking about wanting to find the perfect version of his body for what he wants to do on the pitch. His determination was noticed by Norway's former assistant manager Per Joar Hansen.

> We noticed very early that he had started wearing goggles in the evening that kept the blue light out, which can help him sleep better at night. I can tell you very few players were doing that. So he was ahead of the game there, in the sense that as a young player he was already taking on things like this. He turned off the Wi-Fi in the apartment at night because he felt that could affect his quality of sleep. He filters his water, all this kind of stuff. He is someone who works to optimise every aspect of every day, in terms of his body.

Relaxing and recharging his batteries is an area of his life where Haaland is, in his own words, 'extreme'. It is also where his fondness for meditation comes in. 'As a striker, I think it's really important that when you're in the game to not think too much,' he told *The Athletic*.

> If I'm going to go into my next game thinking about the chance I missed last game, it's not good. You have to go into the game hungry. It doesn't matter what happened before, if you scored three goals, if you scored zero goals, if you haven't scored in a while. You have to go into the game with

the same mentality. And so I think about not thinking too much about it! It's about using all of it as motivation and not some negative, going into training like this (he puts his head down). You want to be the best in training today. This is also something that helps me a lot, this meditation outside the pitch to just kind of let go of the negative thoughts.

Haaland believes it's what gives him an edge. 'I think you have to be mentally strong today with so much else going on outside the pitch,' he admits. 'You have to have extremely good focus, you have to be strong in your head because it's not easy being a footballer. Everybody thinks it's easy.'

In the Viaplay documentary Haaland spoke about making sure he eats high-quality food.

> I'm interested in looking after my body. To eat food of the highest possible quality, as local as possible, I think is the most important thing. People talk about meat not being healthy. OK, but what kind of meat? Is it the meat you get at McDonalds or is it from a local cow that's eating grass just over there?

He revealed that he eats offal, like heart and liver, but his eating habits aren't all esoteric. In Manchester he reportedly favours the Italian restaurants Vero Moderno and San Carlo, as well as the Manchester branch of Indian restaurant Dishoom. Naturally, he also frequents Pep Guardiola's Catalan restaurant, Tast. According to Paul Hirst, who covers both Manchester City and Manchester United for *The Times*, one of City's nutritionists recommends that chefs give Haaland 200 grams more food than his teammates at mealtimes, and that City have 'imported the best Norwegian salmon that money can buy'. He loves kebabs and kebab pizza as well, but as he explained in an interview with Gary Neville for Sky Sports, 'I can almost never eat it.' And, of course, he eats lasagne. After scoring a hat-trick in his first Manchester derby, Haaland credited his father's recipe for his good run of form. 'I've had it before every home game now and that's turned out fairly well for me in every game,' he said. 'There has to be something special he adds to it.'

Growing up, Erling Haaland idolised his father, and later Zlatan Ibrahimović and Cristiano Ronaldo. He was also, more surprisingly, a big fan of the former Swansea player Michu. He is a big fan of the Norwegian rapper Amara, with whom he later became friends. He is still close with a group of friends from his time in the Bryne youth teams, and spends time with them as often as his schedule allows. Though Haaland doesn't appear to particularly enjoy the limelight, he does have a rather flamboyant dress sense. Now that he is a fully minted superstar, there are elements of him that will inevitably draw criticism in his humility-obsessed home country. In March 2022 Leif Welhaven, a sports columnist in Norway's leading newspaper *VG*, took aim. He called the transfer saga around Haaland's proposed move away from Dortmund 'an extreme example of the financial madness' of international football, and criticised Haaland for arriving in Norway for national team duty in a private jet, for not speaking to the media during that international camp and for taking the number nine shirt with the national team, which previously had been worn by Alexander Sørloth. 'It's not easy to assess how much special treatment it's wise to give this big star. It's definitely important to let the big characters be themselves, but at the same time they have to be part of a group.' National team manager Ståle Solbakken came to Haaland's defence. 'I think it's unfair that we're trying to find faults with Haaland,' he said. Haaland's international teammate Stefan Strandberg was annoyed, and told TV2,

> It fucking pisses me off, to be honest. I know Erling extremely well and in the situation he is in right now, these few months, the least we can do is give him some peace and quiet when he's trying to make a very difficult decision … Why can't Norway just embrace what we finally have? In one moment we're crying out for big characters and stars, and when we have them start complaining about the things they do.

Erling Haaland, for his part, stayed quiet. While he was on national team duty, he played both games, friendlies against Slovakia and Armenia, and scored three goals. A few hours after scoring twice against Armenia, Haaland tweeted, in his very distinctive Jæren dialect: *'Et råd eg fekk frå en bonde for et par år si: Snakk me fødne så går helste alt aent godt. Ok sa eg å gjekk'*, which roughly translates as, 'A piece of advice I received from a farmer a few years ago: speak with your feet, then the rest will take care of itself. OK I said, and left.'

The farmer in question was, of course, his great-uncle Gabriel Høyland. As Erling's performances on the pitch continue to thrill, inspire and excite, there will always be a lot of people who want to know more about who he is, what his private life is like, what he thinks and what he says. One suspects that Erling Haaland himself will always prefer to speak with his feet.

24

CHAMPIONS OF EVERYTHING

On 11 January 2023, Southampton FC knocked Manchester City out of the Carabao Cup. Guardiola would later describe it as 'the lowest game in seven years'. Southampton's season was going terribly, the team was bottom of the league and being led by the former Luton manager Nathan Jones – who was having a rather bad time of things himself. The strange thing about the defeat wasn't just that it happened, though that was certainly very strange, but that it wasn't an unfair result. Most of the time when Guardiola's Manchester City team has suffered surprise defeats, it's been a case of the team producing chances, struggling to put them away and getting caught on the break. Here the players had plenty of possession, but Southampton actually out-shot them 12 to 7. 'Today was not even close to what we are,' Guardiola said after the game.

> We were not prepared to play in this competition to get to the semi-finals. We were not ready. You have to be prepared

for every single game when you play for Manchester City and today we were not. If we perform this way (in the Manchester derby) we do not have a chance. I have the feeling today the line-up doesn't matter, the performance happens. We were not here.

The Carabao Cup will likely have been the lowest-ranked tournament on Manchester City's list of priorities that season, but the performance was worrying all the same. Not least because Guardiola had put out a pretty strong line-up, and several of the big hitters who were rested came off the bench early enough in the second half to make an impact. But Manchester City, in Guardiola's words, simply weren't there.

In the Manchester derby, City again had a lot of possession, but produced only five shots over 90 minutes of football. Things had to change. João Cancelo, who had been one of the best players in City's squad the season before, was no longer being selected to play every game and had reacted badly to this. He was sent out on loan to Bayern Munich. After the dramatic win against Tottenham in the next game, Guardiola made his 'happy flowers' rant in public, and according to *The Times* he issued a more private rallying cry to his players at a team dinner in February. 'If you are not together, you will not win anything and you will give up an opportunity that you will regret for the rest of your life,' he told them. Guardiola had made it clear that he felt the attitude of the squad wasn't quite right, but he was also wrestling with the more specific tactical issue of Haaland. For all the goals, the team had clearly lost something after he'd been introduced. The numbers didn't lie. Without a striker who would drop into midfield, the City machine just wasn't functioning as smoothly as before. It was a complex question that turned out to have a weirdly simple answer: if you no longer have a striker who can be an extra midfielder, why not get one of the defenders to do it? And so Pep Guardiola turned to a most unlikely hero: John Stones.

A technically gifted defender, Stones had been a valued part of Pep Guardiola's squad since he joined in the summer of 2016. But there were always questions as to whether he was reliable enough in the defensive aspect of the game to be a first-choice starter. There were periods where Guardiola didn't seem to fully trust him. But now that Guardiola had a need for a defender who could play in a back four off the ball but then step into midfield when the team had possession, Stones's skill set made him a perfect candidate. He had the technical quality and passing ability to play a role in midfield, and he added an extra physical presence to that area of the pitch. For a while Guardiola used 18-year-old academy product Rico Lewis in this kind of role, and the youngster acquitted himself admirably. But it was in March, when Stones returned from a hamstring injury and started to play in this hybrid role, that things really came together for City.

Some other things had also happened. The day after a limp away defeat to Tottenham, Manchester City were charged with 115 charges of breaching the Premier League's financial rules between 2009 and 2018. The charges were referred to an independent commission, and City released a bullish statement: 'The club welcomes the review of this matter by an independent commission, to impartially consider the comprehensive body of irrefutable evidence that exists in support of its position.' Guardiola adopted a defiant stance in public, which according to *The Athletic*'s Manchester City correspondent Sam Lee led to a 'siege mentality' taking hold and the atmosphere around the club being 'transformed'. The team secured a crucial win against Arsenal on 15 February, which put City top of the league on goal difference – though Arsenal had a game in hand. City, still struggling for consistency, dropped points against Nottingham Forest the next weekend. After the draw, the City players 'had a conversation', according to midfielder Rodri. 'It's not enough to play good, you need to punish. I remember the game in Nottingham, these kind of games cannot happen.' Then, something seemed to click into place, both in terms of the system and the attitude. For the next three months Manchester City won every single game they played in the Premier League.

Erling Haaland played his part in this remarkable run of form. After the draw against Forest, he scored nine goals in his next eight appearances in the league for City. On 3 May he scored his 35th Premier League goal of the season, at home against West Ham, and in so doing set a new record for goals scored in a single Premier League season. By this time, Arsenal's title challenge had been derailed. In April the team drew three consecutive games, against Liverpool, Southampton and West Ham. The north London side was still top of the league, five points ahead of City, but City had two games in hand – and the rejuvenated players were smashing every team in sight. On 26 April Arsenal went to the Etihad in desperate need of a result. It was never close. Two goals from a masterful Kevin De Bruyne, a header from Stones and a late goal from Erling Haaland made it a 4–1 win for City. One of the ways City tormented Arsenal that night was by playing direct balls to Haaland, whose physical power the Arsenal defenders had no answer to. 'They can do different things now, with Erling up front,' Arsenal captain Martin Ødegaard said after the game. 'They can play out from the back and they can go direct as well, so it's difficult to defend.' In an odd way it was as if things had come full circle for Haaland and Guardiola. The first time Haaland had played at the Etihad he was playing for the opposing team, Dortmund, and he caused City problems with his physique. Guardiola had pointed out how Dortmund used Haaland as a target to play over City's press, and affectionately called him 'a bastard'. Now, in one of the defining games of City's Premier League campaign, Guardiola had used this exact tactic to his own advantage against his opponents. Now Haaland was his bastard, and a glorious bastard at that. This use of Haaland also represented another tactical evolution for Guardiola, and perhaps a riposte to the accusations that Haaland had dimished the team. Yes, Haaland was not an extra midfielder, and Haaland could not press in quite the same way as some other forwards had under Guardiola. But as the win against Arsenal demonstrated, there are advantages to having a massive physical presence up front. Even for the high priest of possession football. While critics had focused on what Haaland wasn't, Guardiola had seen what he was and the possibilities he opened up for his team.

With City closing in on the Premier League title, attention fell firmly on another competition: Erling Haaland's favourite competition, the Champions League. For Manchester City, this was the final hurdle. Since the Abu Dhabi takeover in 2008, Manchester City had won everything there was to win, except the most prestigious prize of them all. The club was en route to make it five Premier League titles in six seasons, but there was still no Champions League trophy in the cabinet. Erling Haaland knew what he had been signed to do. It later emerged that in his very first conversation with Manchester City chairman, Khaldoon Al Mubarak, after moving to the club, Erling Haaland had promised his new boss that they would win the Champions League. 'So this was, I think, my first conversation post him signing the contract. But what amazed me about Erling is the confidence. He's got something special, confidence with respect,' Al Mubarak said later that year. For Haaland there was an air of destiny to Manchester City's Champions League campaign, with nearly every opponent holding some kind of extra significance to him. It started in the group stage, where City came up against Dortmund, Sevilla and FC Copenhagen. It was a reunion with his former club, Dortmund; another meeting with Sevilla, a team he had scored four goals against in two games while at Dortmund; and a game against FC Copenhagen, the biggest club in Scandinavia and a club he could have moved to back when he was 16 years old. City went undefeated in the group, with Haaland scoring five goals in the four games he appeared in. But when the time came for the knockout stage, things got serious. It is in these rounds where Manchester City have stumbled before, often in unexpected ways. These were the games that Erling Haaland had been brought in to decide in City's favour. And it got off to a slightly iffy start.

For the round-of-16 tie, Manchester City was paired with RB Leizpig, another team with a special significance for Haaland. Leipzig is the mothership of the Red Bull empire, of which Haaland was briefly a member, and a club he once considered moving to. It is also a club that he had already bullied in a Cup final once before. The first leg of the tie was away in Germany, and for the first 45 minutes Manchester City's players were in total control. But Leipzig improved in the second half, caused City trouble and grabbed an equaliser. As far as results go, 1–1 is not a bad score in a first leg played away from home, but Leipzig had shown enough in that second half to raise some concerns. City, after all, had previous in this competition. In 2020 the club's Champions League dreams ended in a shock defeat to French side Lyon. The season before, City had been knocked out in the quarter-finals by Tottenham. Since 2017 Manchester City had been winning titles and setting records in England, and looked for all the world like one of the best teams on the planet, but something always seemed to go wrong in Europe. Ahead of the return leg against RB Leipzig on 14 March, there was a certain tension in the cold, grey east Manchester air. There was little doubt that Manchester City had the better team, but in 90 minutes of knockout football the best team doesn't always win. There was something about RB Leipzig's energetic approach that seemed to unsettle Manchester City in the second half of the first leg. It had all the markings of a potential banana skin.

At this point of the season Haaland was still causing some debate with regards to how well he was fitting in at Manchester City. The goals were there, of course, but the team was still inconsistent. 'He doesn't conform to what you'd normally think of as a Pep Guardiola striker. But you look at the goals tally and it's ridiculous really,' said *The Times*'s Paul Hirst ahead of the game against Leipzig.

So it seems bizarre to even be saying this, but he's still not clicking 100 per cent. The other ten are kind of adapting to the way he plays. The team is adapting to how Erling wants to play, and you can understand why. He's probably the best striker, or at least the best goal scorer, in the world. You probably should adapt your game to suit him, because he ultimately will win you silverware. I still think there are times when Haaland doesn't really know what he should be doing. At the start of the season, I remember coming here and watching him touch the ball 12–14 times, and scoring three times, which is incredible, and he was happy with that. But lately, you see him dropping deep and try to link up play, like Harry Kane. And I'm not sure that's really playing to his strengths.

But while Haaland was still working out how he fitted into the City team, it was clear that playing in England suited him like a glove. 'What has been most striking for me is that he's a really emotional person,' Hirst says.

> You can see the emotion, he doesn't hide anything. I think he really enjoys the physical aspect of the game. It's a cliché, but you can see that he's tailor-made for the Premier League. The rough and tumble of it, he actually enjoys that. And with the emotion, you do see when things don't quite go his way he gets exasperated really quickly. I've seen a couple of times ... if he loses the ball, he'll go and kick someone. It's quite nice to see really, because everyone thinks of him as this kind of super-athlete who is made in a laboratory and is a perfect striker. But when things don't go his way there is a human side to him where he will just go and kick someone because he's really angry.

With Haaland and the team still adapting to each other, an unfancied but potentially dangerous opponent, and residual memories of previous Champions League failures in the backs of everyone's minds, the second leg was bound to be eventful. It was one of those nights that would define both City's and Haaland's season – one way or the other. Early in the game one thing was clear: Erling Haaland was switched on. In the tenth minute he showed his otherworldly physique by accelerating past Leipzig's central defenders to reach a long ball, and nearly managed to poke it past the goalkeeper. The sprint left ripples of murmurs, chuckles and conversations all around the stadium, as thousands of fans turned to the person next to them to ask, 'Did you see that?' There are times when Haaland's movements seem to defy nature. After many years of watching untold numbers of footballers play the game, we have a clearly defined understanding of what the athletic capabilities of the human body are. Haaland regularly smashes these unconscious expectations, creating an odd kind of cognitive dissonance. A player that size simply should not be moving at that speed, yet there he is, zooming along. In the 18th minute a Manchester City corner bounced off the outstretched hand of a Leipzig defender, Benjamin Henrichs, and after consulting the video monitor the referee gave a penalty. There was no chance of Haaland letting anyone else take it, and even less chance of him missing it. He hit it firmly into the bottom corner: 1–0. In the 23rd minute – only a minute following kick-off after the first goal – Haaland got on the end of a long ball and left it for Kevin De Bruyne. The Belgian cracked a shot off the bar, and Haaland – who was sniffing around for a rebound – headed it in. The score was 2–0.

Just before half-time, City got another corner. Ruben Dias clanged a header off the inside of the post, and the ball bounced along the goal line. A Leipzig player attempted to clear it but only succeeded in hitting the ball off Haaland and into the net. A first-half hat-trick – a scruffy one – but also a fine showcase of Haaland's predatory instincts in the box. After half-time İlkay Gündoğan added another goal, and then Haaland took control again. In the 53rd minute he made it 5–0 following a goalmouth scramble, and just three minutes later another rebound dropped to his feet and he produced an instinctive finish. It was 6–0, with five goals from Haaland. With the game emphatically won, Guardiola looked to manage Haaland's minutes and took him off with just over an hour on the clock. Haaland was not entirely happy, but accepted his standing ovation. In the dying minutes of the game Kevin De Bruyne scored the team's seventh of the night. Any talk of City potentially slipping on a banana skin that evening had been made to look foolish. Yes, Leipzig collapsed; yes, the German side's goalkeeper, Janis Blaswich, had a night to forget, but scoring five goals in a knockout game in the Champions League is still really rather special. The only other player to have done it is Lionel Messi.

After the game, a delighted Haaland spoke to CBS Sports and their panel of pundits, which consisted of Micah Richards, Jamie Carragher and Thierry Henry. 'It's an amazing feeling,' Haaland said, before turning to Henry. 'I think you're the only one maybe that knows how to score a lot of goals,' he said, aiming a fine dig at the more defensively inclined Richards and Carragher. Haaland, laughing along with the panel, has come a million miles from his days of providing mostly yes or no answers. 'To win 7–0, to give a statement in this tournament, the Champions League, which is a tournament I love … that we can actually score seven goals. It's not easy to score seven goals. So it's an amazing feeling.' Henry suggested that if he had stayed on the field he could have scored six or seven, to which Haaland replied that he could have done that anyway.

In the first half I could have scored more. I was alone with the goalkeeper with the ball from Nate [Nathan Aké], I had the rebound with Gündo, I thought he was going to play the ball, that's why I went a bit more. If I had dropped down 2 metres I would have scored because he shot at the keeper. So I could have had two more goals in the first half, and there were also crosses from Kevin I could have been at. So there were possibilities. If I stayed on the pitch no one knows what would happen, but in my mind I think I always have to look to the next and to try to always reach more. To stay hungry. Maybe someone if they score five goals they would be happy, you have to be happy, but you have to want more of course.

Only minutes after full-time in this remarkable 7–0 win, in which he had tied the Champions League record for goals scored in a single knockout game, Erling Haaland's focus was on what he could have done better and what he could improve for next time. He also accepted and embraced that the Champions League was a big part of why he had been brought to the club. 'They won the Premier League four times out of the last five years so they didn't bring me in to win the Premier League – they know how to win the Premier League,' he said. 'So you can read between the lines. But I'm here to try to help the club develop even more, to try to win the Champions League for the first time.'

Next up in the tournament was another old enemy of Haaland's in the shape of Bayern Munich. Although it was now a Lewandowski-less Bayern Munich, who were having a slightly tricky time of it in the Bundesliga. Julian Nagelsmann had recently been sacked and Thomas Tuchel had been brought in. While there was a sense that Bayern were not at their best, they were still Bayern Munich. With the first leg at home at the Etihad, Manchester City took control of the tie in the 26th minute when Rodri curled a left-footed shot into the top corner. The 69th minute saw typical team roles reversed as 6-foot-4 Erling Haaland played a cross for 5-foot-8 Bernardo Silva to head home. Just six minutes later it was Haaland's turn, as he popped up in the box to make it 3–0. It had been a lively game, with chances at both ends of the pitch, but City had taken three of theirs and Bayern had taken none. 'It was not comfortable, no. Emotionally, I'm destroyed,' Guardiola said after the game, and suggested he had aged ten years during the match. In the return leg Bayern again created many chances but struggled to put them in the net. At the opposite end, Erling Haaland made it 1–0 in the 57th minute, which effectively ended the tie. A late penalty goal from Joshua Kimmich didn't matter much, and City were ready for the semi-final. Awaiting them there was more European royalty: Real Madrid.

The Spanish giant was another opponent that held extra significance for Haaland, as Real Madrid was one of the teams he had strongly considered joining before moving to City. For City, Real Madrid was in many ways the Manchester club's opposite. First of all, Real Madrid is the ultimate example of European football's 'old money'. It is a club with long traditions of success and a certain level of entitlement, which has nevertheless seen its status and prestige be challenged on the European stage by the newfound wealth of Manchester City and Paris Saint-Germain, as well as the ever-increasing wealth of the Premier League clubs in general. Yet Real Madrid's recent competitive record is in a way a polar opposite to Manchester City's. Between 2013 and 2022, Real Madrid won the Champions League five times and won La Liga three times. For all of Manchester City's dominance in the domestic league, the club had never reached the pinnacle and won the Champions League. Guardiola's teams were known for their intricate systems, in which the team plays and moves almost like a living organism, and in which individual players have to subject themselves to the demands of Guardiola. Real Madrid, by contrast, is not closely associated with any particular tactical system and utilises a number of different ways to win matches, relying on brilliant individuals to tilt games in their favour. The theory had always been that this is what gave them an edge in the Champions League, that players like Luka Modrić and Karim Benzema simply knew how to get it done in these knockout ties, whereas Manchester City's brilliant system had shown a propensity to malfunction when it really mattered. That was the conventional wisdom, at any rate.

The first leg, played in Madrid on 9 May, provided few conclusive answers. The City players were well on top in the first half-hour, but against the run of play Vinicius Junior scored with a beautiful strike from the edge of the D. When the teams left the field at half-time, Real Madrid had had just 32 per cent possession and taken one shot to City's six, but it was the Spanish club that was 1–0 up. It seemed to be exactly the kind of thing Madrid specialised in, and exactly the kind of game that has left City undone in the past. But in the second half the roles were reversed. Real Madrid now had more possession, City took fewer shots, but crucially one of them struck home. In the 66th minute Kevin De Bruyne hit a thumping low drive into the bottom corner to make it 1–1. City came away from the Santiago Bernabéu stadium with a draw, which meant the English side was just one more home win away from the final.

City had reason to be confident going into the second leg. The team was unbeaten in 22 games and had been particularly strong at home. But as the former Barcelona manager Ernesto Valverde once said about Real Madrid: 'The moment when you think you're closest to beating Real Madrid is the moment you're closest to losing to them.' Madrid have a history of comebacks, of rescuing difficult situations, evidenced in a game against City only the season before. In the semi-final second leg, in Madrid, on 4 May 2022, City thought they were through until two goals from Rodrygo in injury time sent the game into extra time. There, Karim Benzema scored the winner from a penalty. That canny old fox Benzema was still there in 2023, and Real Madrid had another attacking superstar in Vinicius Junior. The Spanish team had a rugged defence and some ageing but still brilliant midfielders. City had looked unstoppable of late, but if there was a team that could stop them Real Madrid would be the one. Before the game Pep Guardiola's message was clear. 'This is one of the most important games since I've been here, we cannot deny that,' he said in the pre-match press conference. 'I've told the players to enjoy it.

We're incredibly lucky to be here. It's in our hands, and we just need to win one game to reach the final.'

The players certainly enjoyed it. Manchester City overwhelmed Real Madrid like a steam train smashing into a loosely assembled collection of empty barrels. The game ended 4–0 to City, and it could have so easily been more. 'Ultimately only the flailing fingertips of Thibaut Courtois prevented this from becoming a total humiliation, the sort of scoreline that eventually earns a game its own Wikipedia page,' wrote Jonathan Liew in the *Guardian*. 'It was probably City's greatest performance under Pep Guardiola, a kind of footballing perfection, a museum piece, not merely a lesson but a scolding, sport as scorched earth strategy'. City had too much energy, the players moved too much and they moved the ball too quickly. Real Madrid simply had no way to keep up. City was like a dog picking up a stuffed toy and shaking it until dead, the stuffing spread out all over the carpet. The visiting side's most potent attacking weapon, Vinicius Junior, was totally nullified by the remarkable athleticism of Kyle Walker. Kevin De Bruyne, eagle-eyed and with surgical lasers for boots, pinged brilliant balls around and recorded two assists. Jack Grealish was effervescent and a joy to watch. Bernardo Silva, who had spent quite a lot of the season on the bench, displayed his uncanny combination of technique and scrappiness. Haaland was thrice denied by Courtois, but Silva, Manuel Akanji and Julián Álvarez stepped in to provide the goals. It was a demonstration of footballing power and excellence rarely seen against this calibre of opponent, and it made Real Madrid look like a team belonging to a bygone era. 'These guys have done it for many years and today they got the reward they deserve,' Guardiola said after the game about his squad. Whether it was City's best performance under Guardiola is hard to say. There have been quite a few good ones but, given the stakes, the opponent and the occasion, it must be one of the most impressive and most significant. It left City with just one more hurdle between them and the trophy they coveted the most: a Champions League final against Inter Milan.

Before that, though, there was the small matter of a Manchester derby in the FA Cup Final. After beating Arsenal in the fourth round of the Cup, Manchester City had been favoured by the Cup gods and received a fairly kind path to the final. Bristol City, Burnley and Sheffield United were all dispatched with a minimum of fuss, to set up a final against Manchester United. 'I don't recognise my team,' Pep Guardiola had complained back in January. After the loss to Manchester United back then, Arsenal had been eight points clear at the top of the league and City had been knocked out of the EFL Cup by Southampton. They were the 'happy flowers' team, one that lacked aggression and hunger. Just a few months later, the club was on the verge of a treble.

Though he didn't score against Real Madrid, Erling Haaland had played his part, with his goals, his physical presence and his determination. In May he was voted the Football Writers' Association Footballer of the Year after taking a record 82 per cent of the votes. 'I also owe so much to Pep and the team behind the team here at City,' he said. 'Everybody has been so good to me since I joined and I have never worked with such top professionals.' The 'team behind the team', as Haaland put it, has certainly played a big part. The injuries that troubled him at Dortmund had not been a problem at City. 'I don't know what he's done in Dortmund but we take care of him 24 hours,' Guardiola said back in April.

We have incredible doctors and physios. They are behind him every second of the day. It's difficult to understand why you'd spend a lot of money and then leave them [the players],

but I don't know what the other clubs do. With this demanding schedule of games every three or four days we have to
take care of them – with nutrition, rest, sleep, food. For the
training, how many minutes – there is data. Sometimes
they cannot train more than 10 or 15 minutes. People say
'Why was he subbed against Leipzig when he'd scored all the
goals?' but then he was injured after the Burnley game. He
could not play with us against Liverpool or for Norway. We
know we have to keep a watch because he's so big. Physios,
massage, backs, shoulders, tendons, everything. He works
so much inside the training centre, much more than on the
pitch. Today in modern football, players train more behind
the scenes than on the pitch.

City even dispatched a member of their medical team, Mario Pafundi,
to work with Erling Haaland and the Norwegian national team
during international weeks. The Norwegian FA insisted, however,
that Pafundi was there to work with the team in general, not just
Haaland. Manager Ståle Solbakken acknowledged, though, that 'of
course, it's no coincidence that he comes from Manchester City and
that Erling is a part of that.'

The flip side of staying fit was that, when it came down to the last
two games of the season, the two finals, Erling Haaland had more
minutes in his legs than in any other season of his life. Significantly
more. In the 2019/20 season he completed 2,751 minutes, spread
across the Austrian Bundesliga, the German Bundesliga, the two
countries' respective Cups and the Champions League, but with a
COVID-19 break thrown in. In his first full season with Dortmund,
playing at lower intensity in empty stadiums, he played a total
of 3,540 minutes in all competitions. In his second season with

Dortmund, injuries meant he only played 2,388 minutes all in. At the end of his first season in England, with the two finals left to play, Erling Haaland had already accrued 3,951 minutes in his legs – and most of those in the more physically demanding English league. Perhaps it's no wonder that his goal output tailed off a bit towards the very end of the season.

On FA Cup Final day, 3 June, Manchester United were desperate to stop Manchester City from potentially winning the treble. The treble, of course, was an achievement closely associated with United themselves, being so far the only English team to win the league, the FA Cup and the Champions League. United wanted to keep it that way. City had finished 14 points ahead of United in the 38-game 2022/3 Premier League season, more than enough evidence that the Guardiola-led side was a significantly better team. But local derbies can have a life of their own, as can Cup finals. So with a local derby in the FA Cup Final, surely anything could happen? This theory survived a full 13 seconds of the actual game itself, before İlkay Gündoğan smashed a volley past David De Gea and into the United net. Oh well. Erling Haaland, again fulfilling the role of Pep Guardiola's unlikely target man, had won the long ball that eventually ended up with Gündoğan. City continued to look the better team in the first half, but United were handed a chance to equalise when the ball bounced off the arm of an unwitting Jack Grealish in the box. The referee, after consulting the monitor, gave a penalty. Bruno Fernandes kept his nerve and made it 1–1. It set things up for an exciting second half, but just six minutes after the break City struck again. Even though he'd already scored one volley, Gündoğan was left completely unmarked on the edge of the box when Kevin De Bruyne was taking a wide free kick. De Bruyne spotted the lonesome German and lofted the ball in his direction, and Gündoğan managed to direct a bouncing volley towards goal. There wasn't that much speed on it, but De Gea couldn't get across fast enough and it snuck in by the post. City were back in charge, and stayed there. At the final whistle the City players could celebrate a domestic double, but cameras caught Haaland sending a clear message to his team-mates 'One more!' According to Guardiola after the game, he wasn't the only one. 'All the players were telling each other "one more to go" as they were hugging each other.' He said that the players 'feel we are in a position which we may never be in again.' He called what they had done as a team during his tenure 'incredible, five Premier League titles, two FA Cups, Carabao Cups, but we have to win the Champions League for us to be recognised how we deserve'. Everything now came down to just one game in Istanbul.

Going into the big final, Erling Haaland was actually now on something akin to a goal drought. At least a drought by his almost superhuman standards. He had scored just one goal in seven games. 'You can think of it as one goal in seven games, or 52 goals in 52 games and eight assists,' he told the *Guardian*. That number of goals in all competitions was comfortably a new record for a player in the Premier League era. The only other player to score more in the history of the English top division was Dixie Dean, who scored 63 in all competitions for Everton in the 1927/8 season. The game has changed so much since then as to make any comparison largely meaningless, but records are records, and Haaland is no doubt aiming to break that one next. 'I didn't expect to score this many goals but, again, I could have scored more. I've been missing a lot of chances, so I could have scored more. That's the truth,' he said. In an interview with UEFA's matchday programme for the final, he praised his manager and his teammates.

Pep, his coaches and all the staff behind the scenes do every-thing to try to help us bring the best version of ourselves onto the pitch. I've already learned so much from Pep and I'm sure there is more to come. I knew I had to adapt to a new coach, new staff, new team-mates and environment, but I feel like I've adapted well and I've loved every single minute.

He also described the squad as 'Absolutely incredible'. Which, given they were on the verge of a treble, it would be hard to disagree with.

The Champions League final, while being the biggest game in club football's calendar year and one of the biggest events of the global sporting calendar, is not always a swashbuckling affair. Sometimes there's just too much at stake, too much pressure and tension, for the swash to buckle. For Italian club Inter, just being in the final was an unexpected delight. The club had finished third in Serie A and had won the Coppa Italia two seasons in a row, but theirs was not a team that would be immediately and universally acknowledged by most observers as one of the very best in Europe. Yet here they were, in the final. The most pivotal results in Inter's run to the final actually came early on in the season, when the team beat Barcelona 1–0 at home and managed to get a 3–3 draw at the Camp Nou. This set Inter up to progress from the group in second place, behind winners Bayern Munich and ahead of the Catalan giants. Inter then embarked on what one might respectfully describe as not the hardest route to a Champions League final anyone has ever had. The first knockout round was against Porto, then Benfica – which had a squad riddled with defensive injuries in the first leg – and then cross-town rivals AC Milan in the semi-finals. Milan had to fend off Inter without the team's attacking fulcrum Rafael Leão in the first leg. There is no such thing as an easy route to a Champions League final, but it's not unfair to suggest that Manchester City, having smashed both Bayern Munich and Real Madrid, arrived in Istanbul with slightly more solid credentials. But Pep Guardiola knew better than to underestimate Inter. In the build-up to the game he made several references to the fact that his side was coming up against an Italian team. Inter, managed by Simone Inzaghi, didn't exactly follow the old Italian *catenaccio* school of football. But still, there is a certain mythos that surrounds Italian teams, especially on occasions such as this. Their capacity for being tactically careful, cagey and even downright sneaky should not be underestimated. Guardiola would see this as the complete antithesis of his own football, and thus something to be taken very seriously.

One thing Guardiola was definitely not going to do was repeat his wild gamble from the last time he was in the Champions League final with Manchester City, when he inexplicably decided to play without a holding midfielder. Over the years Guardiola had earned a reputation for 'overthinking' on these big occasions, because of his tendency to pick unexpected line-ups in big games – and the fact that some of those big calls ended up backfiring. This particular line of criticism, whether justified or not, is something Guardiola has clearly become sensitive to. Ahead of a match against Atlético Madrid in the previous season, Guardiola had sarcastically announced that 'In the Champions League I always overthink.' He also explained why he makes changes.

> I always create new tactics and ideas, and tomorrow you will see a new one. I overthink a lot, that's why I have very good results in the Champions League. I love it. It would be boring if I always played the same way. If people think I will play the same against Atlético and Liverpool, I don't think like that because the movements from Liverpool are completely

different than Atlético – especially because the players are all different. Every player has a mother and father, and the mother and father give different personalities to the players. That's why I love to overthink and create stupid tactics, and when we don't win I am punished. Tonight I will take inspiration and I'm going to do incredible tactics tomorrow. We play with 12 tomorrow!

For the avoidance of doubt, he did not, in fact, play with 12 men. And Manchester City won the game and knocked out Atlético Madrid. Still, there have been some odd calls over the years, such as no holding midfielder against Chelsea in the 2021 final, or the unexpected back three against Lyon in 2020. Guardiola no doubt had perfectly logical reasons for making these decisions, but sometimes there is a thing to be said for just playing your best 11 players in positions they know, in a system they're familiar with. Which, after settling on this hybrid defence/midfield role for John Stones, is mostly what Pep Guardiola did in the spring of 2023. For the final against Inter, there was very little doubt over who would be starting.

The only real question would be whether or not Kyle Walker would have a place in the starting line-up. In the end, Guardiola went for Manuel Akanji, Nathan Aké and Ruben Dias, with John Stones in his hybrid role. Rodri, one of City's best players throughout the season, anchored the midfield, with Jack Grealish on one flank and Bernardo Silva preferred over Riyad Mahrez on the other. The captain, İlkay Gündoğan, and the creator-in-chief Kevin De Bruyne filled attacking midfield roles, while up front the inimitable Haaland would roam free. The game was cagey, as expected, and far from City's best work that season. City's passing was unusually stodgy in the first half, a problem that was made worse when Kevin De Bruyne had to come off with a pulled hamstring in the 36th minute. It was his 49th game for City that season, and he had played a further eight with the national team. It was one game too many. Perhaps he wasn't the only one who had neared the end of his physical capacity. City lacked aggression and tempo. Was it because of the occasion, because of the disciplined work of determined opponents or because of accumulated fatigue after a very long season? It is impossible to know for certain, but the answer is more than likely a combination of the three. Haaland toiled. He was played through on goal in the 26th minute, but it was a difficult finish on the run and he hit it straight at Inter goalkeeper Andre Onana.

Phil Foden, on for De Bruyne, added something to the game. Not everything he tried came off, but at least he had a sense of urgency and invention to him. City's opening goal, when it arrived, started with Foden. He attracted the attention of a pair of Inter players before moving the ball on to Akanji. The defender carried the ball forward and slipped it through to Bernardo Silva. One Inter defender tried to intercept but didn't get there. Another slipped and fell over. Suddenly Silva had some space in the area just wide of the six-yard box. He played an instinctive cutback, which took a slight deflection off an Inter player and landed in the path of Rodri, who put the ball in the net with a controlled finish. Just like against Bayern, City's holding midfielder had come up with a huge goal for the team. Inter threw bodies forward, and Romelu Lukaku missed a massive chance to equalise. In the end Inter didn't have enough, and City held on. Whereas the semi-final win against Real Madrid had been footballing shock and awe, an outrageous demonstration of what this City team can do at their best, the final was a scruffier affair altogether. But as Guardiola's footballing nemesis José Mourinho once said, 'finals are not for playing, they are for winning.' And City had won.

Amid the celebrations, a reporter from Norwegian TV2 managed to grab hold of an emotional Erling Haaland. 'It's totally insane,' he said before composing himself. 'A boy from Bryne wins the treble. It's not so bad in the first season in the Premier League,' he continued, speaking with the kind of understatement one would expect from a true son of Jæren. 'It shows that it's possible for everyone. Even for a boy from Bryne who strolled down to the sports hall and played football there. It shows that it's possible.' Back in Norway, TV2 had moved the entire studio broadcast for the game to Bryne's main square, where thousands had gathered to watch the game on a big screen. When asked if he has a message to the people at home, Haaland struggled to hold back the tears. 'I just want to say thank you for the support. I saw there were a good amount of people in Bryne today, and if you're seeing this now thank you so much for your support, this is just unbelievable.'

As City's captain İlkay Gündoğan lifted the trophy, Haaland was stood right at the back of the team, his face a grimace of sheer emotion. Confetti was launched towards the sky, fireworks went off, and Haaland's beloved Champions League anthem rung out across the stadium. There was a moment when Haaland seemed to step back, slightly detached from the rest of the team, shaking his head repeatedly as if struggling to fully absorb the moment. His eyes closed and his grin widened, and it seemed like the exterior of his body was having a hard time containing everything that was going on inside. Haaland can be a man of few words, but there are moments when words are of no real use anyway. Some moments, some emotions, go beyond our vocabularies and powers of expression. So the only thing to really do is stand back, to take it in, and then the truth of the moment can only be expressed through the look in your eyes and the tears running down your face.

EPILOGUE

Even in June, you can never really trust the Jæren weather. Cold, wind and rain can come sweeping in from the North Sea at any moment and immediately make summer feel more like late autumn. But when TV2 moved their entire studio set-up to Bryne to broadcast the Champions League final from the main square, the elements obliged. The sky remained gloriously blue throughout the evening. Several thousand people gathered to watch the game on a big screen and provided a live studio audience. Erling Haaland's grandmother Inger Åse Høyland Braut and her brother Gabriel Høyland were there and celebrated the win with everyone else. 'It wasn't the best game, but the important thing is that Manchester City and Erling Braut Haaland won,' she told *Stavanger Aftenblad*. 'He was marked very closely throughout the game, but there were some moments when he was dangerous. To experience this in the main square, with so many people and everyone behaving themselves, it was a great experience.' There are traces of Erling Haaland all around downtown Bryne. There is a giant mural of him in a Dortmund shirt, painted on the side of the old dairy. It's a big building, but Erling is an even bigger man, so to fully do his massive wingspan justice a bit of arm had to be added to the top of the building. Two of his favourite places to eat are just a few hundred yards down the road. First is the Wen Hua House, a Chinese restaurant known for serving absolutely massive portions. On the walls there are signed Erling Haaland shirts and pictures of Haaland and the owner. On the back of the Manchester City shirt, aside from Haaland and the number nine, it says 'To Zhu, the best Chinese food in the world!' followed by Haaland's signature. On one of the walls outside Wen Hua is another Haaland mural, this time depicting him in a City shirt, in the lotus position. Just up the road is a fast-food place called Yummy Time, where Erling used to go for one of his rare guilty pleasures, the kebab pizza.

The giant mural of him in a Dortmund shirt was done by a Norwegian street artist who goes by the pseudonym 'Pøbel', which loosely translates as 'Hooligan'. When it was finished Erling Haaland posted a photo of it to his millions of Instagram followers. 'Insane @Pobel.no !', he wrote, adding, *'Husk: Alre gløm kor du kjæme frå'*. Remember: Never forget where you come from. Erling Haaland doesn't, and won't. He still visits Bryne as often as his schedule permits, though sometimes his villa in Marbella takes priority. Life is about finding a balance, after all. In June, after recovering from his treble celebrations, Erling made a surprise visit to his old stomping ground, Jærhallen. He took his time, posing for selfies and autographs with the kids who were there.

> This place made me the footballer I am, but also the person I am. That can be as important. Football is one thing, but it's also about the people around it who I appreciate a lot. The hall was a place where we met and had good times.

During this visit, he took a shot on goal against the youngest goalkeeper he has faced in quite some time, and he drove the ball into the bottom corner with such force that his left sneaker went flying – much to the delight of the kids. 'Sorry, mister, but I had to score,' he explained to the pint-sized goalkeeper. 'Was it fun to win the Champions League?' one of the kids asked. 'It was *grœvla* fun.' Erling Haaland doesn't get a lot of time off, but he stayed a while to watch the kids train. 'I was one of these boys not that long ago,' he said. Outside of Jærhallen, on the side of the building, it says *'Dæ æ jabbnå så drœge'*. It's an almost entirely untranslatable local proverb, but it means something along the lines of 'slow and steady wins the race.'

Right next to Bryne Stadium the road passes under a railway overpass, and on the overpass the club motto is written in stern black letters: *'Ett liv – En klubb'*. One life, one club. With the dilapidated main stand of the stadium in the background, the sight has a melancholy tinge to it. After all, the man in the murals outgrew the club before his career had even begun properly. Bryne FK are scrapping away in the second tier. Attendances are down, and the average age of the attendees is up. There is even ominous talk of local youngsters preferring to take the train to Stavanger to watch Viking. But Jærhallen is full of kids, teeming with talent, joy and life. And on the wall inside is another huge image of Erling Haaland in a Norway shirt, celebrating a goal. Next to his mighty frame, it says 'We will sow the joy of football, cultivate talent and reap miracles.' It would sound contrived if the evidence wasn't right there next to the words. When asked what he wants the kids to think about when they see his image up on the wall, Haaland says the answer is simple: 'That anything is possible. A boy from Bryne can win the treble, become the top scorer in the Premier League and Champions League in the same season. It shows you that it's possible for everyone.'

ACKNOWLEDGEMENTS

Getting this chance to present my hometown Bryne and the rise of our greatest hero Erling Haaland to an international audience has been an incredible privilege for me, so I'd like to thank Ebury and Charlotte Hardman in particular for giving me the opportunity to do so. I'd also like to thank Michelle Warner, Jessica Anderson and everyone else at Ebury who worked on the book and turned it into the finished product you are currently holding in your hand.

None of this would have happened without the efforts of my agent, David Luxton, who put everything together. This being my first book, David's experience and guidance was particularly appreciated.

There is a long list of people to whom this book owes a debt. People who have informed my efforts and steered me in the right direction either through casual conversations, formal interviews or simply through their work. Of particular note are, in alphabetical order: Alf Ingve Berntsen, Andy Brassell, Andreas Vollsund, Archie Rhind-Tutt, Bjørn Hagerup Røken, Jan Åge Fjørtoft, Jim Fossheim, Joachim Baardsen, Joakim Bjerke, Jonas Giæver, Karan Tejwani, Kevin Hatchard, Kjell Olav Stangeland, Martí Perarnau, Nick Ames, Nick Miller, Nils Henrik Smith, Ole Jonny Eriksrud Hansen, Oliver Müller, Patrick Owomoyela, Paul Hirst, Per Joar Hansen, Raphael Honigstein, Reidar B Thu, Rógvi Baldvinsson, Sam Lee, Sid Lowe, Silo & Saft, Stein Ivar Langhelle, Sven Bisgaard Sundet, Tete Lidbom, Torbjørg Haugen and Uli Hesse.

Additionally, work from the following outlets are either quoted or have formed part of the research process: *Aftenposten*, BBC, *Bergens Tidende*, *Bild*, Bleacher Report, *Dagens Næringsliv*, Deutsche Welle, Eurosport, *Football Italia*, France Football, Goal, *Heute*, Idunn.no, *Jærbladet*, Kapital, *Klokkepodden*, *Manchester Evening News*, *MARCA*, *Mundo Deportivo*, *Nettavisen*, *New York Times*, NRK, Reuters, Sky Sports, *Stavanger Aftenblad*, Store norske leksikon, The Athletic, the *Daily Mail*, the *Evening Standard*, the *Guardian*, the *Heia Fotball* podcast, the *Independent*, the *Mirror*, *The Spanish Football Podcast*, the *Telegraph*, *The Times*, the *Topp 3* podcast, *Tuttosport*, TV2, VG and Viaplay.

When it comes to dates, lineups and details from specific games, the archives of the Transfermarkt website have been an invaluable resource.

On a more personal note, everyone who does this sort of thing for a living has had at least one person in their lives who has gone above and beyond to help them have a career. In my case that person is Frode Lia, the founding editor of *Josimar*. Thanks for dragging me out of the forest, boss.

More specifically with this book I'd like to thank the good people of Lydbrook, in particular Nick and Isla, as well as the pub hive mind and landlord Andy at the Forge Hammer.

Those were good days, and I'd like to think a good book came out of them.

IMAGE PERMISSIONS